IMAGES of America

Calhoun County

ACKNOWLEDGMENTS

The staff at the Calhoun County Museum was invaluable in the creation of this book. They are George Anne Cormier, director; Buelah Cox, research; Debbie Stovall, genealogy; and Vicki Cox, administrative assistant. We would also like to thank the editorial team at Arcadia Publishing for their patience and gentle prodding to get this book done! All images, unless otherwise noted, are from the collections of the Calhoun County Museum.

Introduction

The area that became Calhoun County has a long and rich history. A Clovis point from prehistoric times indicates that it was inhabited by Paleo-American groups. Later, the territory of the Karankawa Indians covered the area from Galveston to Corpus Christi and inland almost 150 miles, an area of which Calhoun County is in the center. The Karankawa roamed this territory and met the first European incursions. Unfortunately, by the Civil War, they had disappeared.

The Spanish explorer Alvarez de Pineda explored the Gulf Coast area and drafted maps for governor Francisco de Garey of Jamaica. Then, in 1528, Cabeza de Vaca used the area as a base of operations for his explorations. Because there was no easy wealth to be found here, the Spanish were not as interested in it as they were in the gold- and silver-rich areas of Mexico and Central America. Later, the French became interested in the central Gulf Coast area.

In February 1685, the French explorer Rene Robert Cavalier Sieur de la Salle entered Pass Cavallo with his ship, the *Belle*, while hunting at the mouth of the Mississippi River. He lost another ship, the *Amiable*, on the shoals of the pass. It is believed that he first set foot near what is now Powderhorn Lake, and there is now a statue of him there, in Indianola Park. After exploring the area, he built a fort on Garcitas Creek, which is now part of Victoria County. After the fort was abandoned because of disease and Indian attack, it was taken over and built upon by the Spanish.

The Spanish, realizing that the French might have wanted to claim the area for themselves, started searching for La Salle's colony. In 1689, Alonso de Leon found what was left of the fort. Eventually, a Spanish presidio was built over the ruins, burying the fort until it was uncovered in recent excavations.

The first Anglo settlement in the county was the town of Linnville. It was established in 1831 by German immigrant John Linn, who built the first wharf and warehouse approximately three miles from the current site of Port Lavaca. The colony grew as goods made their way here from New Orleans and New York. It became the port that supplied much of the interior with necessary goods.

As important as Linnville was, it could not withstand an attack by the Comanche Indians in August 1840. The settlement was raided and burned by a group in retaliation for unjust treatment by whites in San Antonio. Many of the inhabitants escaped by boat and were welcomed by men operating a warehouse in the area that became Port Lavaca.

When the Spanish first came to the bay, they found thousands of bison roaming the area. Having no word for the animal they saw, they called them *la vaca*, "the cow." The site of Port Lavaca was laid out in 1842. Although an important port, Lavaca was not able to hold up to the growing town of Indianola. The seeds for the growth of Indianola were sown by Prince Carl Solms-Braunfels when he and 100 German families landed on Indian Point in 1844. The original tent city built by those who remained with him became known as Karlshaven, and eventually Indianola.

Other towns in Calhoun County were also settled in the 1840s. The town of Seadrift was begun in 1848 by a group of Germans who decided against moving inland. In the 1850s, many Polish immigrants came to Indianola. Olivia, however, was settled as a large Swedish colony. Port O'Connor, originally called Alligator Head, was named in honor of Thomas O'Connor. Many native Tejanos were granted land in the county and built ranches on the prairies.

Texas became a state in 1845 and Calhoun County was organized from portions of Victoria, Jackson, and Matagorda Counties in 1846. It was named after John C. Calhoun, who had been vice president under John Quincy Adams and Andrew Jackson. Lavaca became the county seat, but because of the railroad and the growth of Indianola's port, the county seat was transferred there in 1852. In 1857, the county courthouse in Indianola was completed, traces of which remain today—about 50 feet out in the bay.

The chief exports from Calhoun County during this period were cotton, hides, tallow, pecans, and cattle. For a time, canned beef was shipped from Indianola, mostly for use on ships. The Civil War began in 1861 but did not affect Calhoun County until around 1862, when Port Lavaca was shelled by Union gunboats anchored at Gallinipper Point. Although cannonballs damaged many of the homes, the parrot gun on the *Westfield*, a union gunboat, exploded and the vessel could not move closer into the port for continued fire. The Clifton and Westfield battle prompted the creation of the underwater mine by Capt. Edgar Collins Singer and the Singer Company of Port Lavaca.

Fort Esperanza, on Matagorda Island, was under the control of the Confederate army until 1863, when it was captured by Union forces. The one and only land battle in Calhoun County, the Battle of Norris's Bridge, was won by Union troops, who then marched on to Port Lavaca. Trenches made by both armies can still be seen on Matagorda Island today.

A highly dangerous hurricane swept through Indianola in 1875. Because the town was so close to sea level, many people died and much property was damaged. Although the town was rebuilt, it never regained its former status. After being hit by a second hurricane in 1886, the town simply passed into history. In 1887, the county seat reverted back to Port Lavaca.

In the early 1900s, although not the bustling port its rival had been, Port Lavaca became a vacation spot for people who lived inland. Excursion trains brought groups to swim and dance at the pavilion that jutted into the bay. It has recently begun to regain its importance as a port city because of a 26-mile ship channel that connects Calhoun County with the Gulf of Mexico.

Today, Calhoun County raises and exports cattle. It also produces sorghum, rice, corn, pecans, cotton, and of course, fresh seafood. The largest companies in the area are Alcoa, Dow, Formosa, and BP Chemical. Gemco of Port Lavaca and Union Carbide are growing industries in the area. The hope of a promising future lives in all who live, work, and enjoy Calhoun County.

One

Early Trials

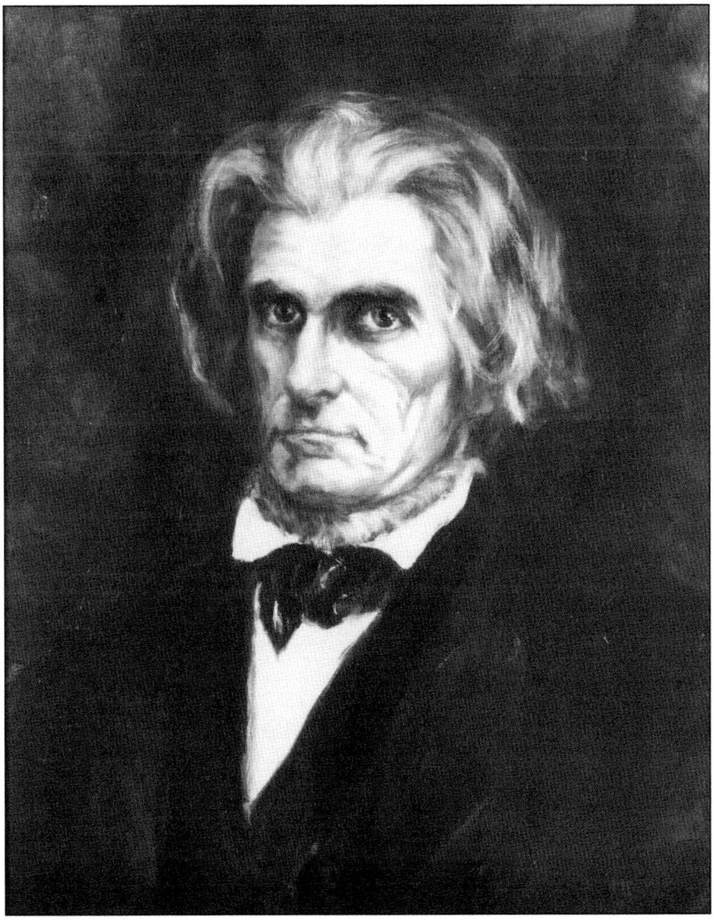

Calhoun County was named in honor of John Caldwell Calhoun (1782–1850), a distinguished southern statesman who served in Congress and was the vice president from 1825 to 1832.

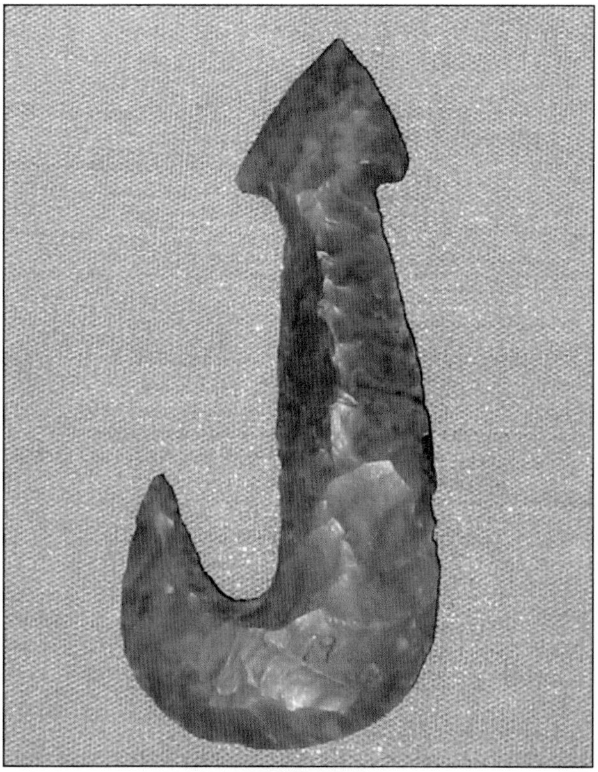

The Karankawa, which meant "dog lovers" in their language, inhabited the Texas coast from Galveston Island to south of Corpus Christi, and as far inland as the current location of Eagle Lake. This old Karankawa fishing hook is housed at the Calhoun County Museum.

The Karankawa used bows and stone arrowheads such as these. With bows said to be almost as tall as a man, and arrow shafts nearly three feet in length, they had amazing skills for hunting and warfare. The Karankawas' ferocious appearance, unpleasant smell, and rumored cannibalism instilled great fear and terror in early settlers.

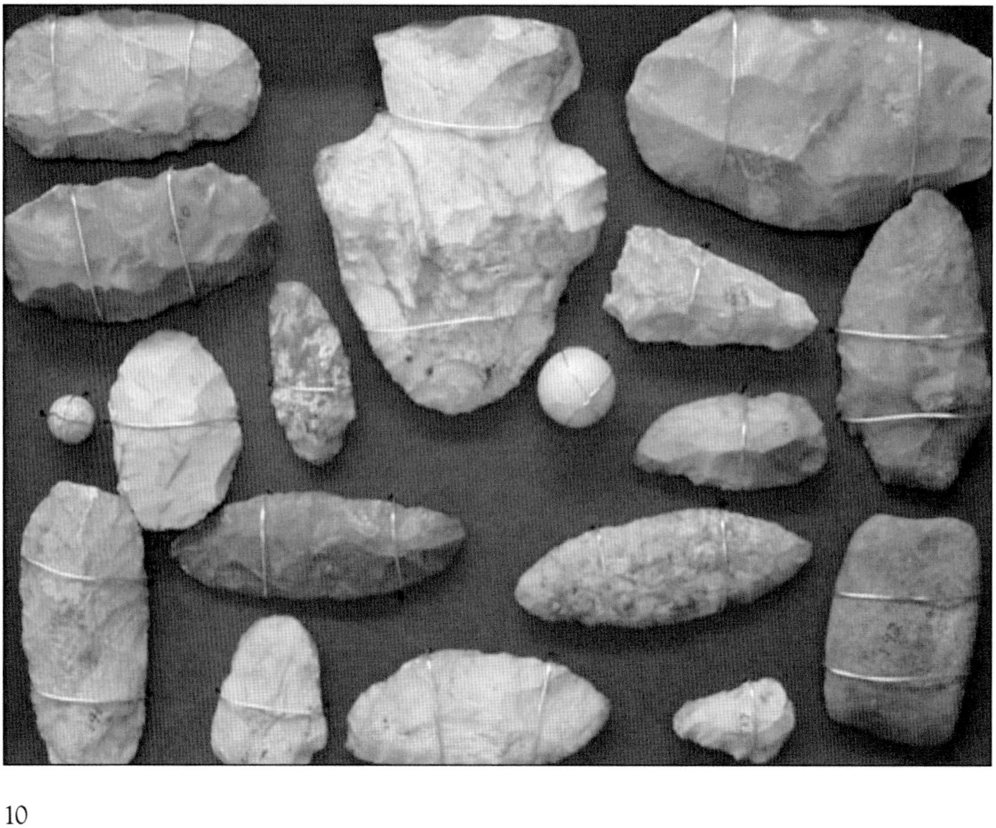

KARANKAWA INDIAN TIMELINE

Pre-European Karankawa ranged from Galveston Bay to Corpus Christi Bay and approximately 100 miles inland, principally near bays and offshore barrier Islands.

1528 Karankawa met survivors of the Narvey Expedition. Cabeza de Vaca lived on Malhado, and after he escaped there, he was enslaved by the Karankawa Indians.

1529 February – Indians moved inland.

1534 Cabeza de Vaca escaped the Karankawa with Andres Dorantes de Carranza, Alonzo Castillo Maldanado, and an African-born slave named Estevanico, and they made their way to Mexico.

1537 Cabeza de Vaca returned to Spain and published an account of this travels.

1685 Robert Cavelier, Sieur de la Salle landed at Matagorda Bay.

1688 After bad relations and killings on both sides, the Karankawa attacked Fort St. Louis and killed all the remaining colonists except for five children. Two Frenchmen who had been away from the fort returned and buried the remains of the dead.

1689 Alonso de Leon found Fort St. Louis and buried three remaining bodies that had not been found previously. He managed to rescue the Frenchmen and bargained for the release of siblings Robert, Lucien, and Magdalene Talon.

1691 Capt. Francisco Martinez was able to purchase Eustace Bremen and the last remaining Talon child, John Baptiste.

1719 Karankawa captured a Frenchman named François Simars de Belliste, who stayed with them for 15 months.

1721 April – In an attempt to bring Christianity to the Karankawa, the Spanish built a presidio and mission at the site of Ft. St Louis. These were called Neustra Senora de Espiritu de Zuniga and Nuestra Senora de Loreto.

1722 April – The missions opened.

1726 Mission de Espiritu Santo de Zuniga moved to the Guadalupe River.

1811 Karankawa were in the center of the Mexican Revolution.

1817 Karankawa had a confrontation with Francisco Xavier Mina at Matagorda Bay.

1818 Jean Lafitte became embroiled in a war with the Karankawa at Three Trees and killed many of the Native Americans.

1821 Stephen F. Austin met with the Karankawa.

1822 Austin met with them again.

1824 Karankawa signed a treaty with Austin, which they did not keep.

1827 May – Karankawa sign another treaty.

1840 Mexico gave the Karankawa permission to move south of the Rio Grande.

1858 They were forced back over the border because they had caused problems for the Mexican government. The remaining Karankawa were killed by Juan Cortina and others.

This timeline traces the known history of the Karankawa people, who disappeared entirely in the mid-1800s. In fact, in 1840, no more than 100 Karankawa were known to be living. By 1860, on the eve of the Civil War, they had disappeared from the Texas coast. The only evidence of the Karankawas' existence comes from the journals of explorers and early settlers and artifacts that have been excavated from long-abandoned campsites.

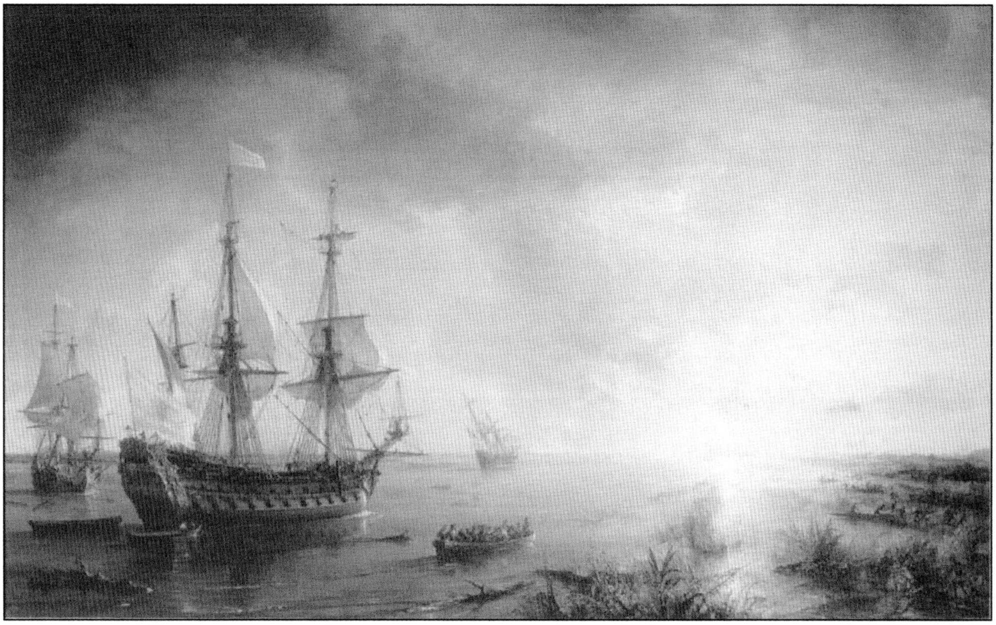

Jean Antoine Théodore de Gudin's famous 1864 work *La Salle's Expedition to Louisiana* is seen here. The painting shows his fleet—*La Belle*, *La Joly*, and *L'Amiable*—entering Matagorda Bay. The *Belle* managed to make it into the bay, but the *Amiable* ran aground, split apart, and lost most of its valuable cargo.

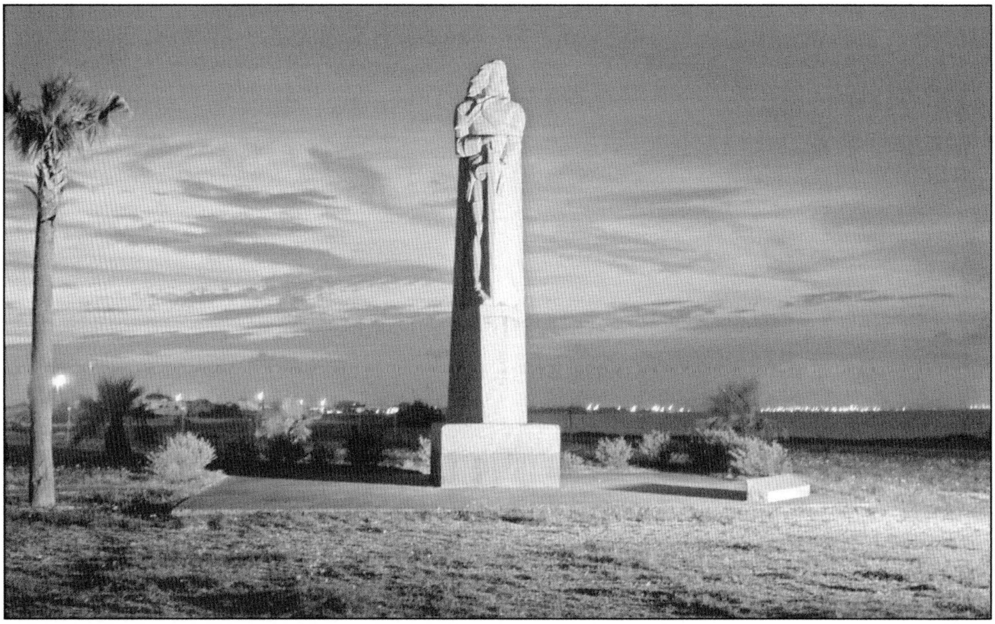

This monument to La Salle stands at the original site of Indianola. Erected in 1936, the historical marker on the side reads in part: "On July 24, 1684 La Salle sailed from France to establish a colony at the mouth of the Mississippi. Landed at Matagorda Bay, February 15, 1685 . . . La Salle's colony on Matagorda Bay gave the United States its first claim to Texas as a part of the Louisiana Purchase . . . America owes him an enduring memory, for, in this masculine figure, she sees the pioneer who guided her to the possession of her richest heritage."

LA SALLE TIMELINE

1643 La Salle is born in France.

1669 Sets out to explore the Ohio Region.

1677 Goes to France to seek official permission to explore western New France from King Louis XVI.

1682 January – La Salle's expedition starts its southward trek along the Mississippi.

April – Discovers the mouth of the Mississippi, and on April 9th, claims all lands drained by it for France and names it Louisiana XIV.

1684 August – Approximately 300 people depart from France aboard four ships, the *Belle*, *Le Joly L'Amiable*, and *Saint-Francois*.

September – Spanish pirates seized the *Saint-Francois* and, a few days later, most of the fleet arrives at Santo Domingo.

November – The remaining ships sail toward what they believed to be the mouth of the Mississippi.

1685 January – First landfall on Texas Coast.

February – The *Belle* safely enters Matagorda Bay through what is now known as Pass Cavallo. *L'Aimable* runs aground trying to enter the narrow channel. The bulk of supplies for the founding the colony are lost at sea.

March – *Le Joly* leaves for France. Approximately 180 people stay behind. La Salle sets out with 52 men in canoes to explore "Baye St. Louis" and to look for a suitable location for the settlement.

April – A permanent location for the colony is found. Fort St. Louis construction begins.

June – A group of 70 colonists depart from the island camp and head for Fort St. Louis.

July – Joutel and his men, who had stayed at the island camp, finally arrive at Fort St. Louis aboard the *Belle*.

October – La Salle and 50 men go in canoes to search for the mouth of the Mississippi. The *Belle* follows with 37 men. There is no contact between the two groups for a month.

December – Capt. Richaud and his men from the *Belle*, who were murdered in their sleep, are finally found by the land party.

1686 January – La Salle leaves again to explore another route.

February – The *Belle* wrecks on a shoal during a storm. Many members of the crew perish. The La Salle party returns to Fort St. Louis after being gone for two months.

May – Six survivors from the *Belle* reach Fort St. Louis in a canoe. The ship had run aground shortly after La Salle's departure and had remained on Matagorda Peninsula near the wreck for three months.

1687 January – La Salle leaves for Illinois with 17 men, leaving only 20 people behind at the fort, illness and hostile natives already having claimed the rest.

March – La Salle is assassinated near present-day Navasota by Pierre Duhaut, Liotot, and L'Archeveque, three of his companions on the trek.

April – The Spanish expedition of Rivas and Iriarte finds the remains of the *Belle*.

1688 December – Weakened by smallpox, the colonists cannot repel an attack by the Karankawa. Indians capture Fort St. Louis. A few children taken captive are later rescued by the Spanish.

1689 April – Gen. Alonso de Leon's expedition finds the remains of Fort St. Louis.

This timeline shows the known history of La Salle's exploration. La Salle's final journey resulted in failure, and only a scant few of the original colonists who started out with him returned to France. We know of his trials and travails from the journal of one such survivor, named Joutel, and from artifacts salvaged from La Salle's sunken ship, *La Belle*.

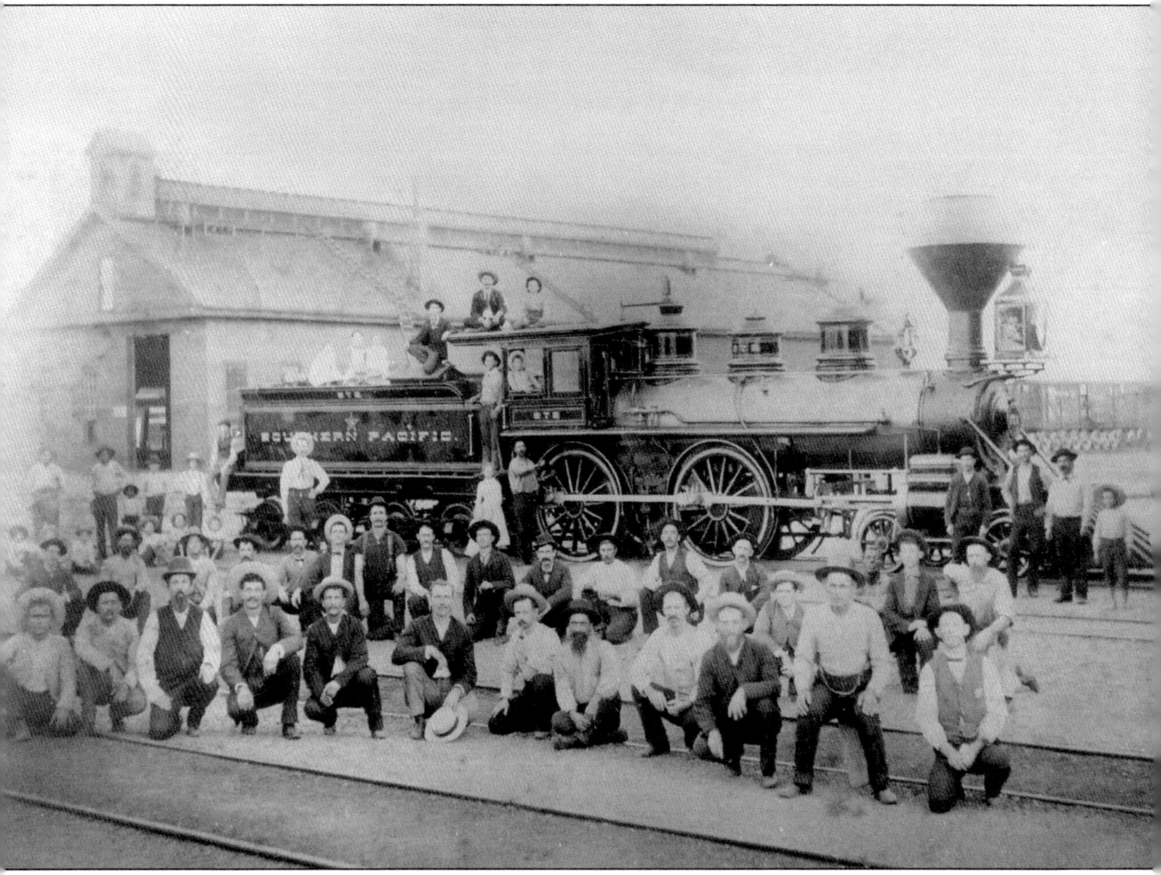

This group poses in front of a Southern Pacific engine and the Indianola roundhouse. In the first row, third from the right, is Peter Clement, who was an agent for the Morgan Steamship Line until after the 1886 hurricane. His home, the port, and the shipping business in Indianola were all devastated by the storm's tidal surge.

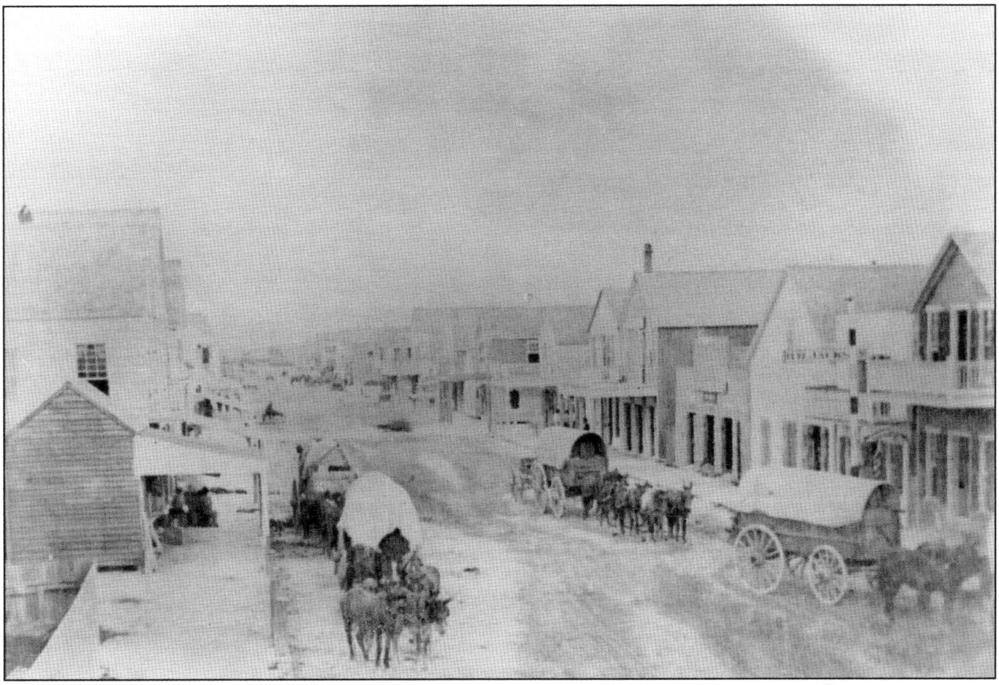

This rare 19th-century photograph of Indianola looks east down the city's main thoroughfare. Conestoga wagons are being pulled down Main Street by teams of mules. Indianola was called by several names, including "Queen City of the West," and later, "Mother of Western Texas." Goods brought to warehouses in Indianola were dispersed throughout Texas. Traveling from Indianola was also one of the shortest routes to the west coast.

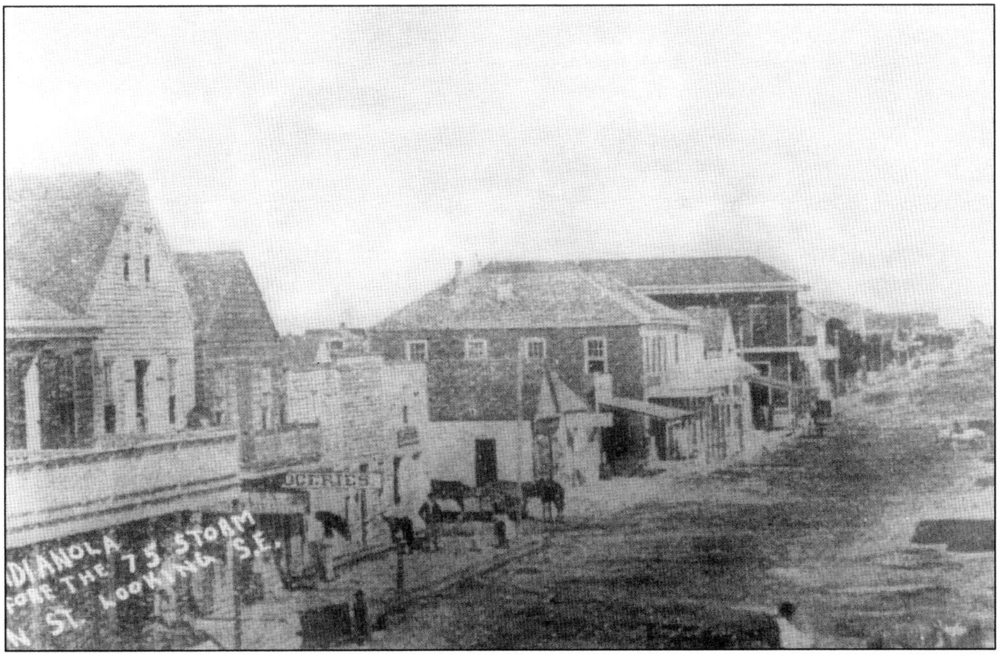

Indianola was at its height when a storm damaged the city in 1875. This photograph was taken before the storm and looks southeast down Main Street.

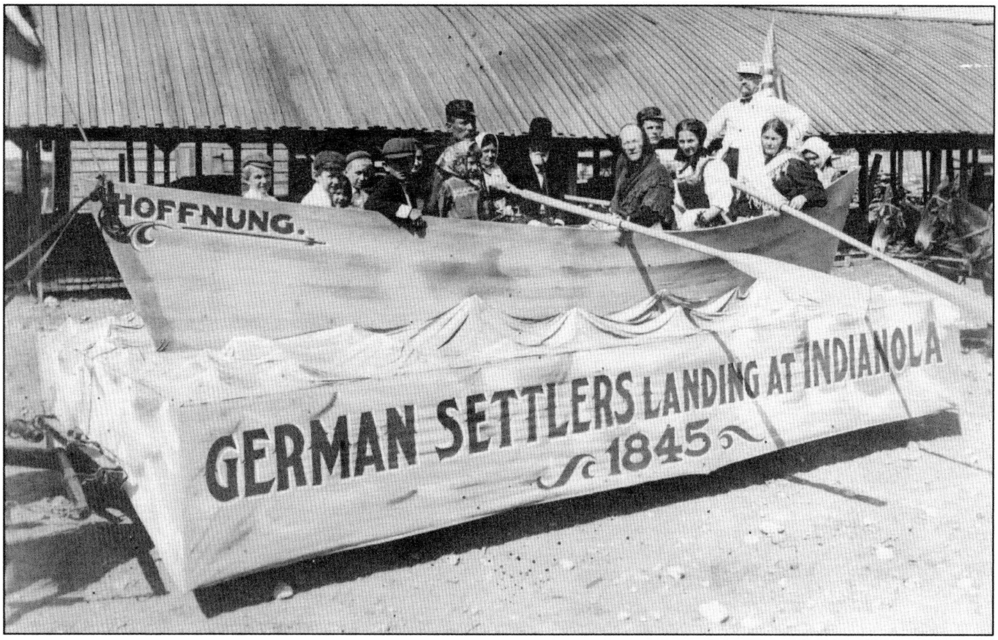

This float from a parade in the early 1900s commemorates the many Germans who immigrated to Indianola starting around 1845.

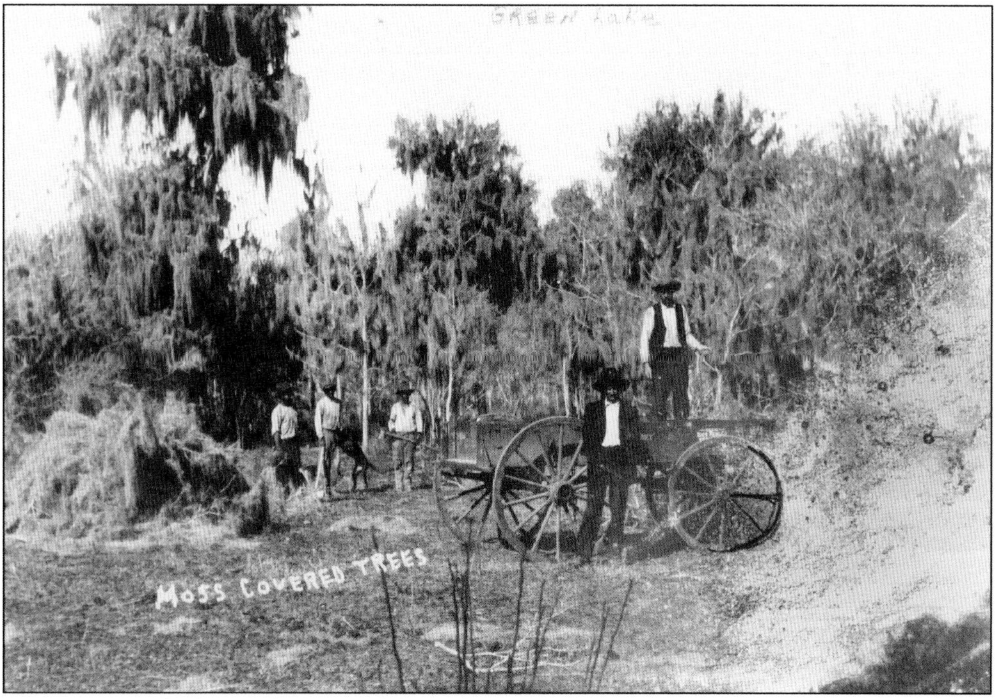

Green Lake is the largest freshwater lake in Texas and was strategically important to both sides during the Civil War. After the war, the area around it, which had been a thriving, wealthy community, was barely populated. It supports a wide selection of waterfowl and wild game.

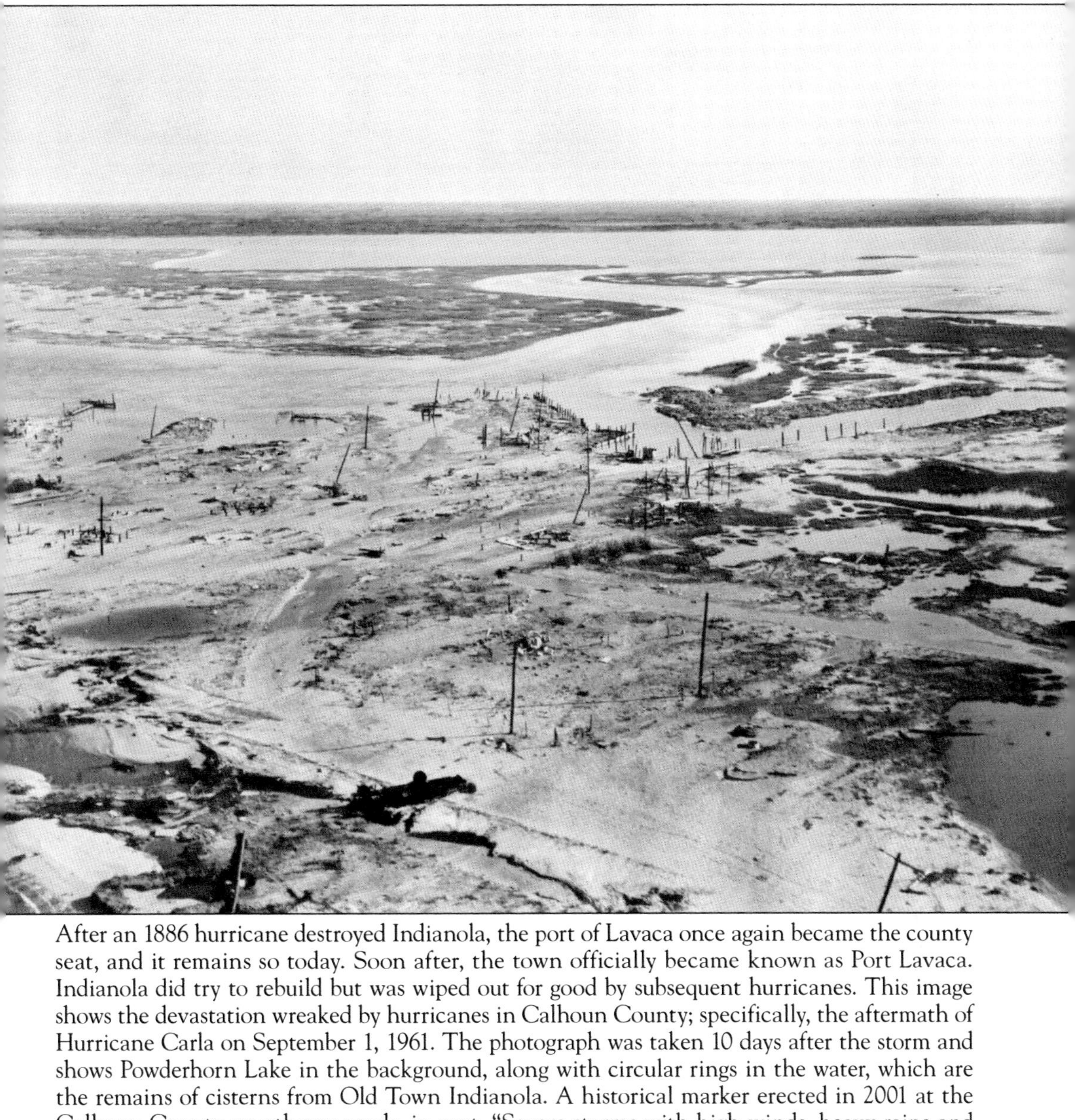

After an 1886 hurricane destroyed Indianola, the port of Lavaca once again became the county seat, and it remains so today. Soon after, the town officially became known as Port Lavaca. Indianola did try to rebuild but was wiped out for good by subsequent hurricanes. This image shows the devastation wreaked by hurricanes in Calhoun County; specifically, the aftermath of Hurricane Carla on September 1, 1961. The photograph was taken 10 days after the storm and shows Powderhorn Lake in the background, along with circular rings in the water, which are the remains of cisterns from Old Town Indianola. A historical marker erected in 2001 at the Calhoun County courthouse reads, in part, "Severe storms with high winds, heavy rains and tidal surges, hurricanes have played a significant role in events that shaped Calhoun County's history. Entire towns, including Indianola (a key Gulf seaport and Calhoun County seat) and Saluria (Republic-era port on Matagorda Island) were destroyed by 19th-century storms. Over the centuries, residents have dealt with wind and water damage to property, and lives have been lost during hurricanes."

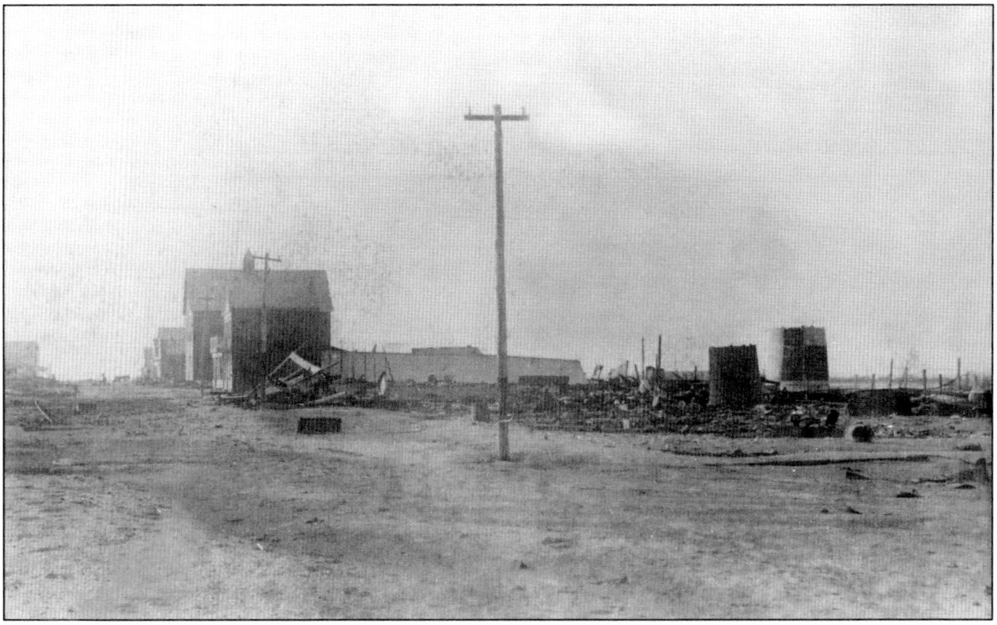

These rare images show more of the devastation in Indianola and other parts of Calhoun County after the 1886 hurricane. It was one of the most intense hurricanes ever recorded in US history. Above, the Runge & Co. store and warehouse were destroyed. Below, the Indianola icehouse, located in the business district, sits in the debris of the storm. The signal building collapsed and caused a fire that burned the area—another reason the county seat was moved back to Port Lavaca in 1887.

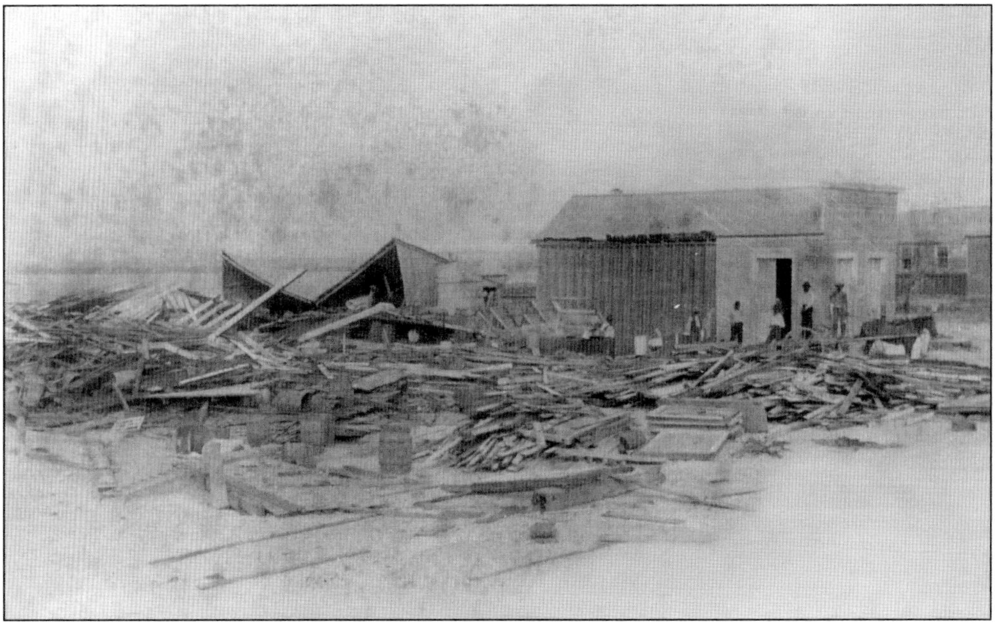

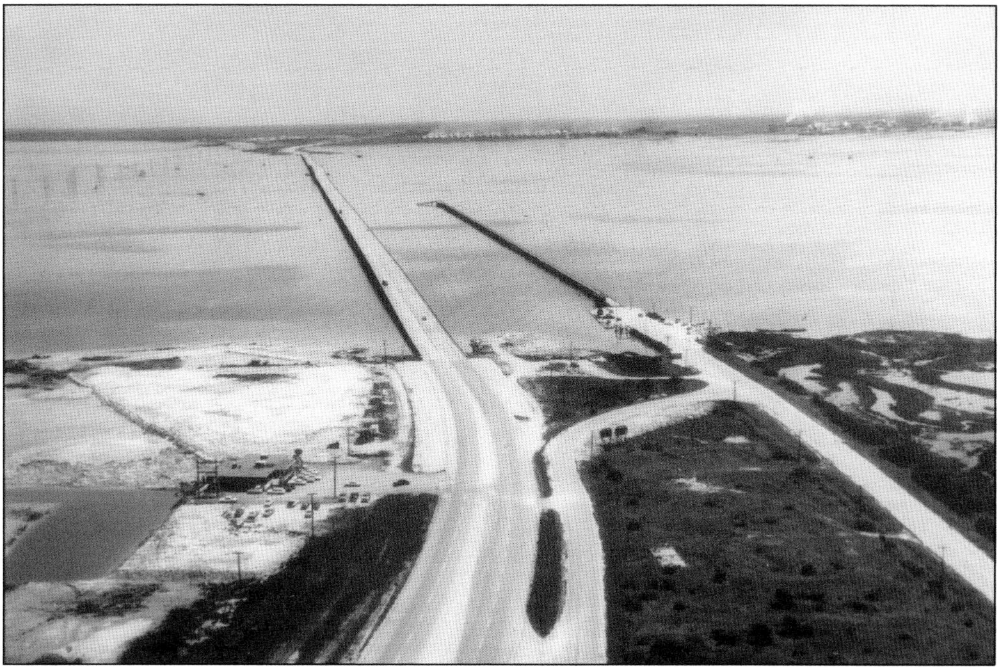

In 1961, the causeway across Lavaca Bay between Port Lavaca and Point Comfort was the longest bridge in Texas. It was damaged in 1961 by Hurricane Carla and had to be repaired. The causeway and the pier are seen here.

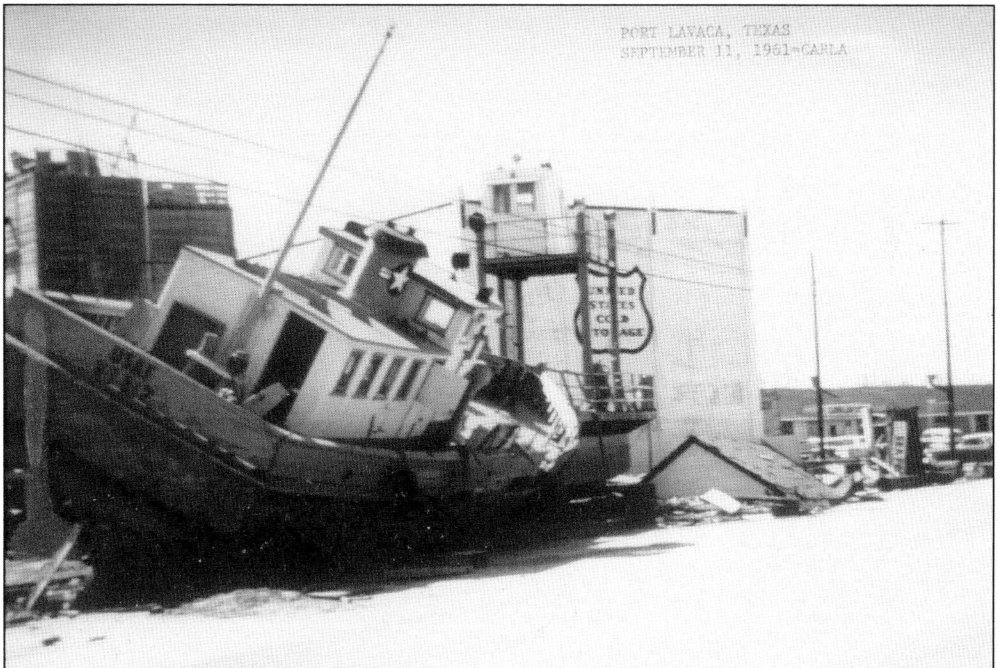

On September 11, 1961, Hurricane Carla did millions of dollars in damage along the Gulf Coast. It landed as a category 4 hurricane, with wind gusts in Port Lavaca up to 170 miles per hour. It lifted this boat straight out of the water and left it on shore.

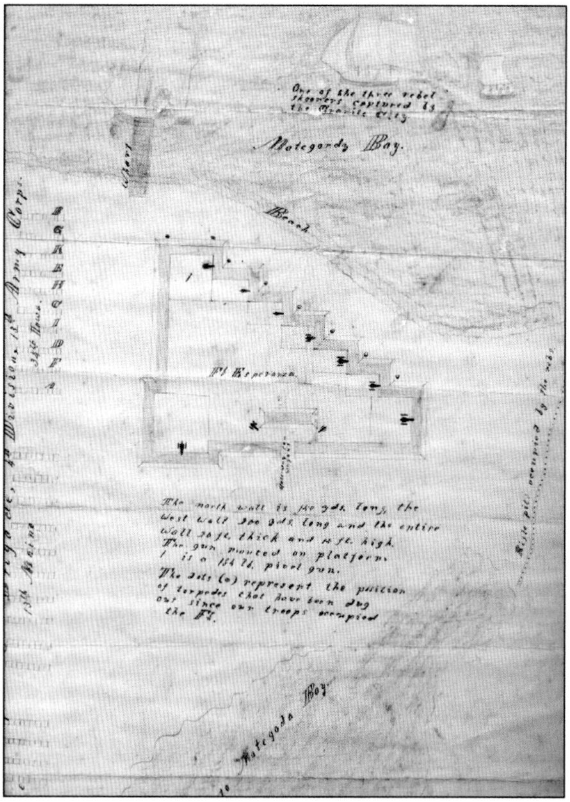

Fort Esperanza was built on Matagorda Island and was hotly disputed during the Civil War. This is a detail of a drawing by Enos Reed of Company K, 34th Iowa Regiment, in December 1863.

The Civil War–era wooden engraving by Thomas Nast below is titled *Union Troops in the Streets of Indianola, Texas.* It was published in the *New York Illustrated News* on April 6, 1861, after the successful capture of Indianola. In 1862, Union gunboats attacked Lavaca. It was defended by two waterfront units, which managed to make the Union ships turn back. Lavaca lost its wharves and its railroad during the war, making Indianola the more important town and the county seat for a time.

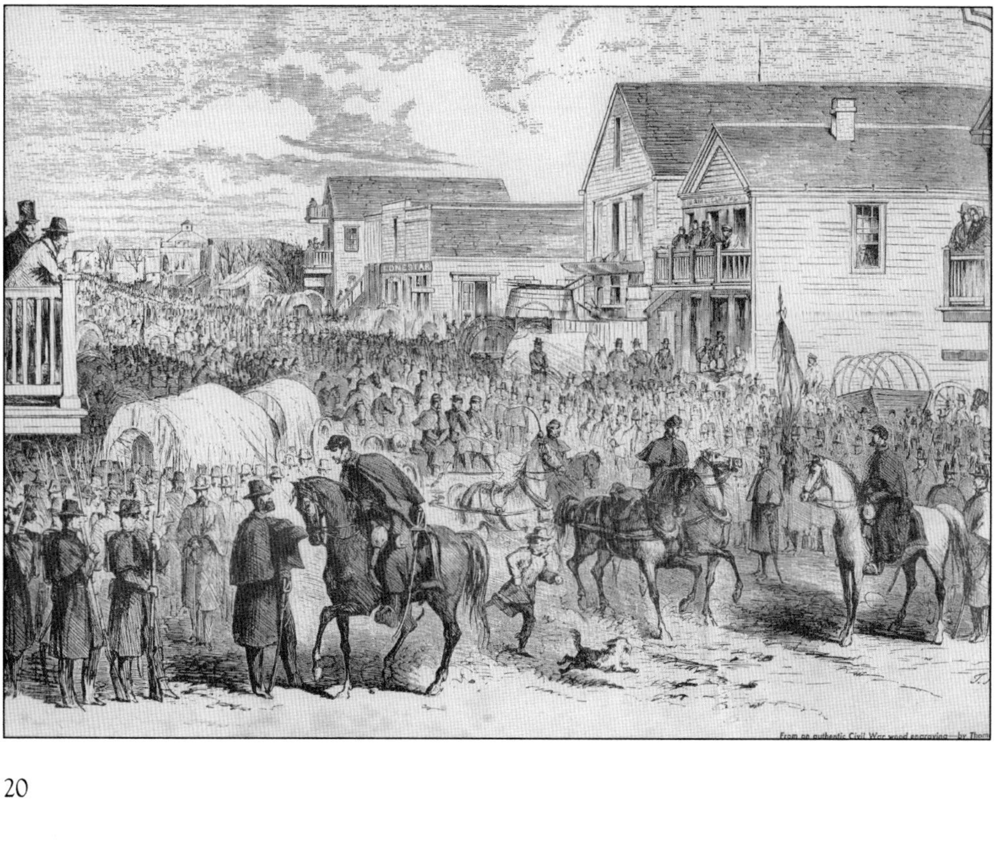

Two

LIFE ON THE BAY

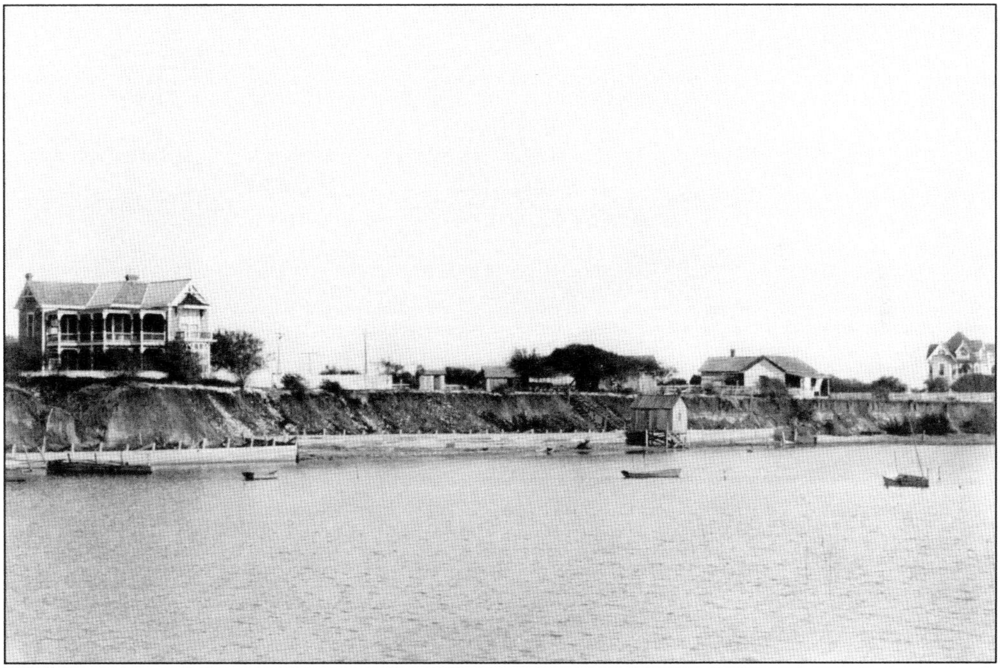

After a raid by Comanche Indians on Linnville in 1840, most of the residents moved to the smaller town of Lavaca. By 1846, when Calhoun County was established, Lavaca had finally become the county seat. By 1900, as seen here, several large homes dotted the Lavaca Bay shoreline. At left was the residence of Champion "Champ" Traylor, who established the First State Bank in Port Lavaca. After his death in 1922, his widow, Maude Berry Wallis Traylor, gave a large donation in his name to the Calhoun County Memorial Hospital.

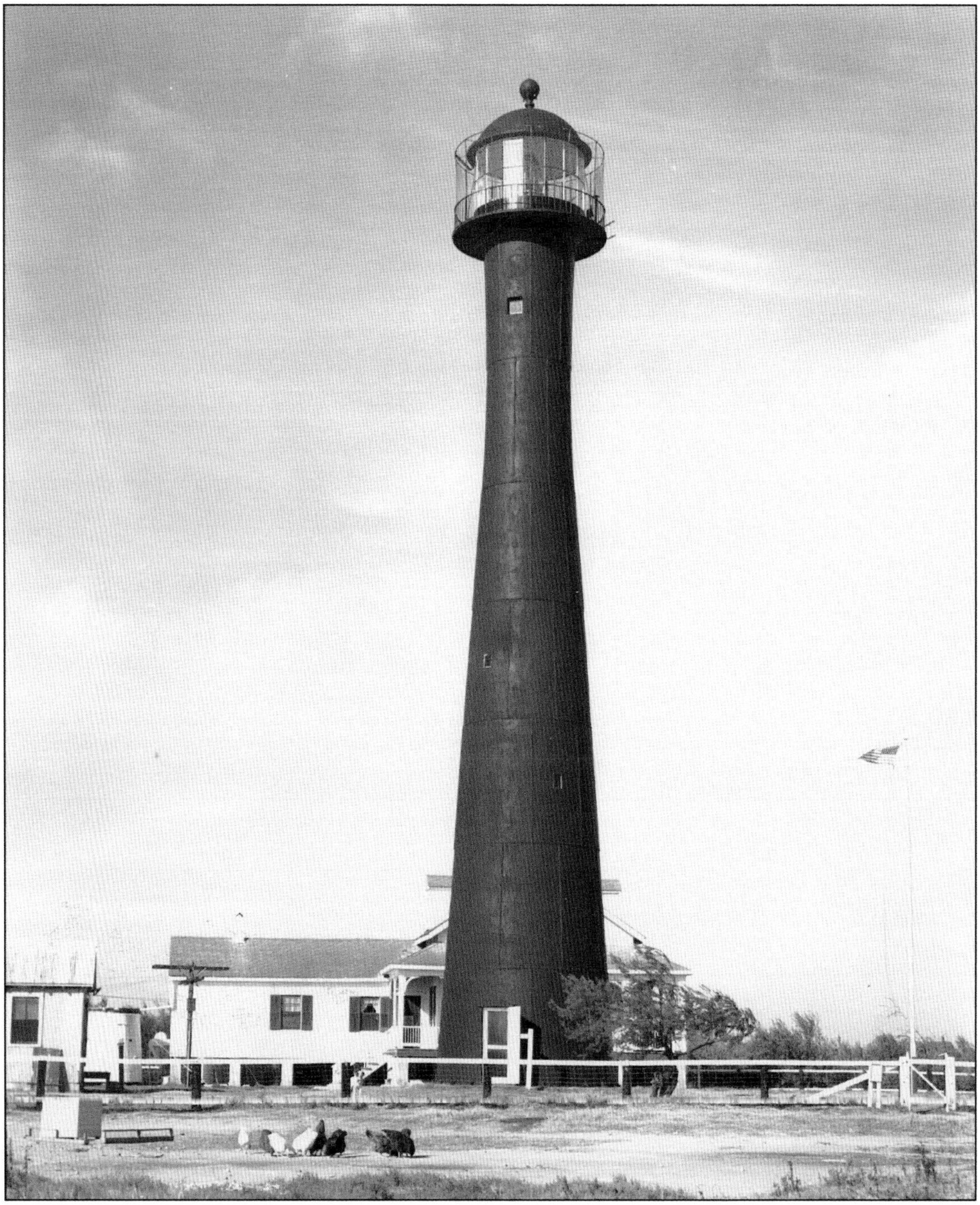

The Matagorda Island lighthouse was built in 1852 and served as a beacon to ships entering Pass Cavallo. That year, there was an outbreak of yellow fever, but workers still managed to build the tower, seen here around 1950. As Indianola grew, Lavaca tried to keep its place as the main port and the county seat, but in 1852, Indianola took both titles from Lavaca. Most of the shipping moved to Indianola as well. (Courtesy Wikicommons/ public domain work of the United States Coast Guard.)

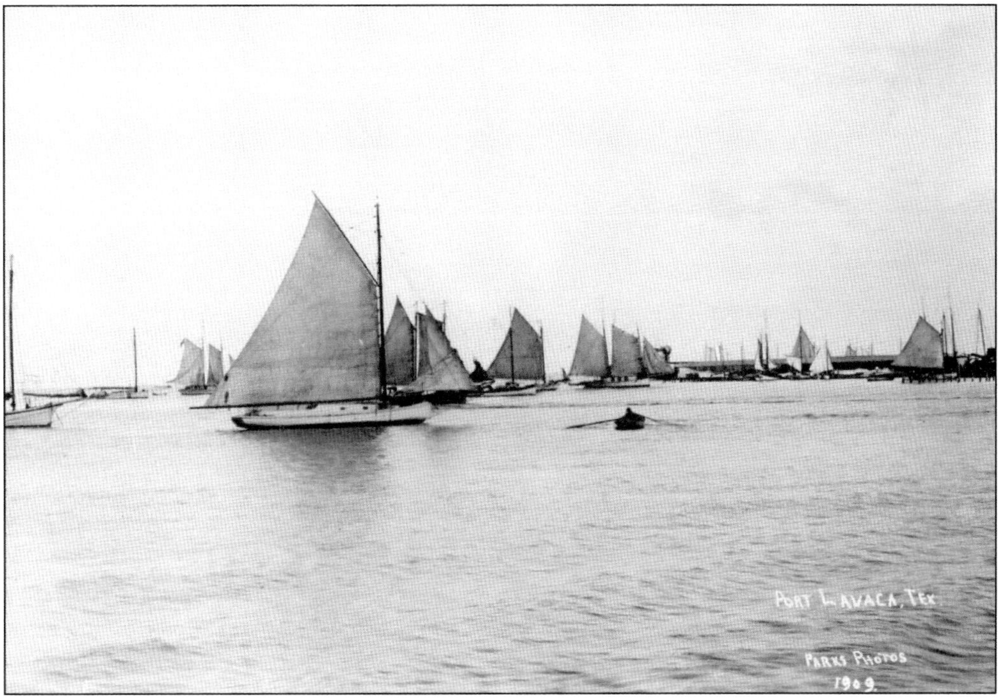

Above, dozens of sailboats maneuver around Lavaca Bay and Matagorda Bay in 1909. Below, the Halfmoon Reef lighthouse, funded by Congress in 1854, is typical of the screw-pile-type lighthouses that served as beacons along Texas's Gulf Coast. It operated from 1858 to 1942.

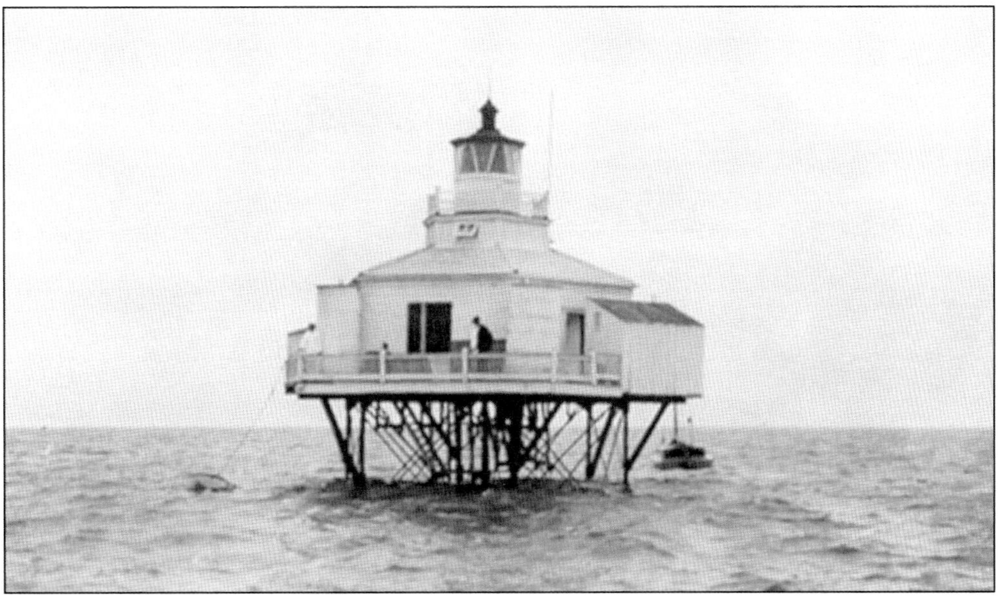

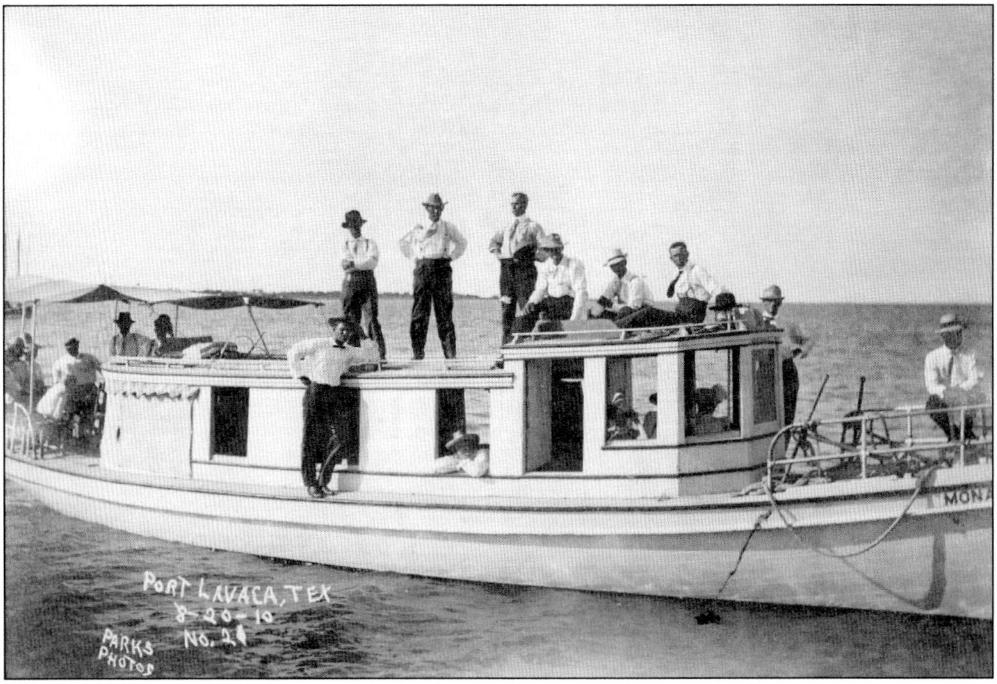

This group, identified as "the Gregory Brothers and Peck party," enjoys a pleasure cruise on Lavaca Bay aboard the *Monarch* on August 10, 1910.

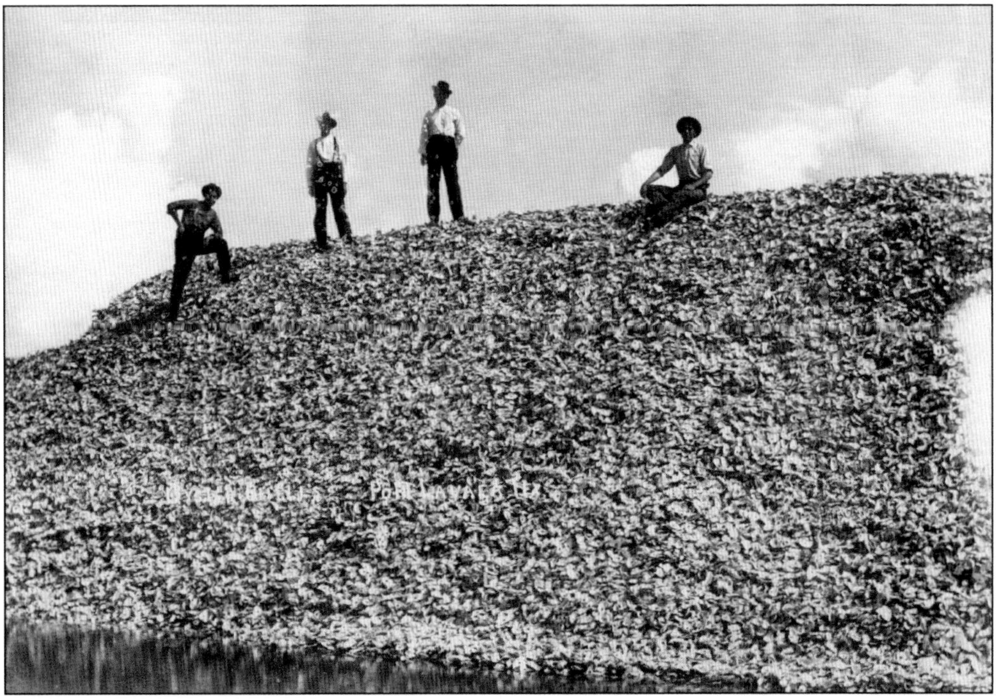

In the early 1900s, oysters were bountifully provided by the bay and were a large part of the Calhoun County economy. These four men pose atop a veritable mountain of oyster shells.

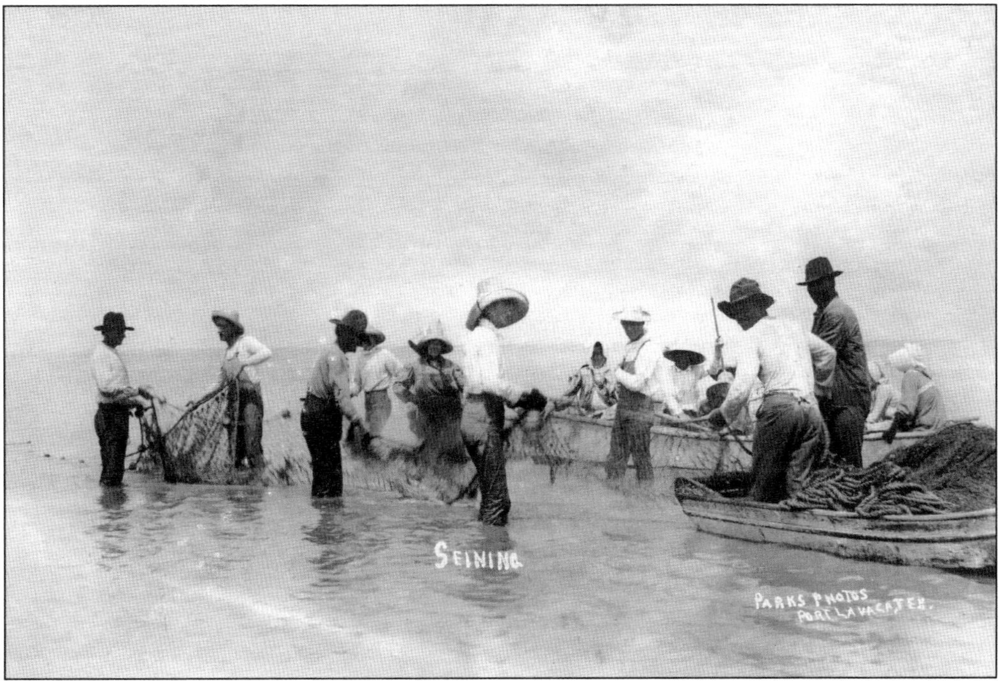

Percy Parks, a local photographer in the early 1900s, took the above photograph of a group of fishermen seining in the bay. Seine-hauling is a simple and effective method of fishing that employs a seine, or dragnet, to hang in the water with its bottom edge weighed down and its top edge buoyed afloat. Below, a boat lies at anchor in front of the shoreline of Port Lavaca.

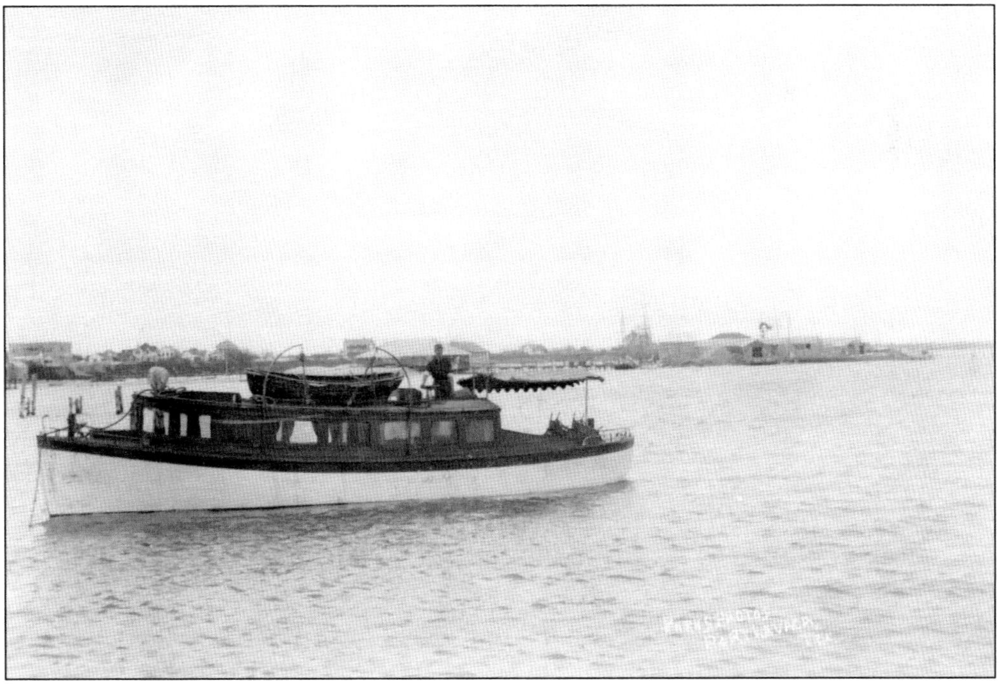

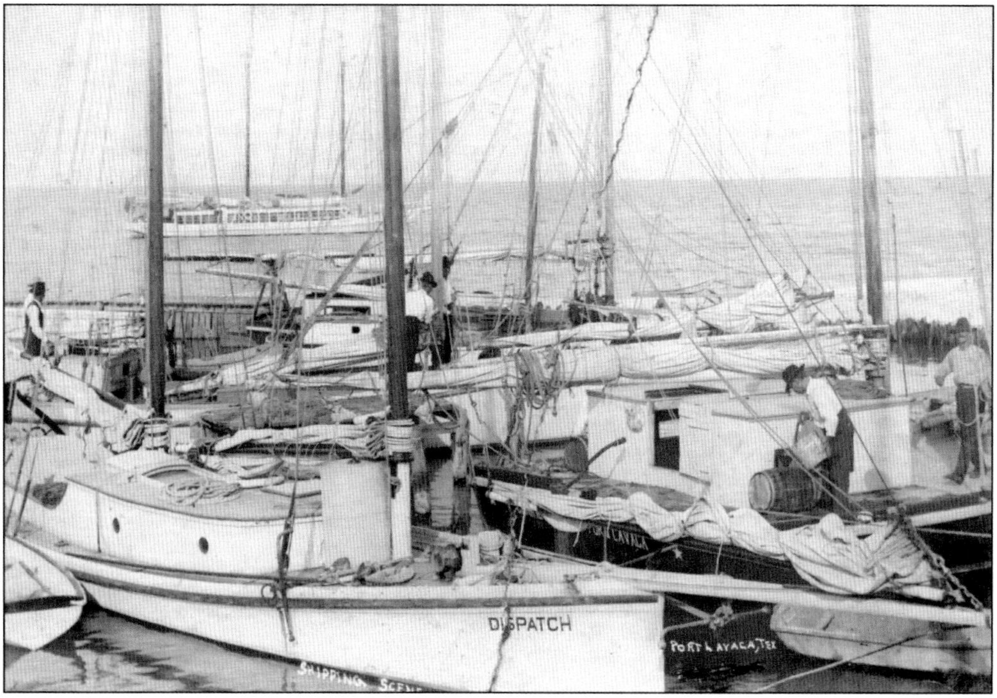

In this shipping scene from 1908, the boat *Dispatch* is in the foreground. This was the typical style of boat that fished Matagorda and Lavaca Bays around that time.

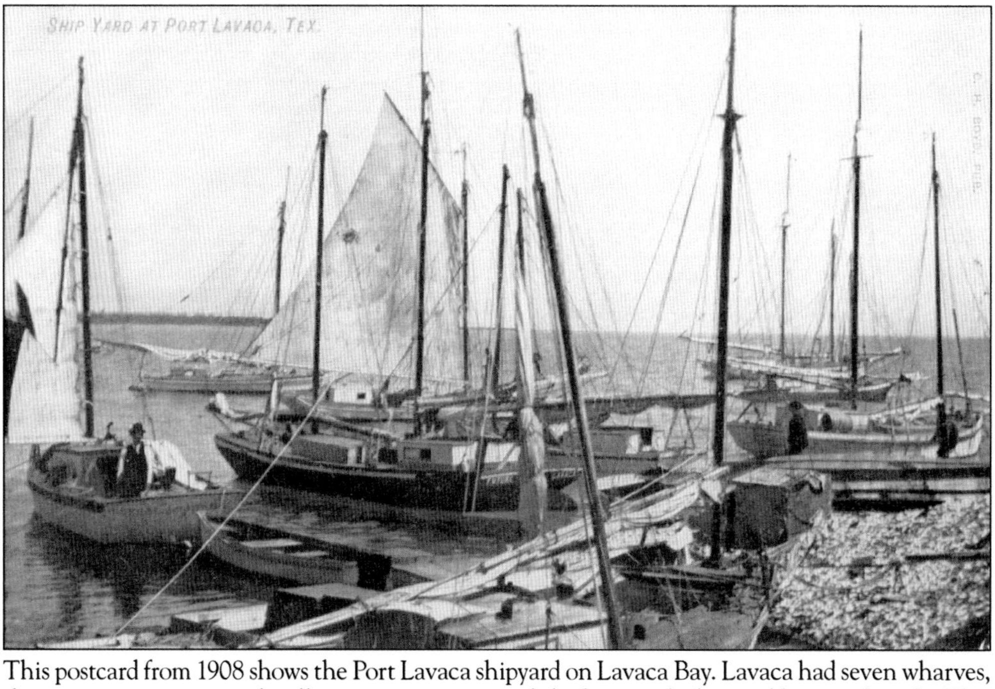

This postcard from 1908 shows the Port Lavaca shipyard on Lavaca Bay. Lavaca had seven wharves, shipping out cotton, wool, tallow, pecans, corn, and the hooves, hides, and horns of cattle. This was a period of great growth for the town.

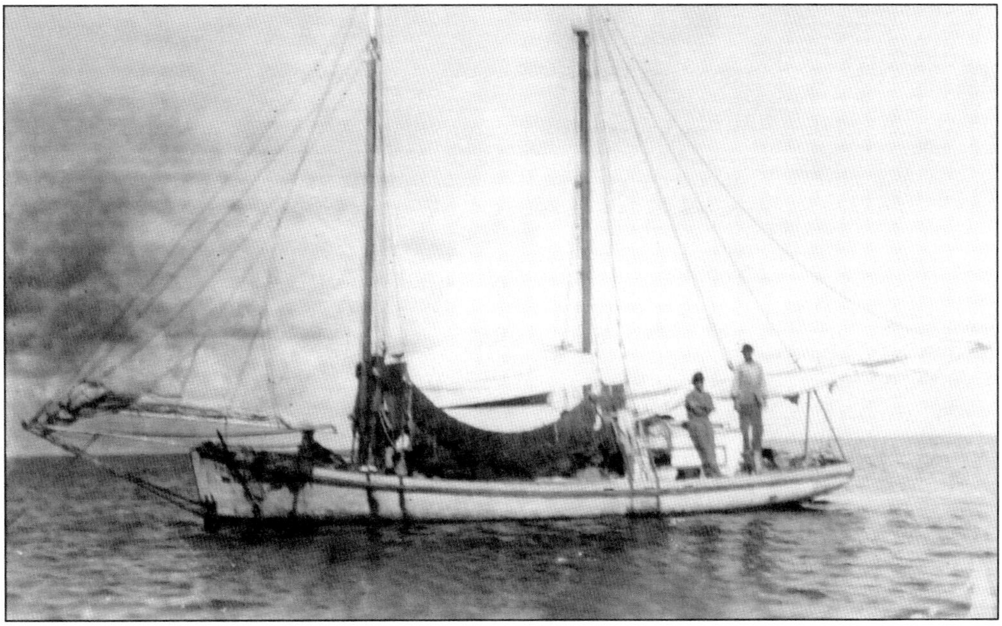

The sailboat above was anchored in Matagorda Bay on August 19–20, 1914. Below is an undated photograph of a sailboat and other small boats in the Lavaca Bay.

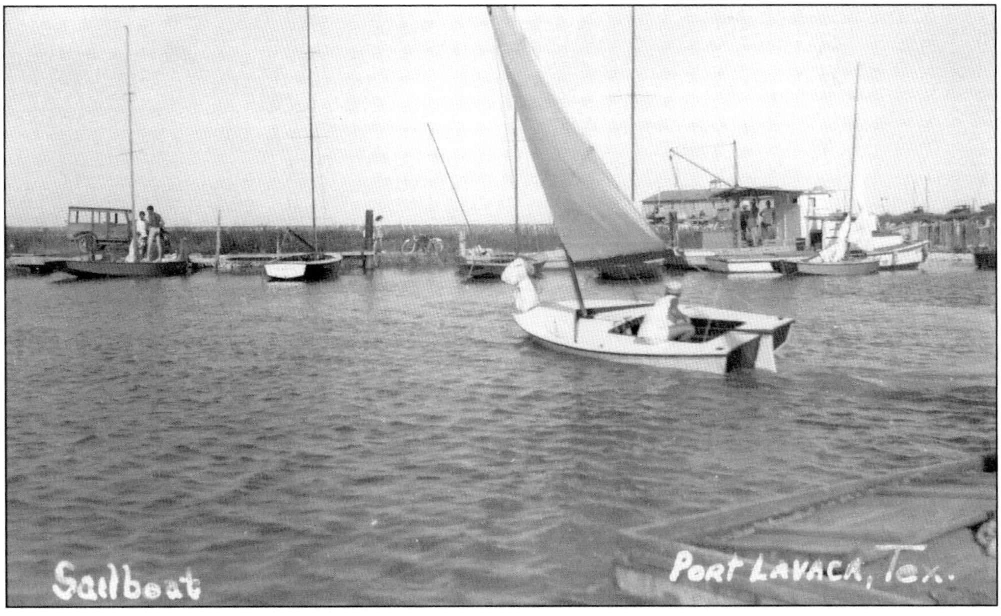

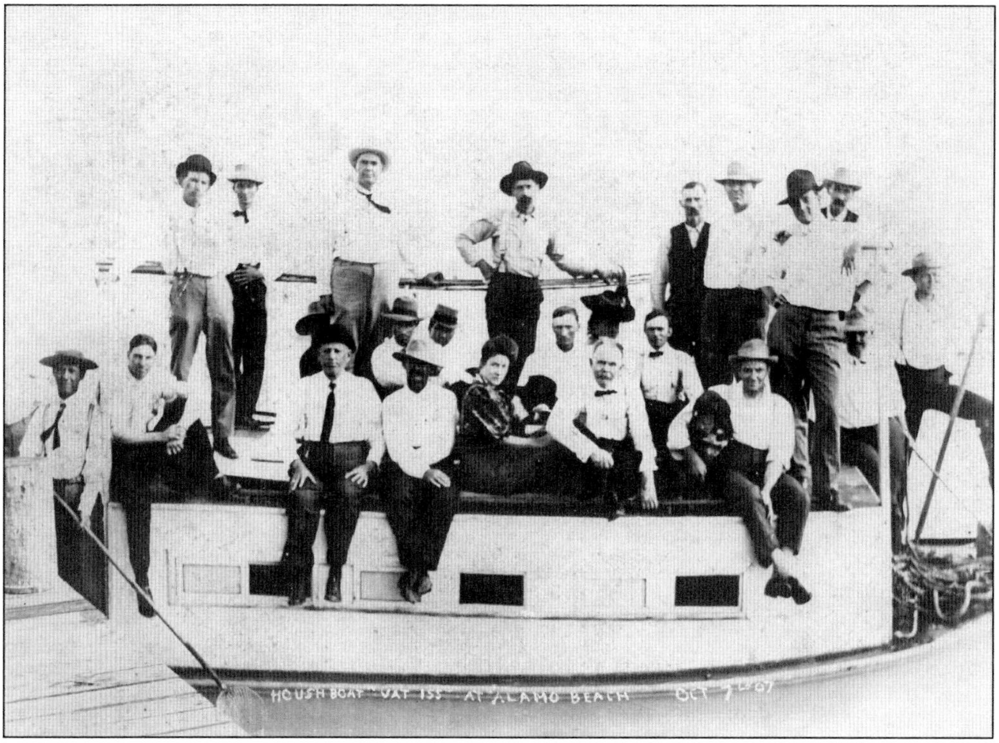

This group poses for a photograph on the houseboat *Vat ISS*, which was docked at Alamo Beach on October 7, 1907.

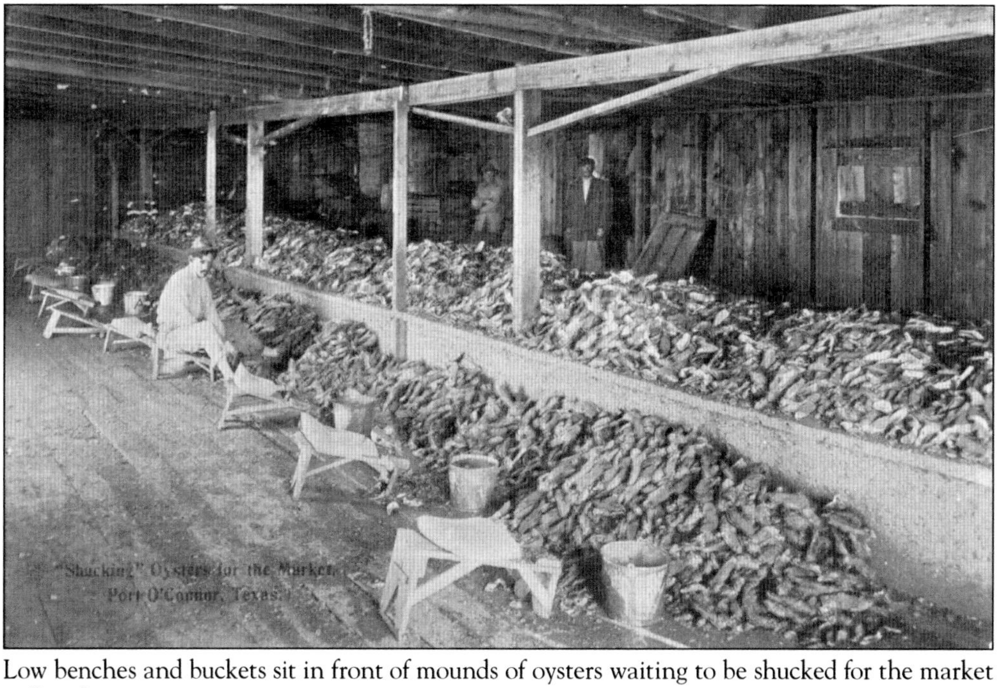

Low benches and buckets sit in front of mounds of oysters waiting to be shucked for the market in Port Lavaca.

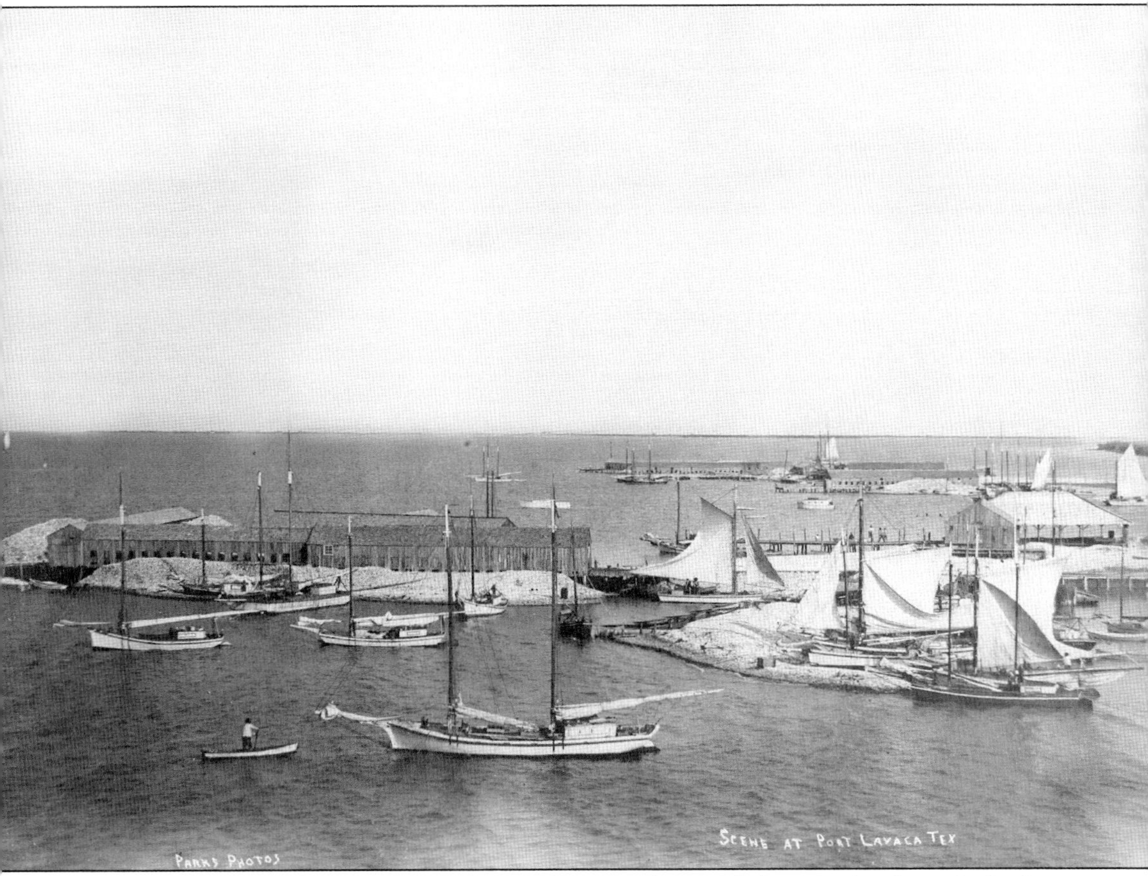

Boats in the harbor and old oyster houses were favorite subjects of photographer Percy Parks. In this photograph, Parks captures sailboats on the bay and the fish and oyster houses dotting the waterfront in the Port Lavaca harbor.

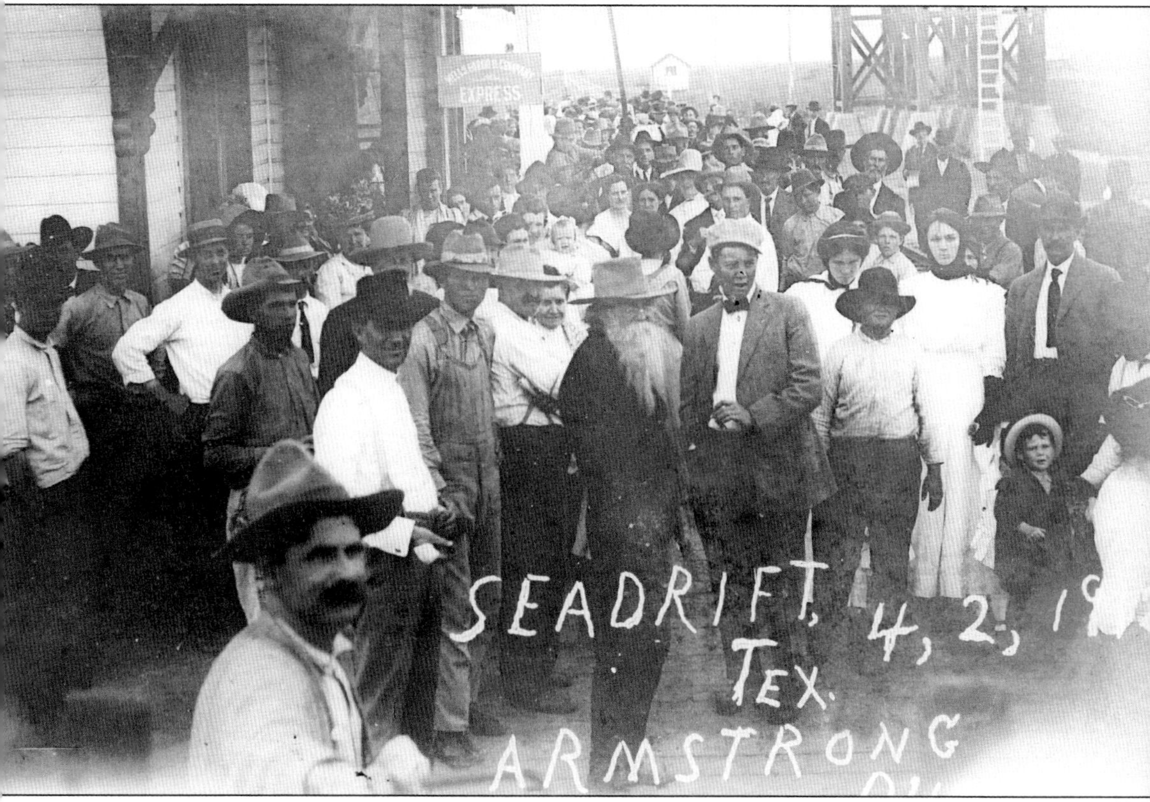

Seadrift is located on the northeast shore of San Antonio Bay, unlike the other towns in the county that are located on either Lavaca Bay or Matagorda Bay. This large group of men, women, and children congregate in front of the Wells Fargo Express in Seadrift on Thursday, April 4, 1912—only 11 days before the sinking of the *Titanic*.

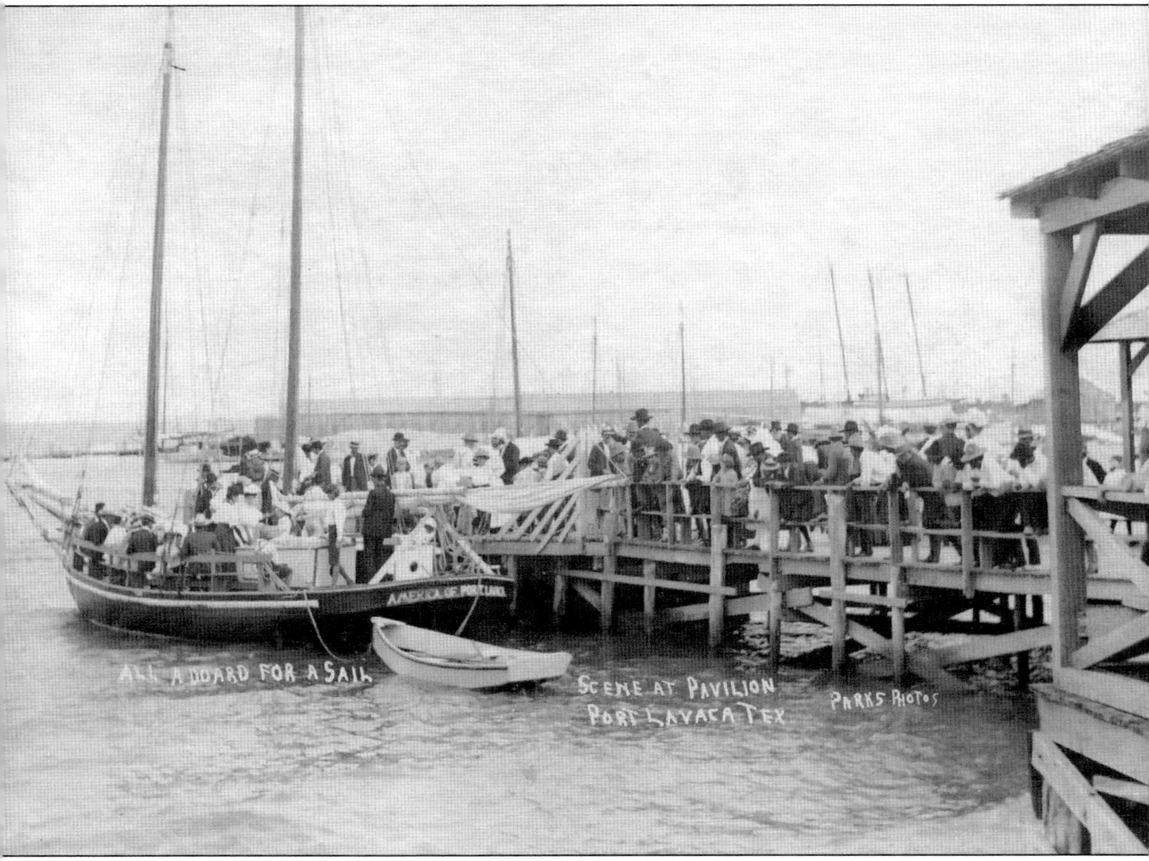

Partygoers at the pavilion prepare to board the *America of Port Lavaca* and other small boats for a sail in Lavaca Bay.

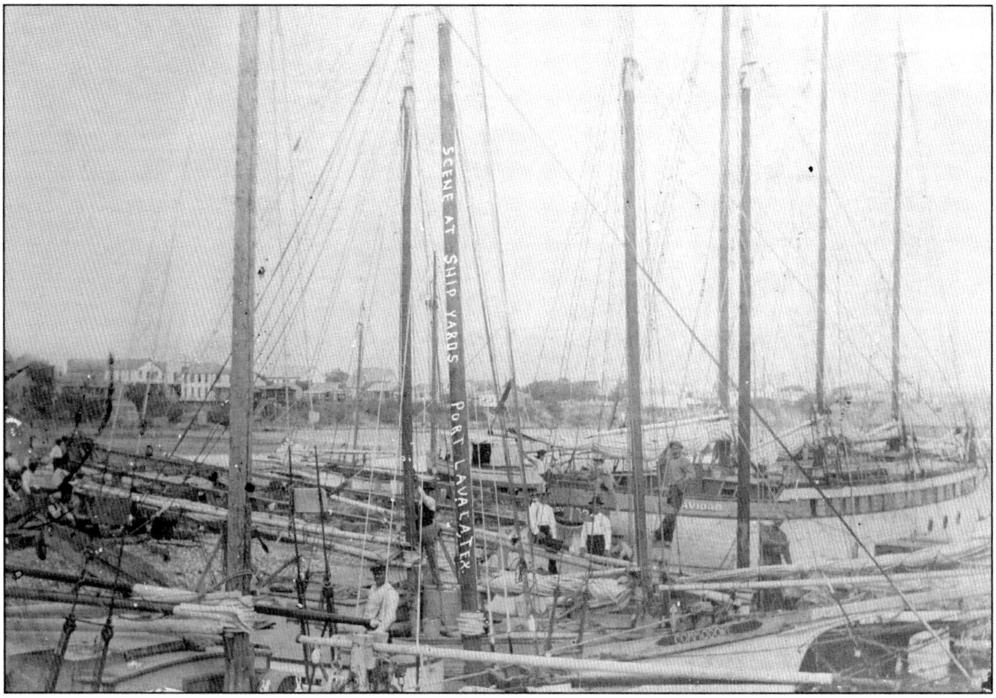

Sailing vessels the *Navidad* and the *Commodore* lie berthed at the shipyard in Port Lavaca.

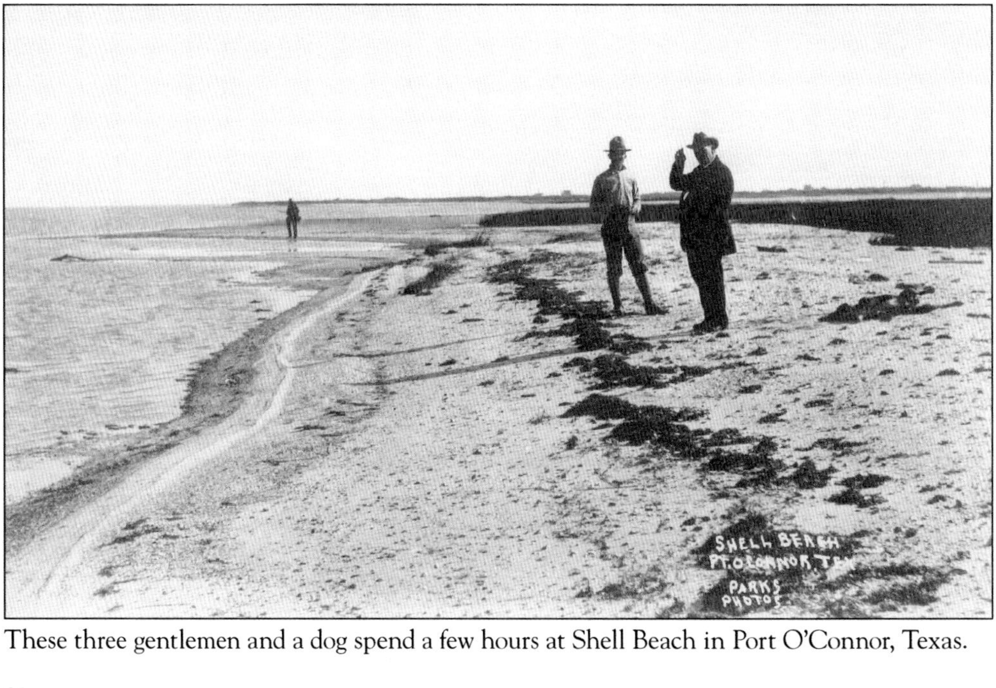

These three gentlemen and a dog spend a few hours at Shell Beach in Port O'Connor, Texas.

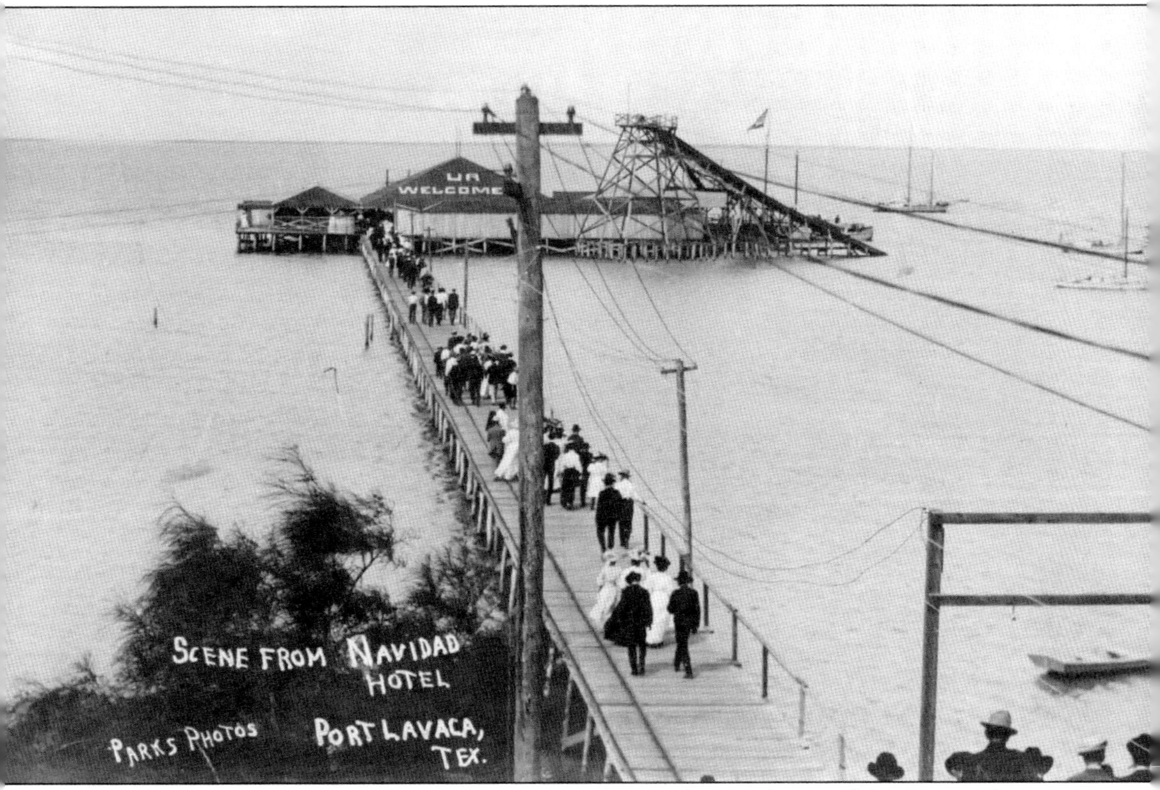

Completed in 1908, the Navidad Hotel was on the shore in line with one of the five pavilions. Near here, at the train depot, excursionists would disembark to enjoy a summer weekend at the beach.

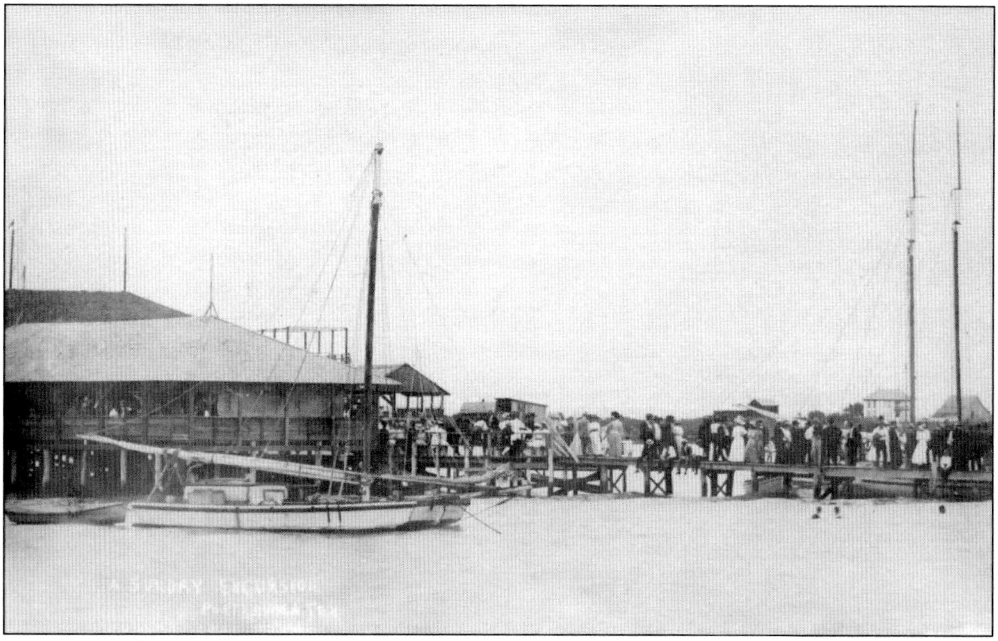

Families out for a weekend excursion stroll down the pier to the pavilion, known as the Shoot-the-Chute. This pavilion was built in 1895 and opened in 1896. Small boats were hoisted to the top of a huge slide and anyone who was daredevil enough got into the boat, which was then released to slide down and bounce across the water.

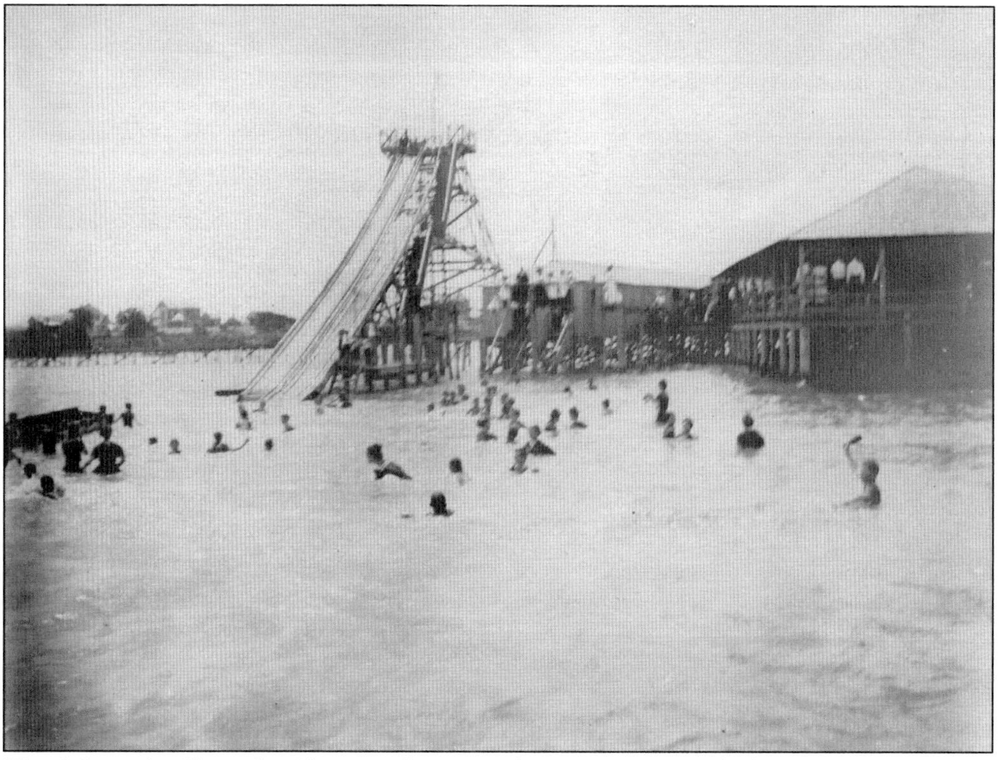

The slide on the Shoot-the-Chute pavilion rises above swimmers in the bay.

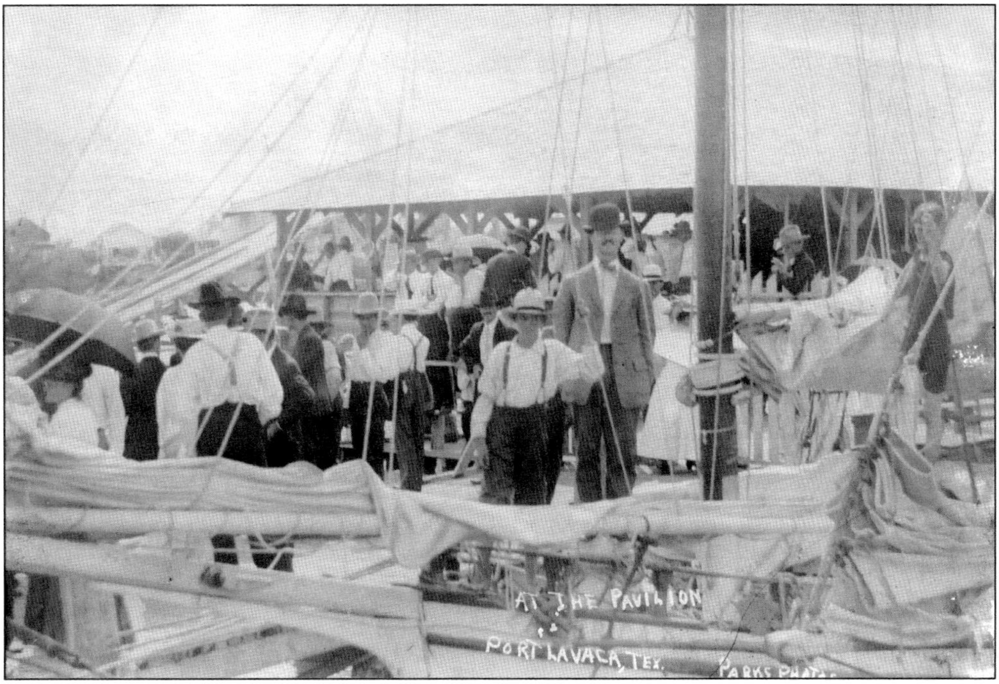

Boats and people gather at the Shoot-the-Chute pavilion to enjoy a day of sailing, feasting, and dancing.

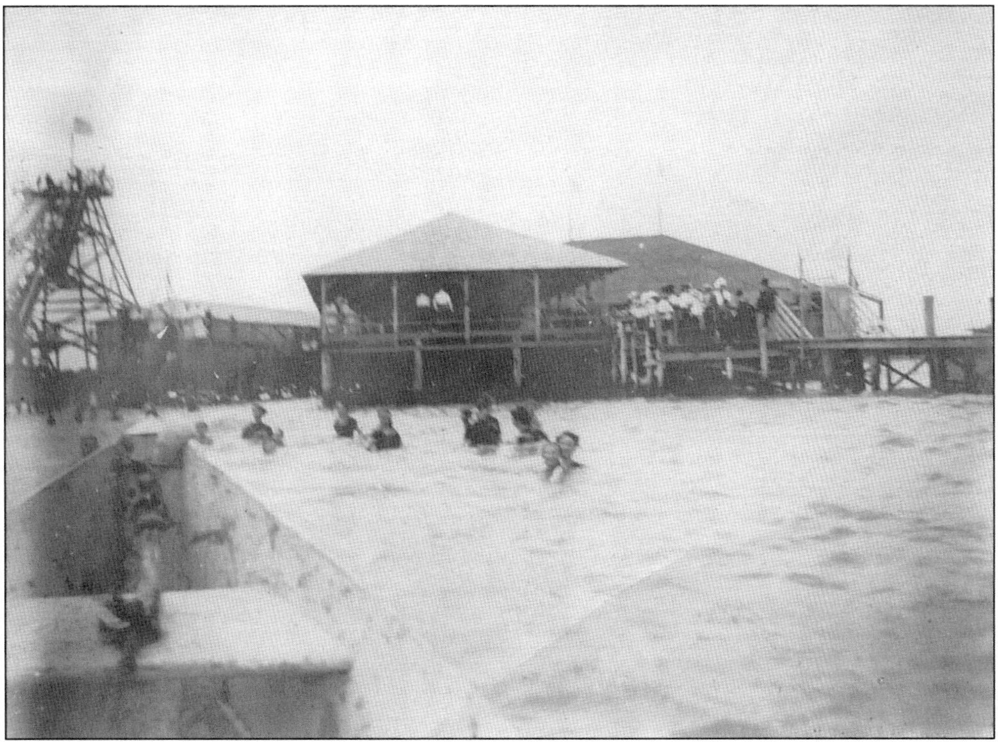

This photograph, taken from a boat in the bay, shows swimmers enjoying the water near the popular Shoot-the-Chute.

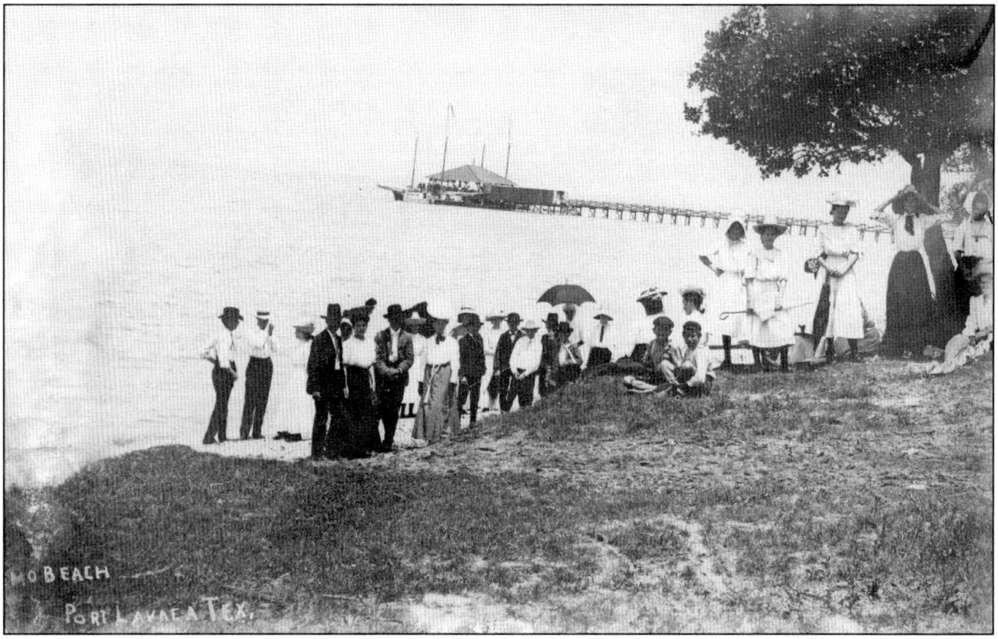

These beachgoers enjoy the pavilion and the beach at Alamo Beach around 1900.

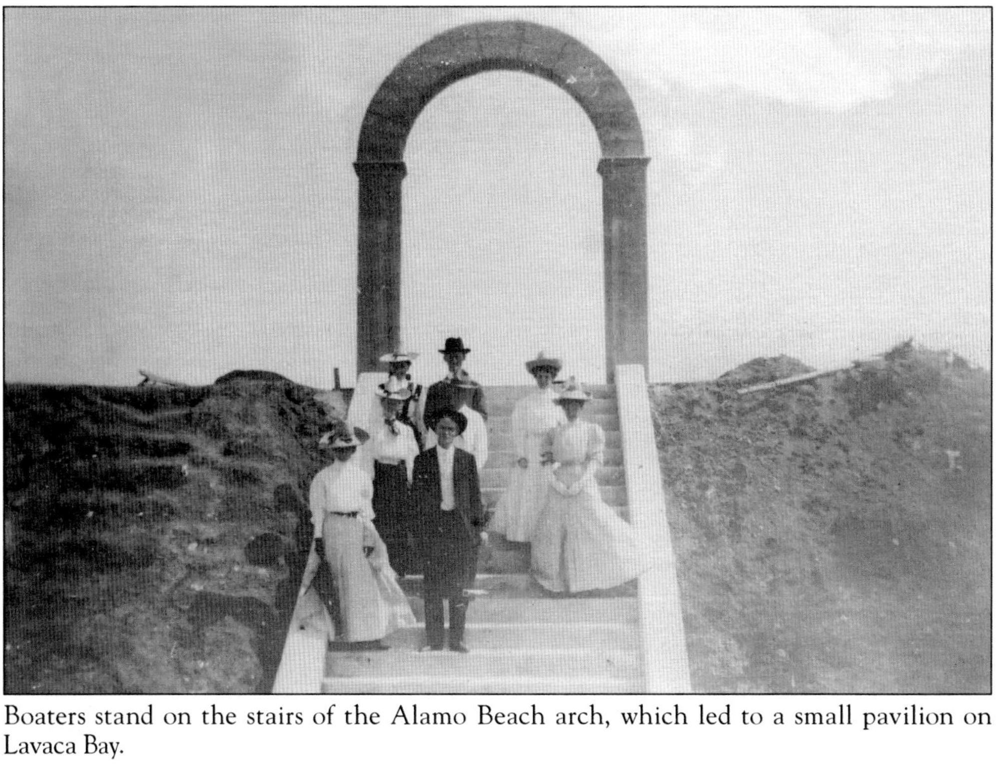

Boaters stand on the stairs of the Alamo Beach arch, which led to a small pavilion on Lavaca Bay.

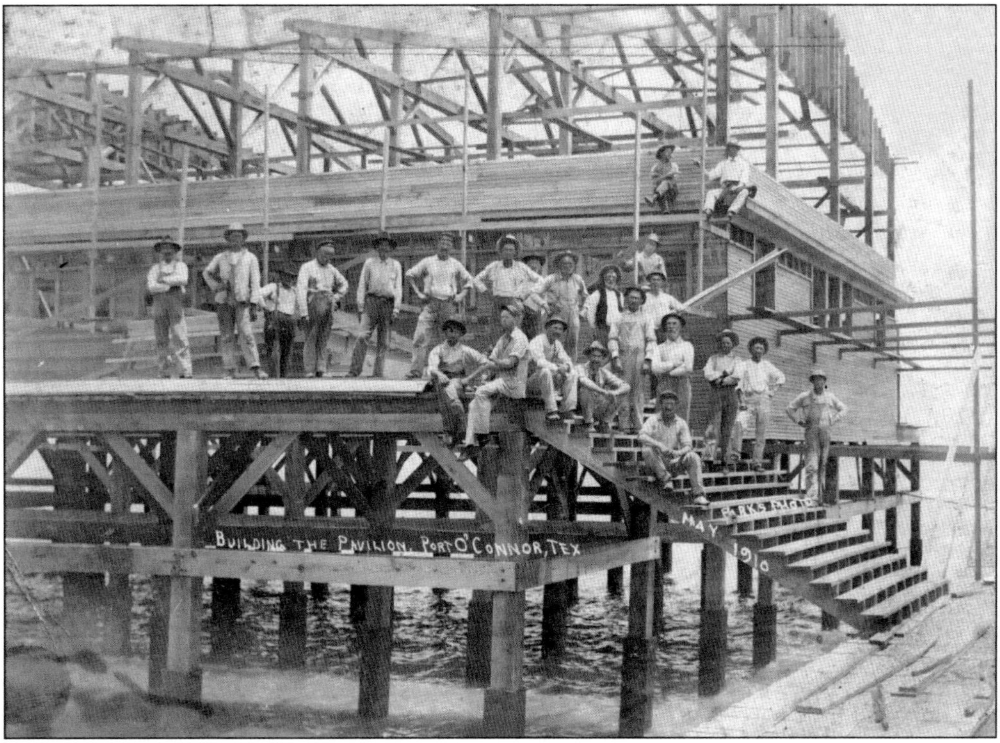

Above, workmen pause for a group photograph during the construction of the Port O'Connor Pavilion in May 1910. Below, the finished product is seen, billed as the "$20,000 Bathing and Pleasure Pavilion." It stood 60 feet by 164 feet and could accommodate about 300 guests with its 180 dressing cubicles and 120 additional "baskets."

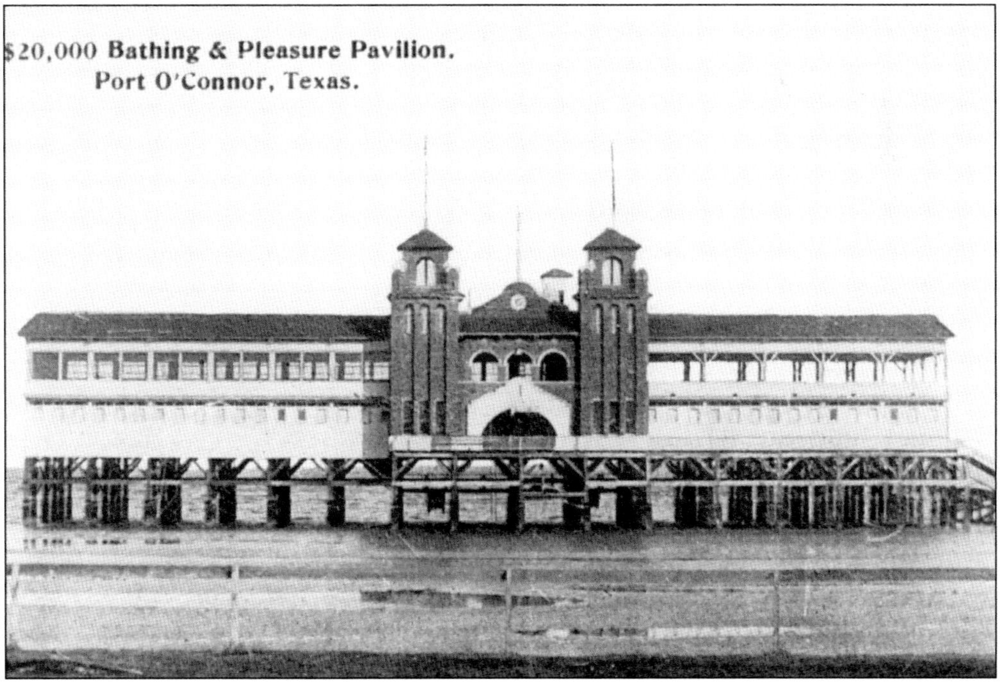

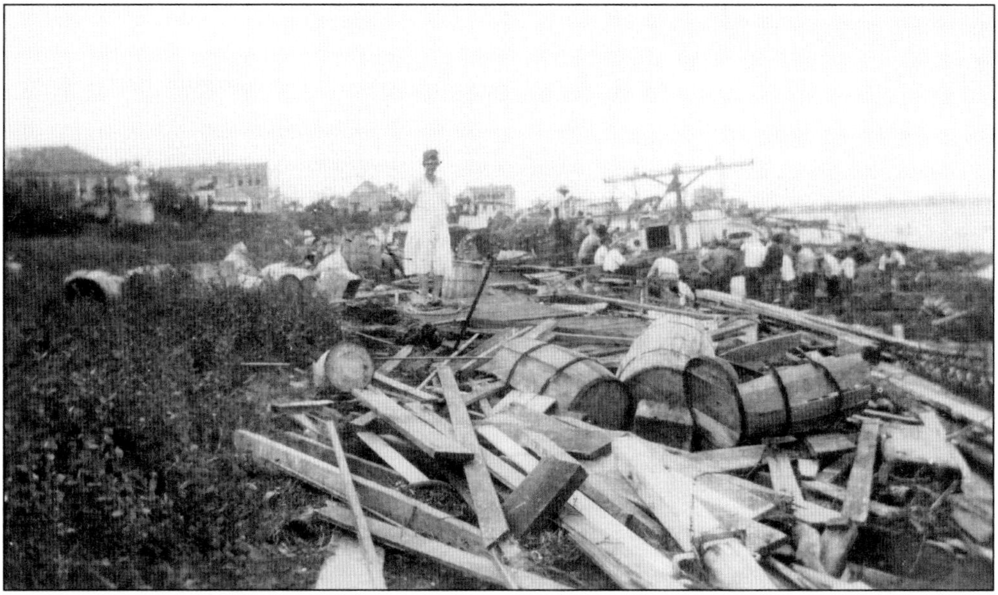

Hurricanes are a constant threat along the Texas coast. The category 4 hurricane of 1886 devastated Indianola and the surrounding area. Here, a woman stands amidst wreckage near the shore from a hurricane that hit Port Lavaca and the coast in the early 1900s.

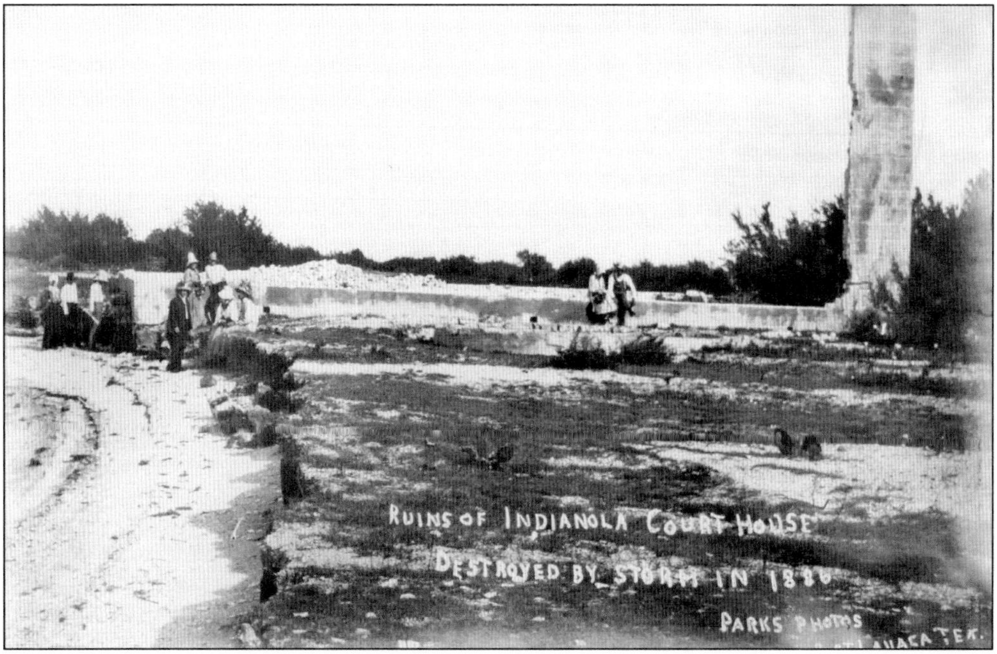

Seen here are the ruins of the once prominent Indianola courthouse in the early 1900s. Neither the 1875 or 1886 storm completely destroyed the courthouse. A resident of old Indianola, Mrs. Henry Sanders, stated, "the court house and jail were little damaged even in the 1886 storm after which the moveable things were taken to Port Lavaca which became the county seat." In the years following the 1886 hurricane, other storms and vandalism took what was left of the building. The foundation, seen here, is now approximately 50 feet out in the water because of erosion and subsidence.

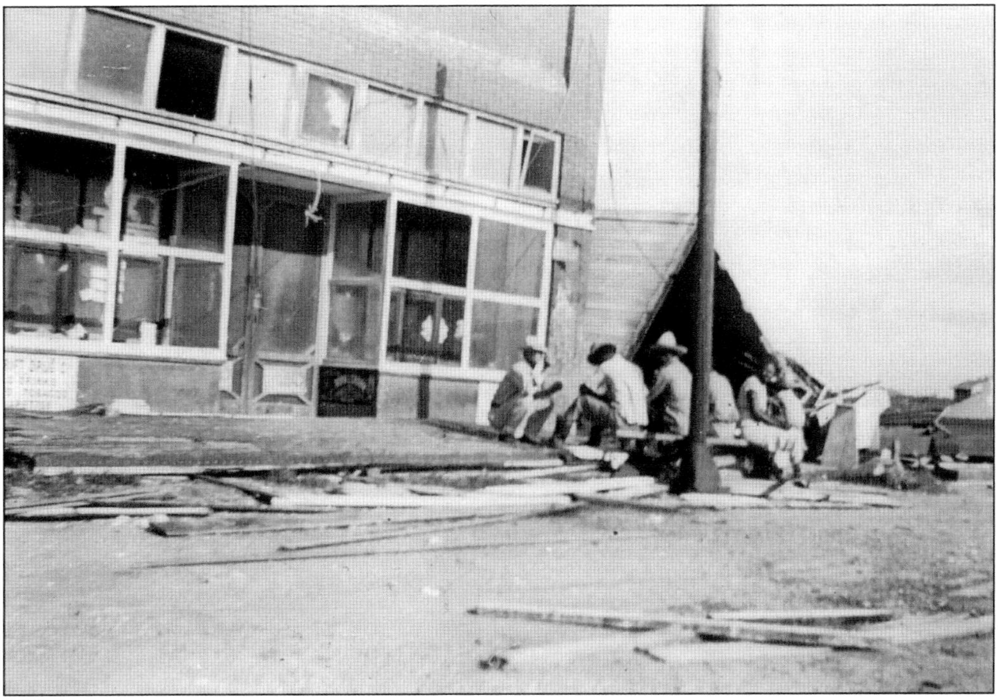

This photograph likely shows the aftermath of the 1919 hurricane. Note the blown-out windows and fallen buildings in the background.

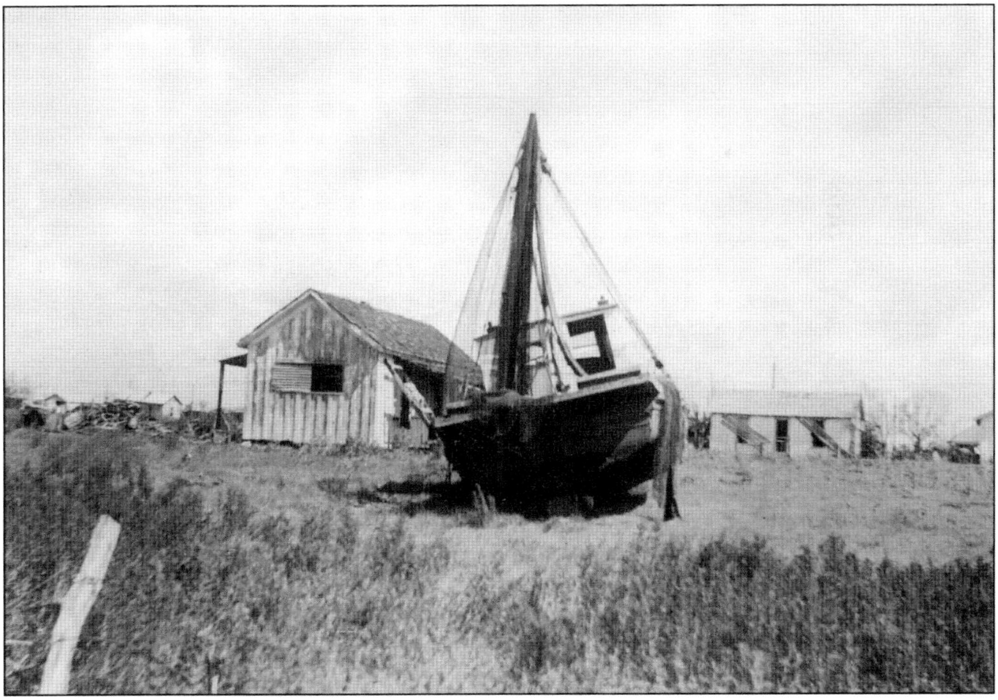

A number of hurricanes came ashore in the early 1900s. During one such storm in the 1940s, this shrimp boat was left high and dry due to the tidal surge.

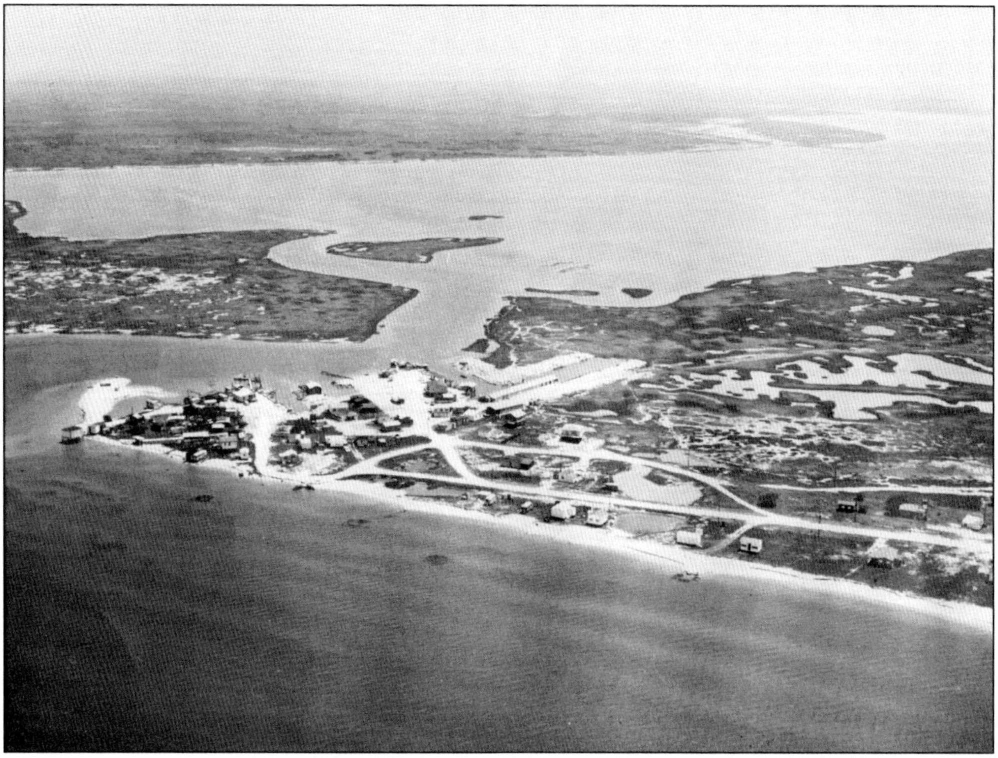

The photograph above is an aerial view of Indianola before Hurricane Carla in 1961. Below, what was at the time the longest pier in the world was damaged by Carla. It used to be the bridge connecting Port Lavaca with Point Comfort before the new causeway was built. About half of the pier was destroyed by a fire reportedly caused by lightning in the fall of 2000. A second fire occurred in June 2003, destroying an additional 350 feet of the pier.

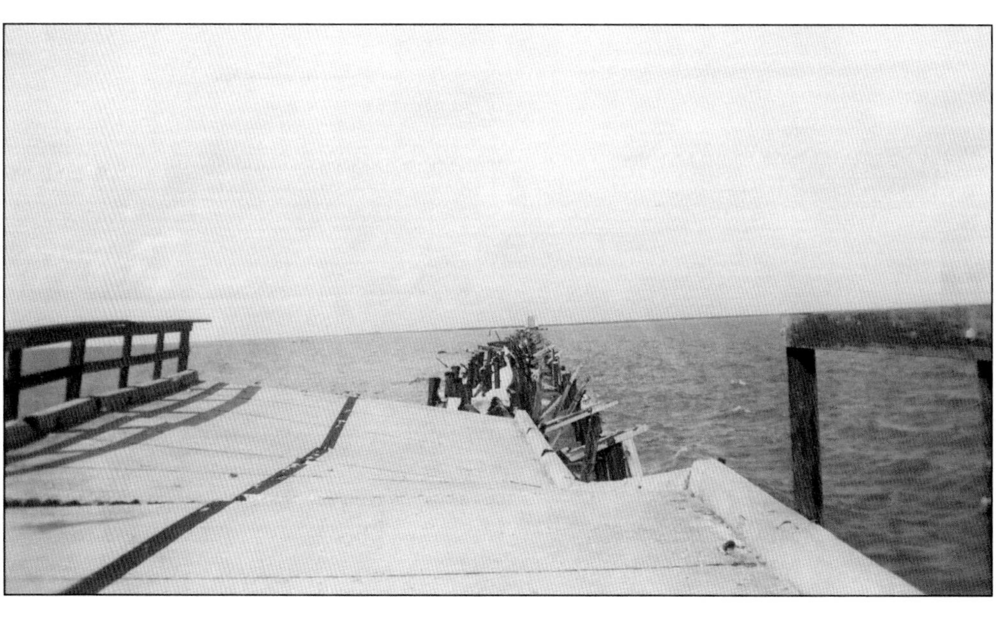

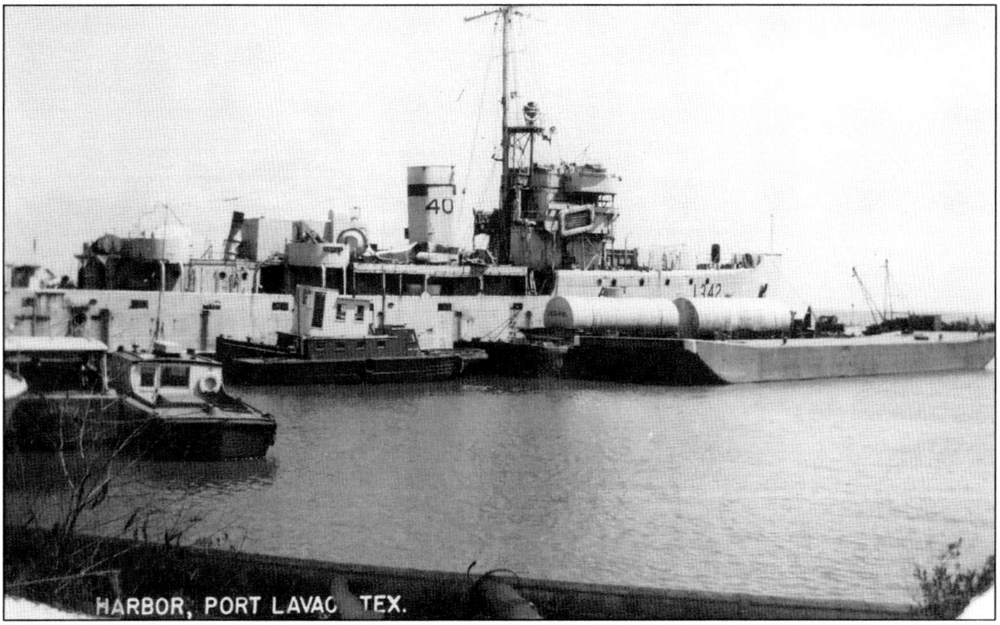

This busy scene shows a barge in the harbor of Port Lavaca. The bay was one of the busier ports on the Texas coast and brought a lot of goods and businesses to Calhoun County.

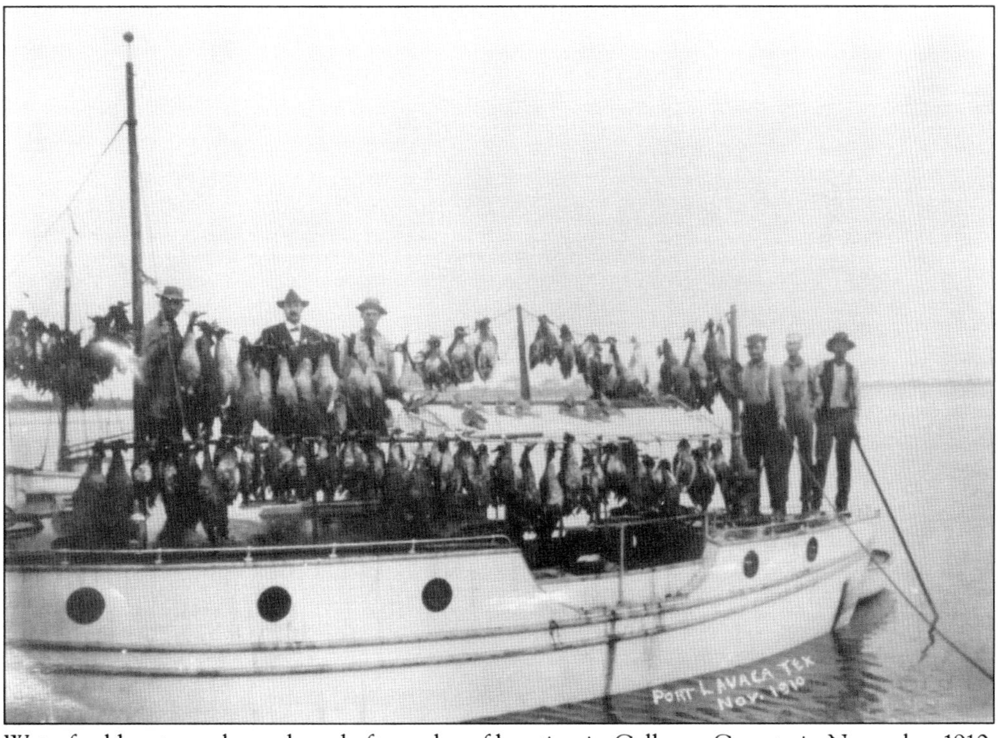

Waterfowl hunters relax onboard after a day of hunting in Calhoun County in November 1910.

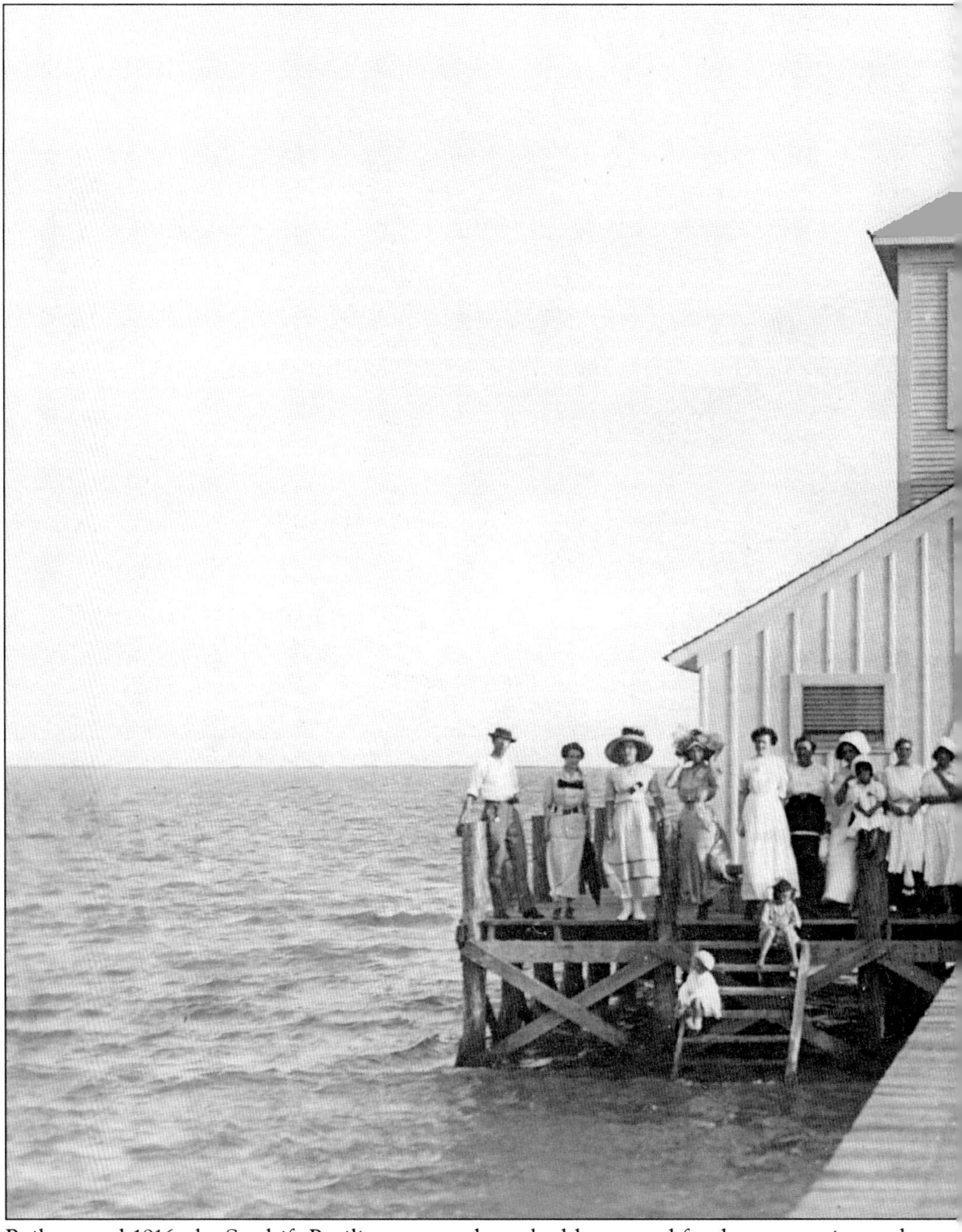

Built around 1916, the Seadrift Pavilion was used as a bathhouse and for dances, parties, and community functions. Along with much of the coastal area, it was destroyed on July 28, 1919. On May 10, 1922, the *Victorian Advocate* noted, "Seadrift Pavilion to Open Tomorrow . . . the formal opening of the Seadrift Pavilion will take place and a number of Victorians are planning to visit

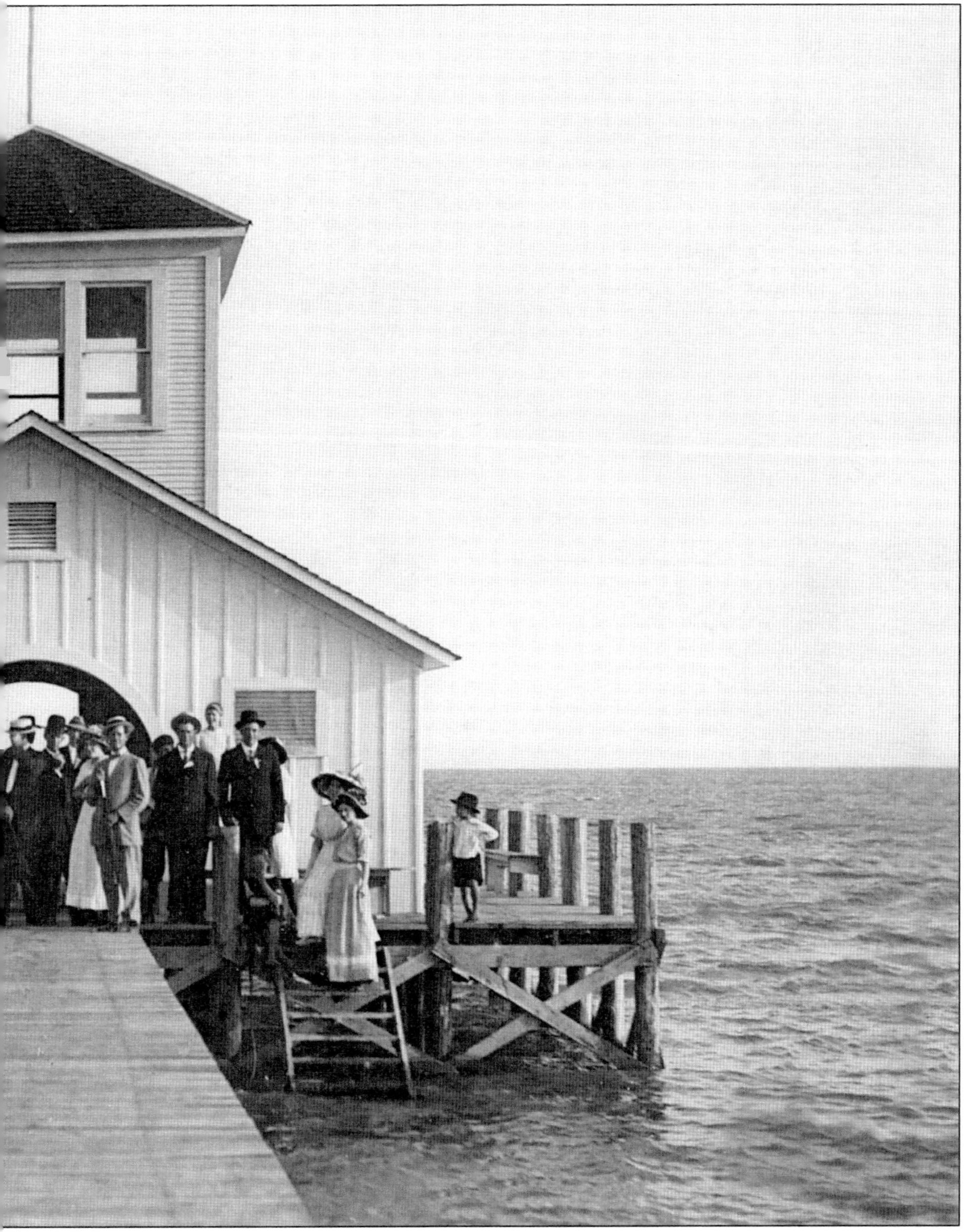

the little coast town and spend the day enjoying the opening day festivities." The article went on to describe the bathing, boating, and fish fry and barbeque at the center of activities, as well as a much-hyped baseball game between the Seadrift Sluggers and the Victoria Boosters. Much dancing also took place, compliments of music provided by the Yoakum orchestra.

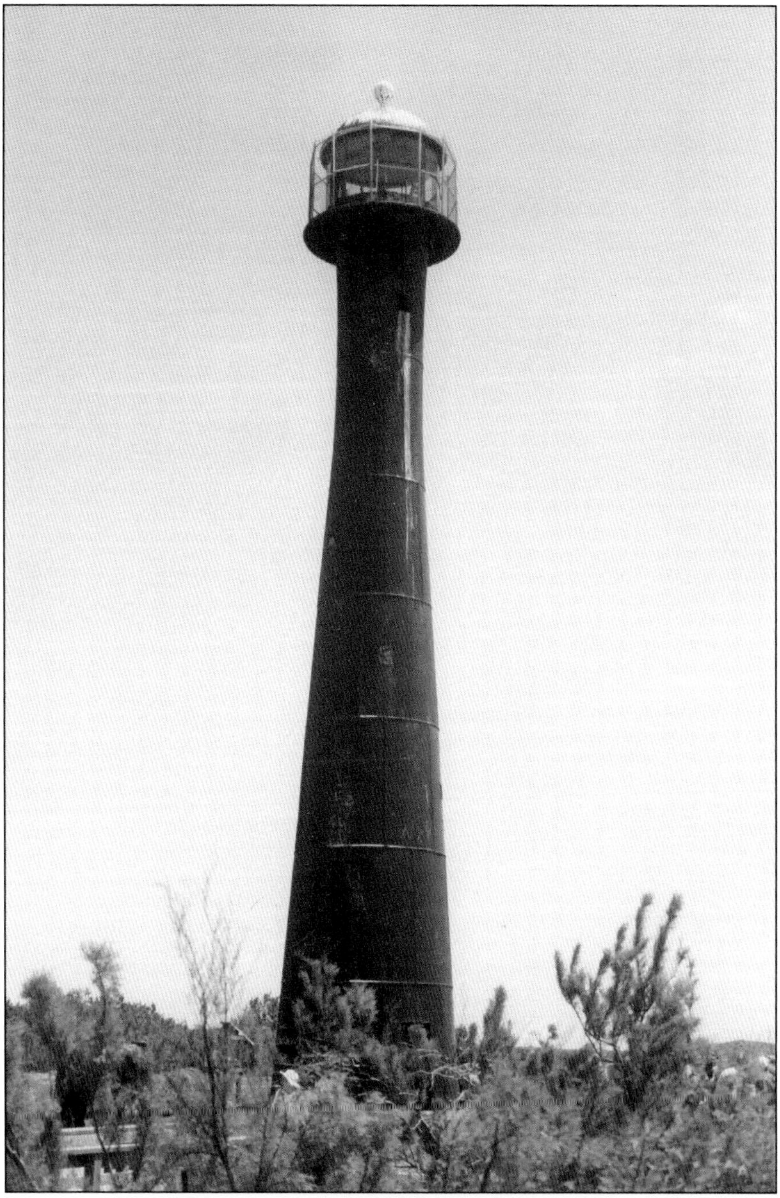

Here again is the historic lighthouse overlooking Matagorda Island. This lighthouse was listed in the National Register of Historic Places on September 18, 1984. The 92-foot-tall, charcoal colored lighthouse is actually the second such structure built on the eastern tip of the barrier island overlooking Pass Cavallo, which leads from the Gulf into Matagorda Bay. The original lighthouse, known as the Matagorda Light Station, was erected in 1852, funded by $1,500 appropriated by Congress. It suffered extensive damage in the early 1860s when Confederate troops removed its Fresnel lens and tried to destroy the tower to prevent the Union army from benefiting from its guiding light. In 1873, what remained of the old structure was dismantled, moved, and rebuilt two miles inland using the same iron plates. At that time, the red-and-white-striped tower was painted black and a new Fresnel lens was installed. That lens, which was removed in 1977, is now on display at the Calhoun County Museum in Port Lavaca. This photograph was taken in 2004 by the author.

Three

AGRICULTURE AND INDUSTRY

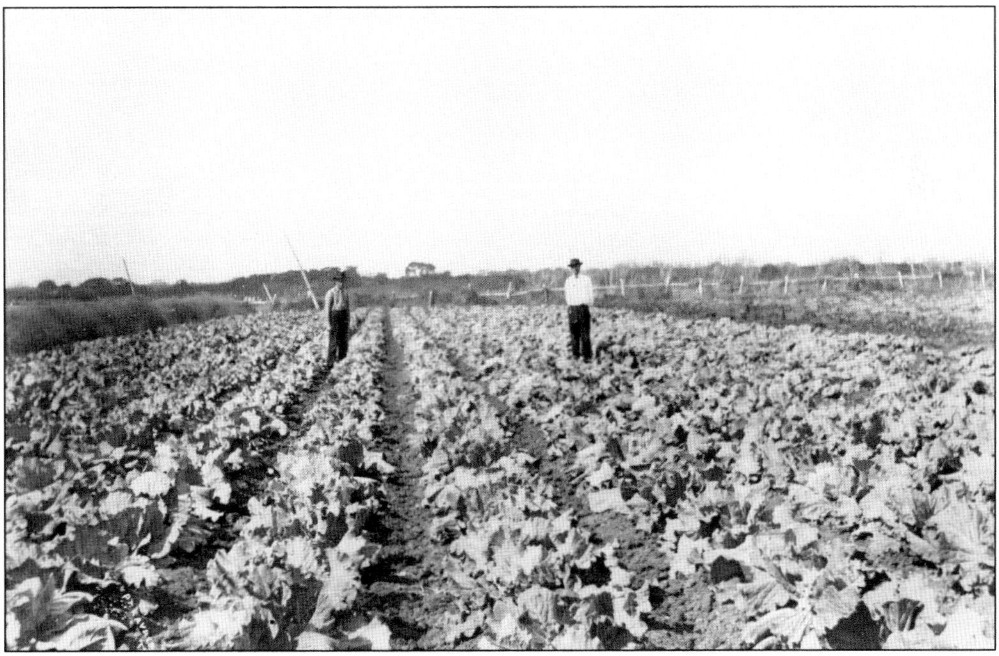

Two men stand in a large cabbage field near Port Lavaca. Cabbage became a staple crop in Calhoun County's thriving agricultural market.

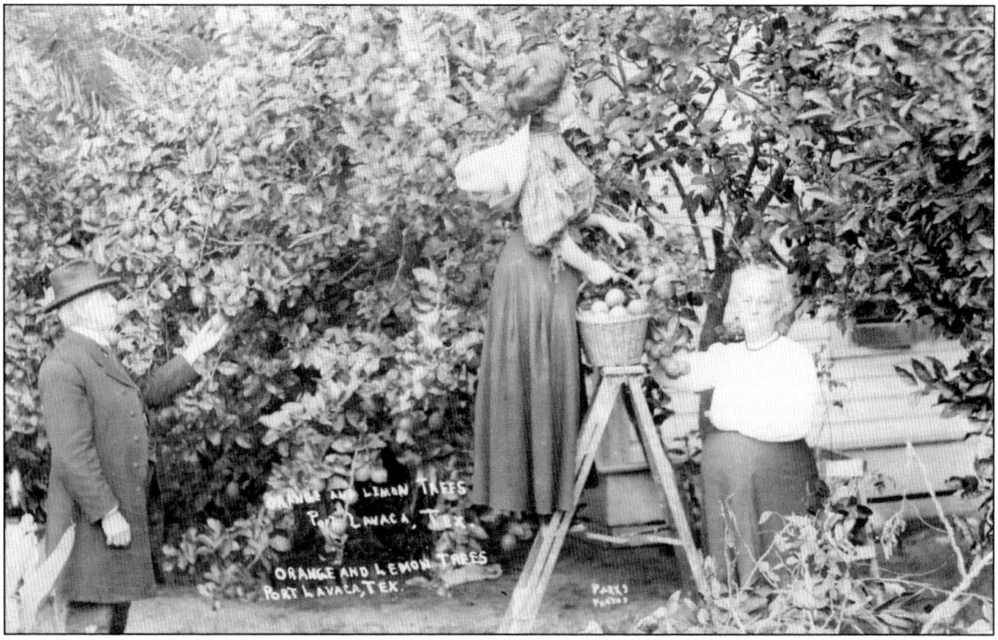

Coastal weather around Port Lavaca allowed for the growing of citrus fruit. Here, a family harvests a portion of their crop—orange and lemon trees ready for the picking.

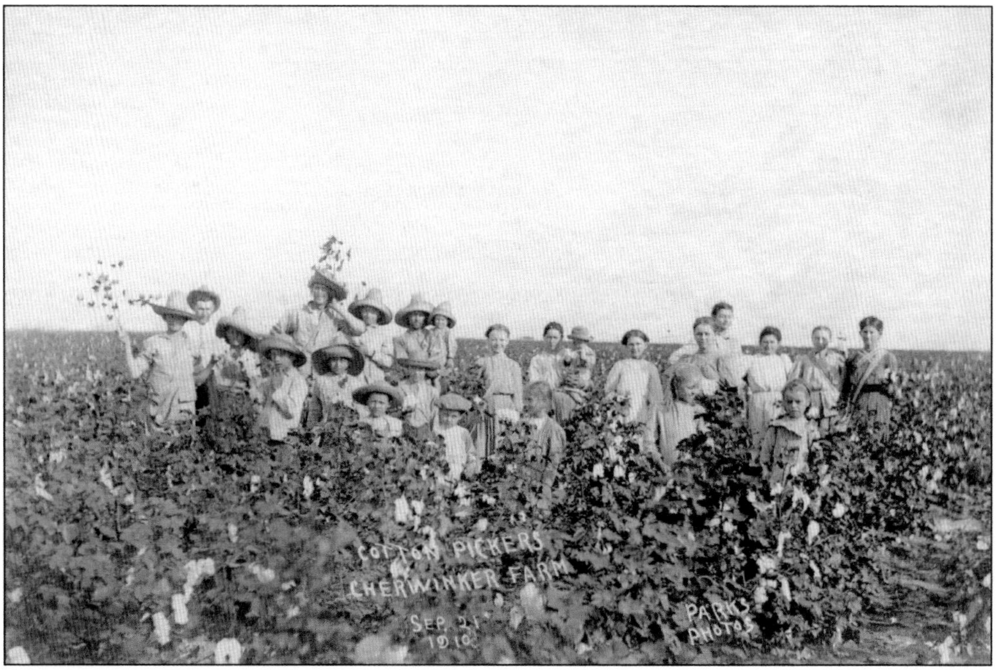

A large group of cotton pickers, mostly children, pose for the camera on the Cherwenka farm on September 21, 1910.

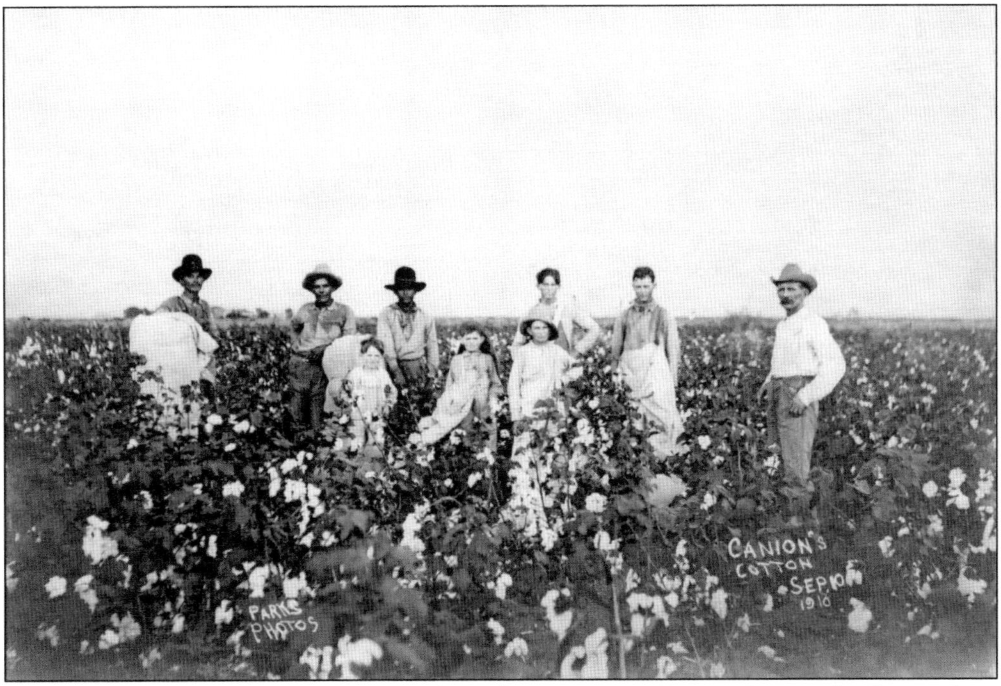

Cotton was and still is an important crop for Calhoun County. Here, pickers on the Canion farm work to harvest it on September 10, 1910.

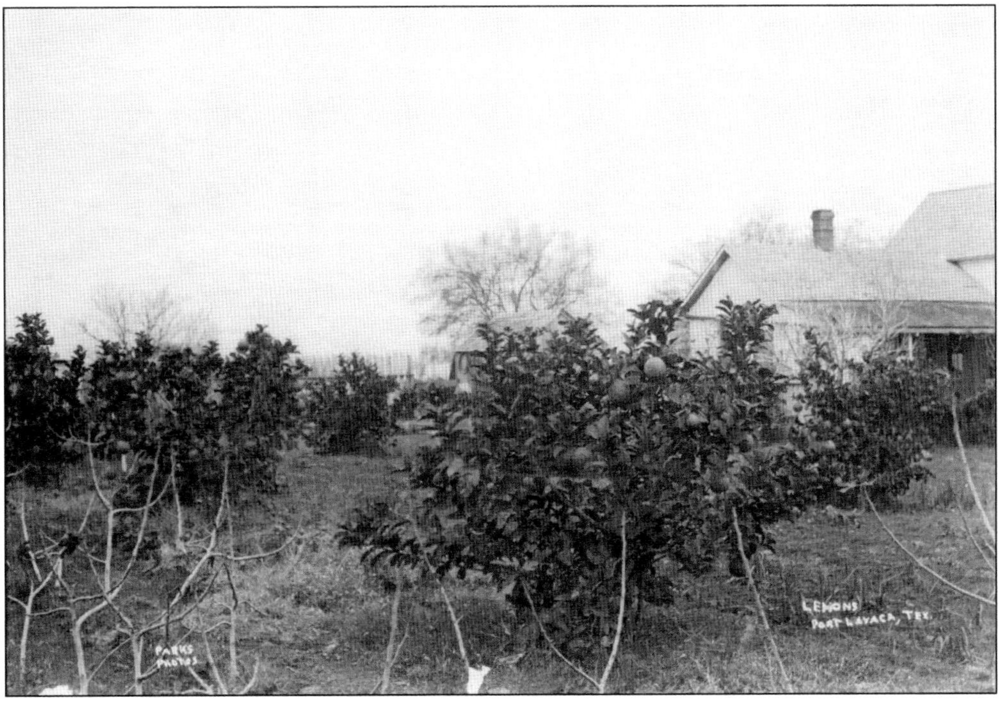

This small orchard of lemon trees appears nearly ready to pick in the early 1900s.

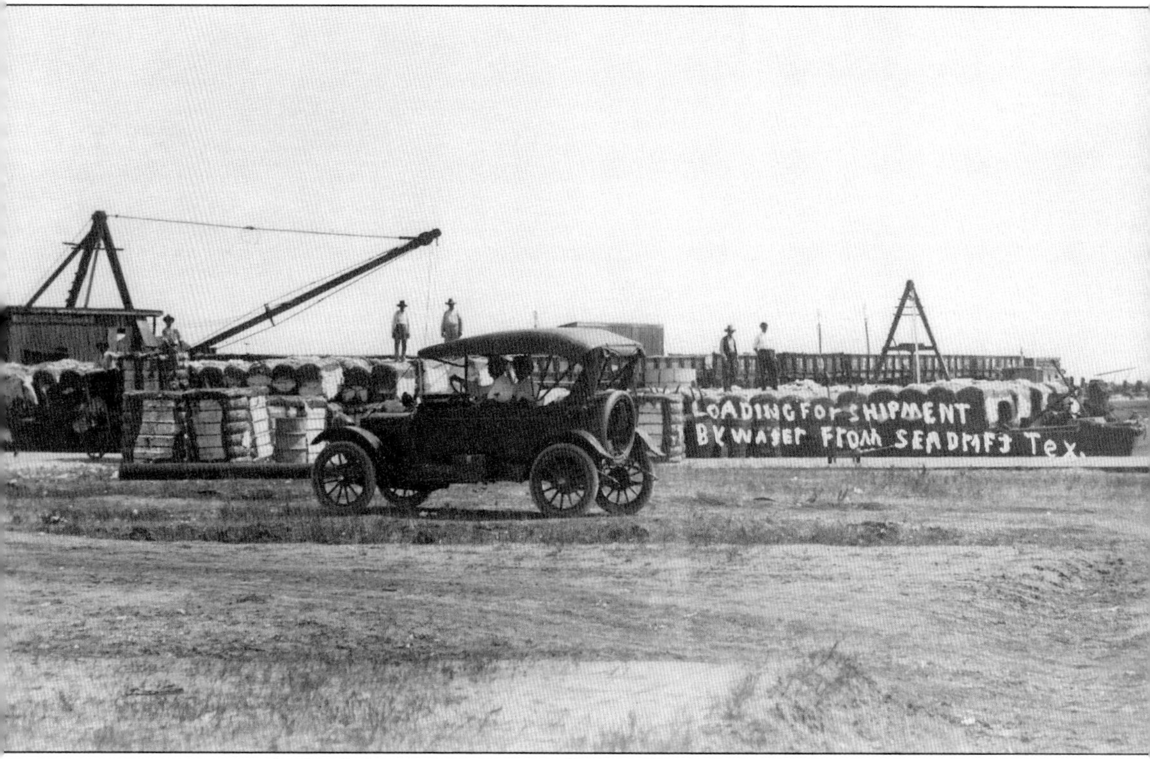

Cotton waits to be loaded onto boats in Seadrift in the early 1900s.

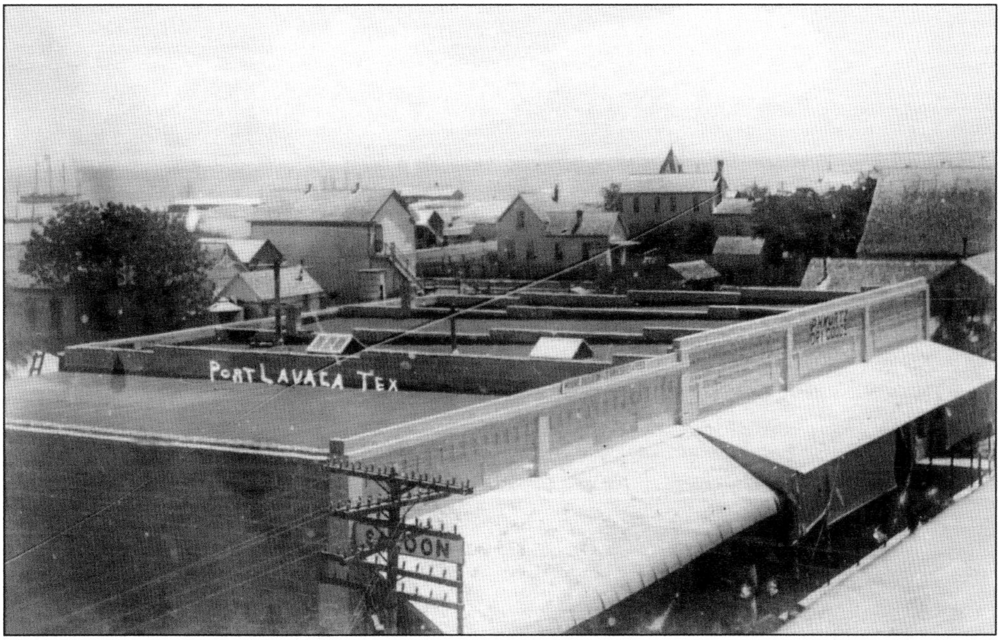

In this elevated view of Main Street in Port Lavaca, a saloon and P.H. Kurtz Dry Goods are in the foreground, with Lavaca Bay in the distance.

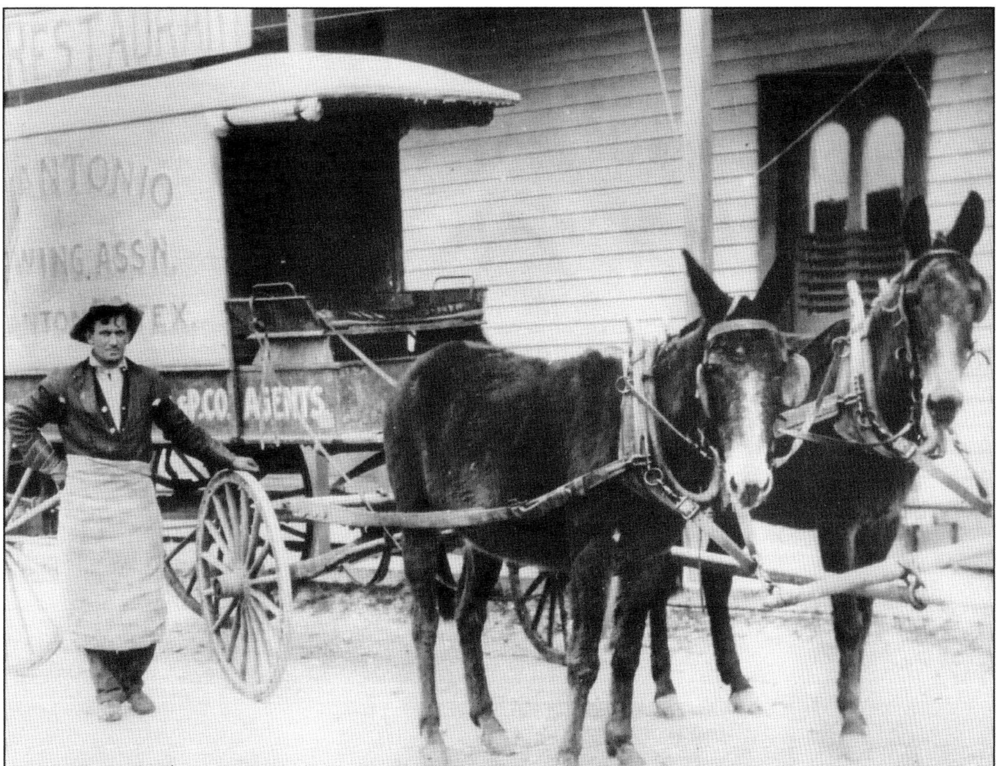

John Boyd stands with his mules at a restaurant and saloon at the corner of South Commerce and Center Streets. The mule-drawn cart was delivering ice.

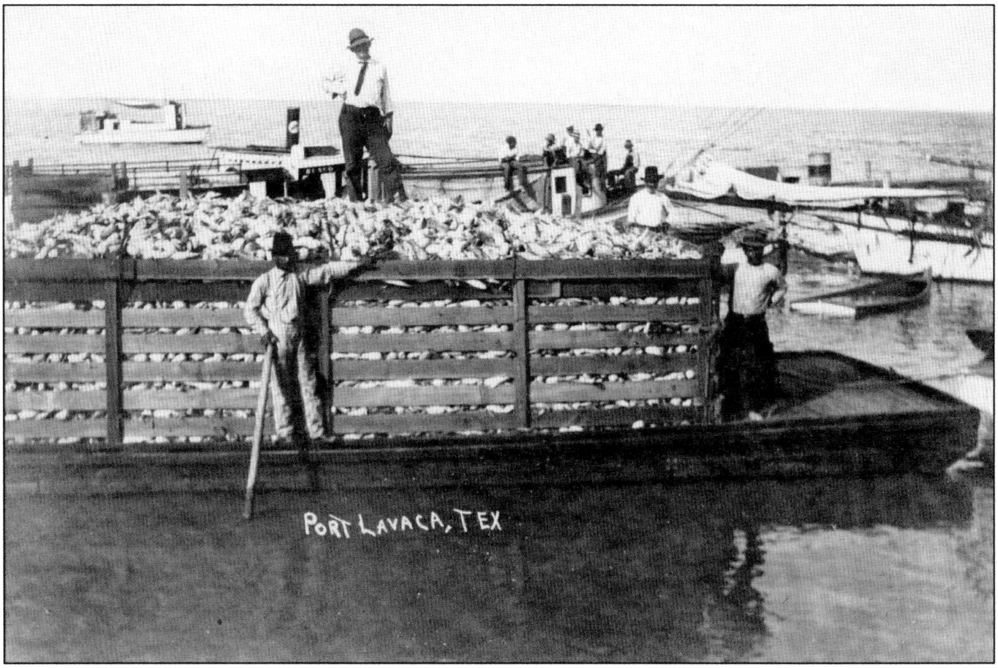

Corn and cotton are still grown in Calhoun County. In the early 1900s, the crops were moved swiftly on the bay by small barges.

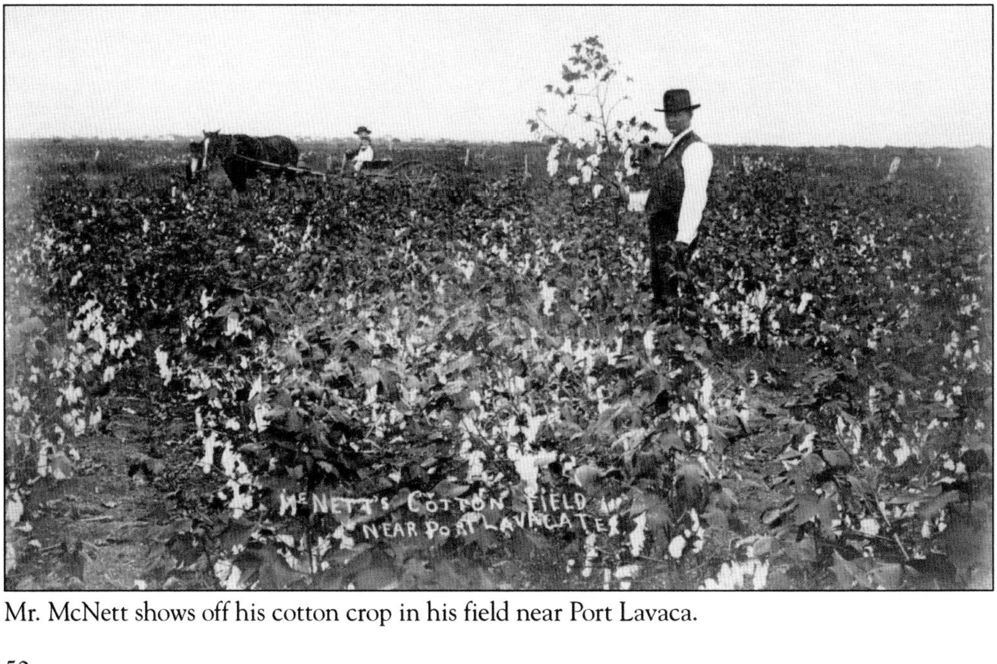

Mr. McNett shows off his cotton crop in his field near Port Lavaca.

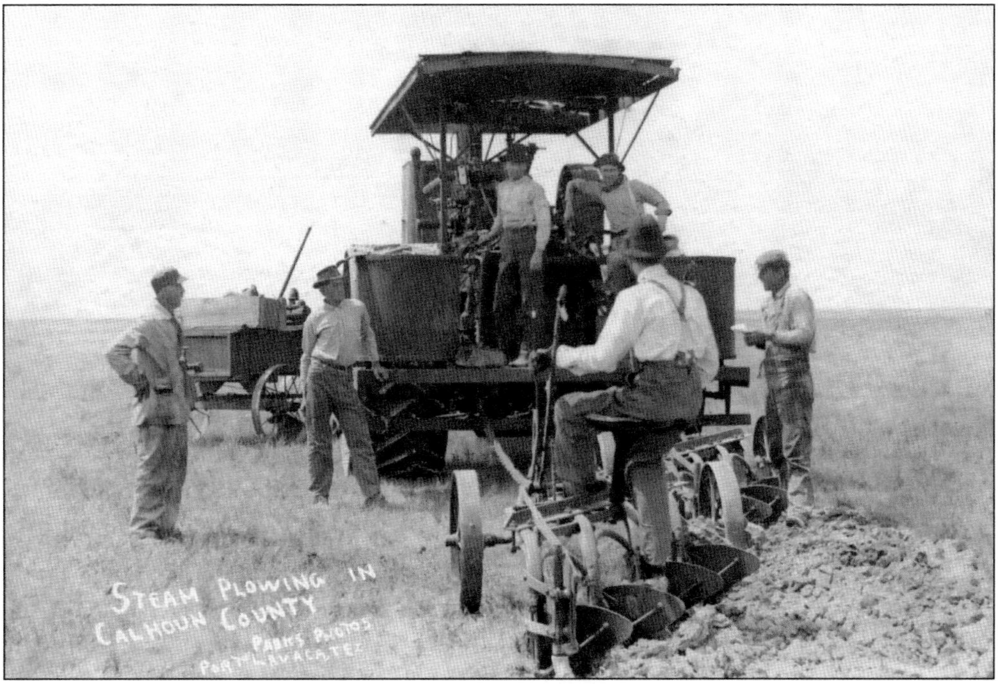

Plowing fields was no easy feat in the early 1900s. Above, Calhoun County farmers use a steam plow to prepare the fields for planting. At right, Joseph Morse Bickford was a teacher at Saluria on Matagorda Island. Bickford also served as a captain in the Confederacy. He started the Lavaca Institute after the Civil War. It soon became one of the best schools in southwest Texas. After 1869, he became a store owner, raised cattle, and was a prominent Mason. As a Mason, Bickford held every office. He was also a school examiner and county treasurer.

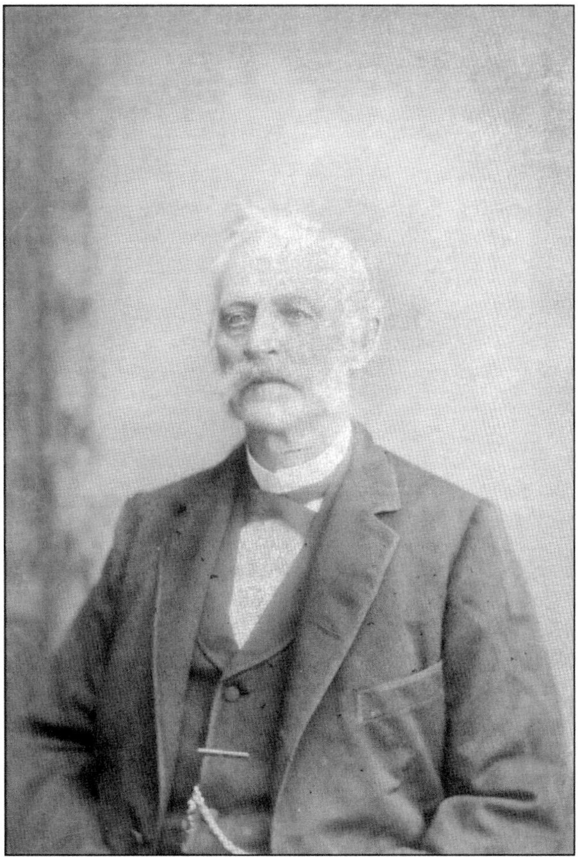

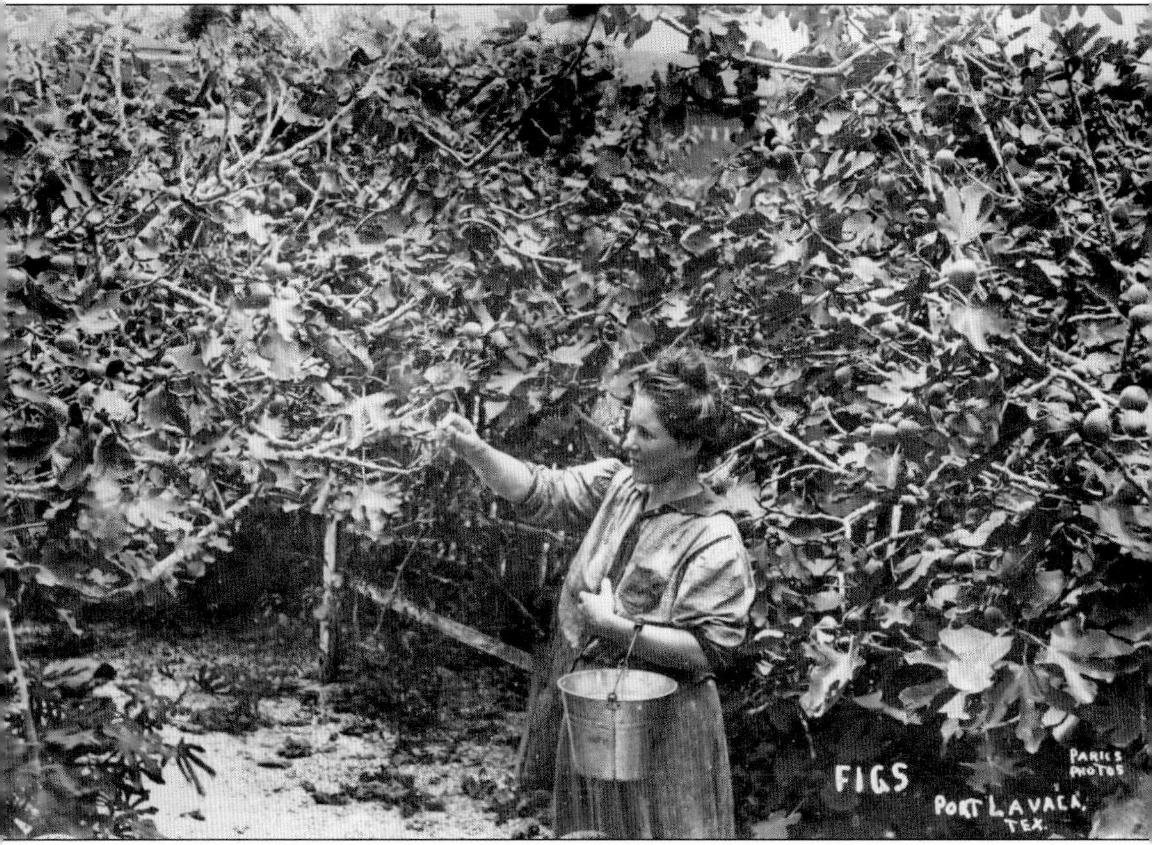

Calhoun County has had several fig farms in its history. In this Percy Parks photograph from around 1910, a woman checks for ripe fruit to harvest.

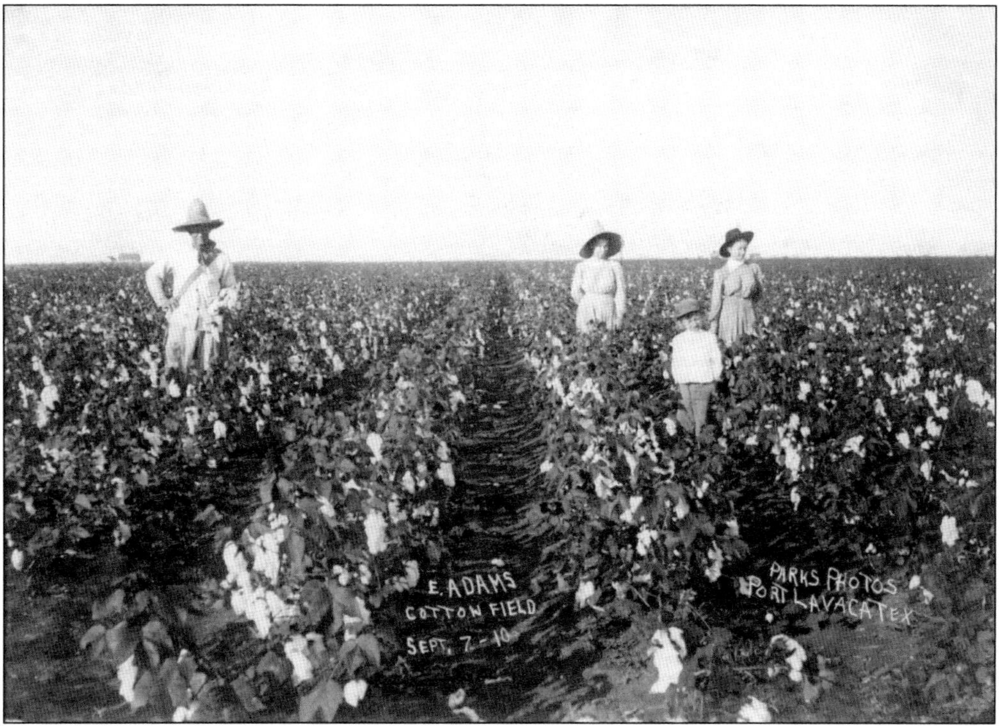

Cotton was an especially important crop in Calhoun County in the early 1900s. The E. Adams cotton field is seen here on September 7, 1910. Cotton is still a large cash crop in the county.

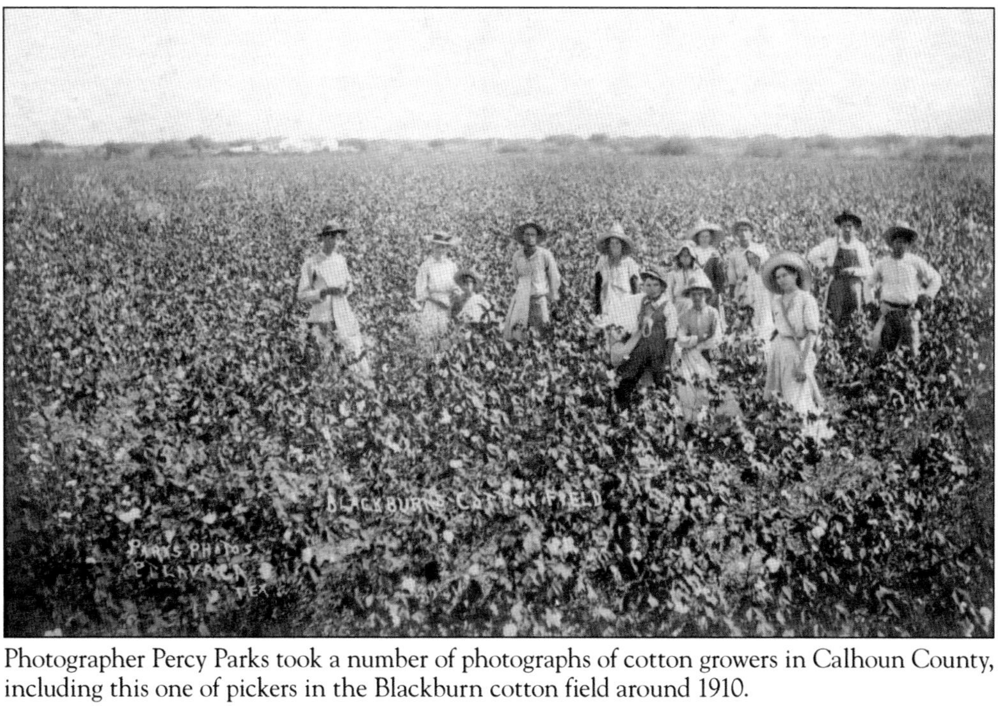

Photographer Percy Parks took a number of photographs of cotton growers in Calhoun County, including this one of pickers in the Blackburn cotton field around 1910.

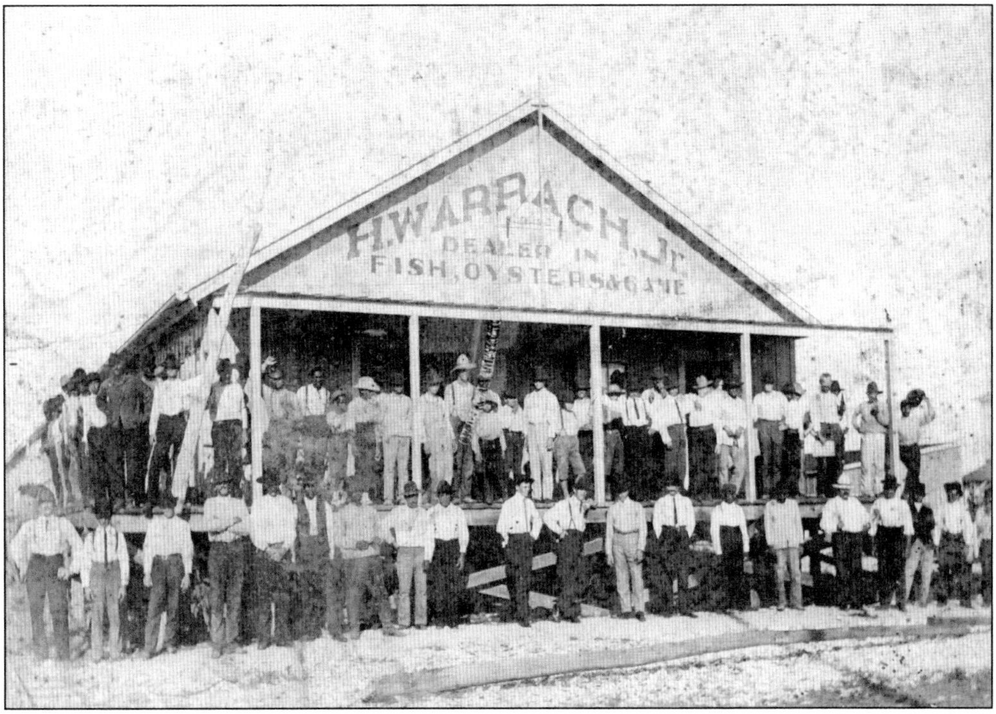

It is presumed that the group of men pictured above worked for Herman Warrach Jr., who dealt in fish, oysters, and game in Port Lavaca around 1900. By the time Warrach was 21 years old, he was already in the wholesale business, selling fish and oysters. The photograph was taken by George Beach, a view photographer and Kodak specialist from Houston. Below is Warrach's small yacht, the *Merrill*.

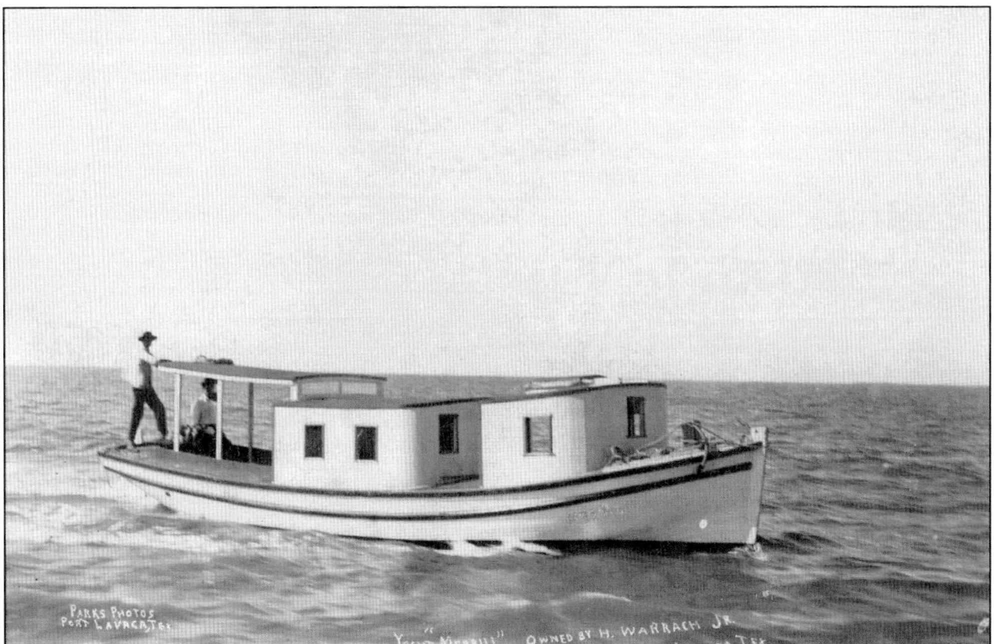

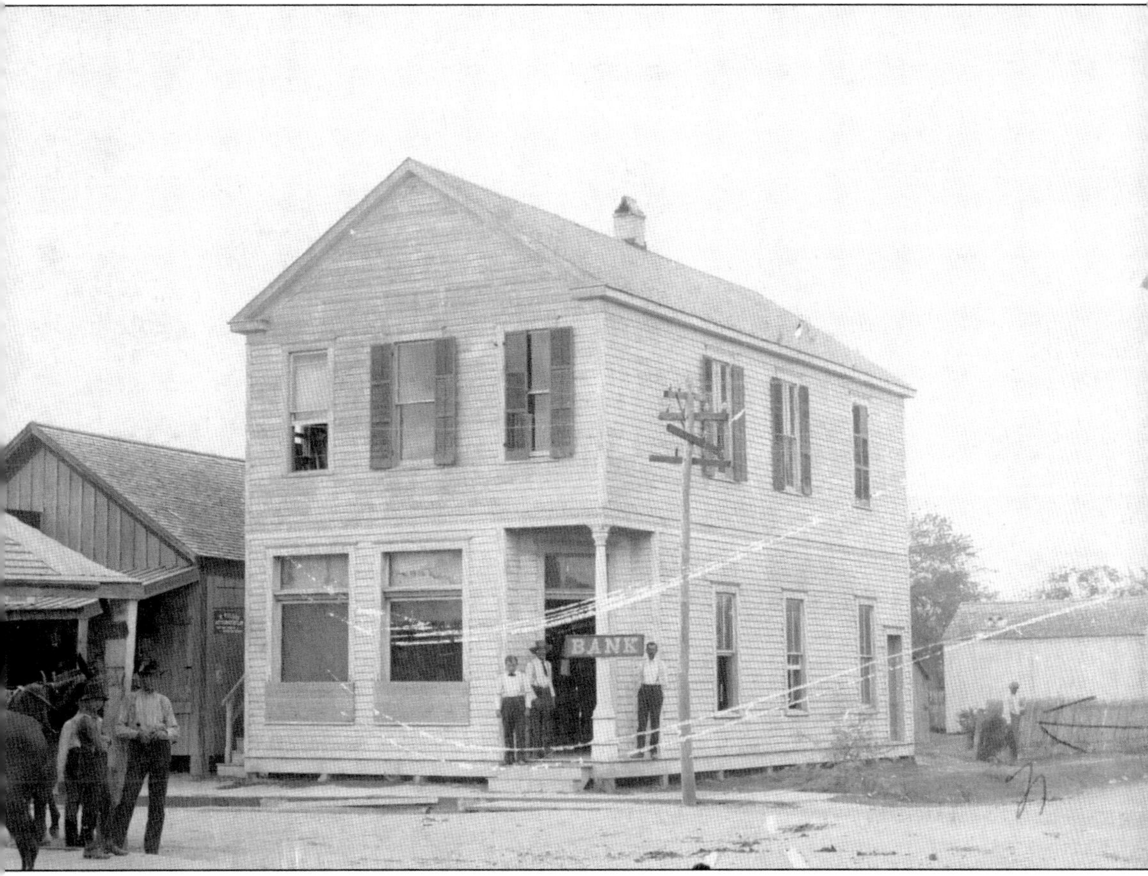

Originally the Bank of Port Lavaca, this bank became known as the First National Bank in 1900. Standing at the right is the cashier, William Calhoun Noble. Harry Bickford, his assistant, is standing to the left on the top step. The open window on the second floor was Willett Wilson's law office, and the building to the left of the bank was Delfres Emile Guidry's first store, commonly called the Racket Store. Across the street, beside the horses, are Duke Whittenburg (the taller boy) and Clark Blardone. Mr. Lacker stands in the far right background, near the small building where Lucille Bickford had a kindergarten. The bank was located on South Guadalupe and Austin Streets on lot seven, block 12 of the original town site. It was originally owned by Felix Jackson before it was bought by First National Bank.

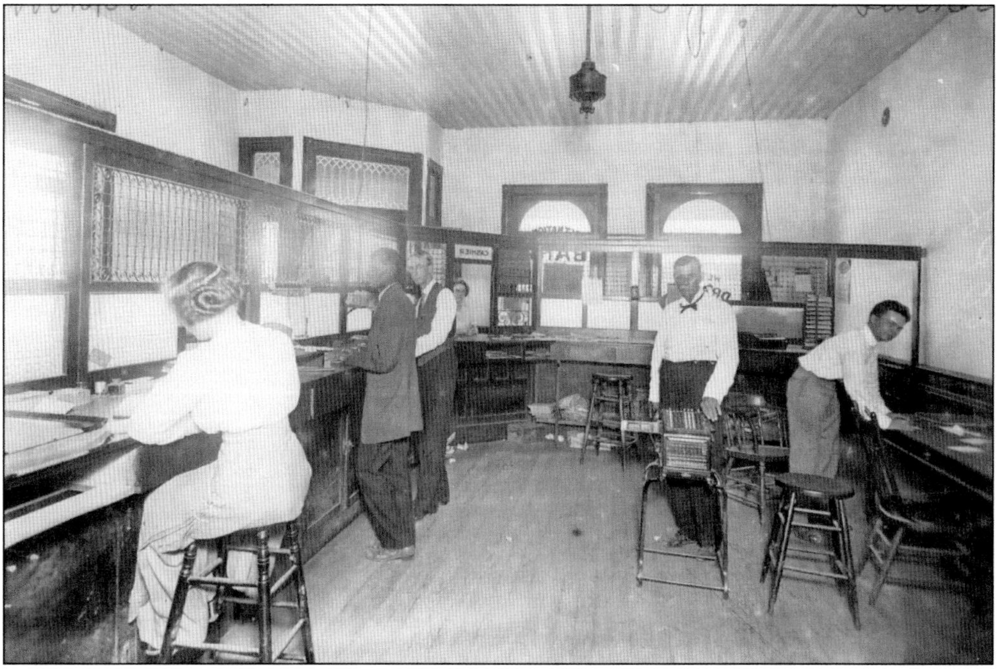

In July 1900, the First National Bank opened its doors. This interior photograph looks out from the point of view of the bank employees, with employees W.C. Noble second from right, Garner McConnico at far right, and Irene Rose "Wink" Michot at far left.

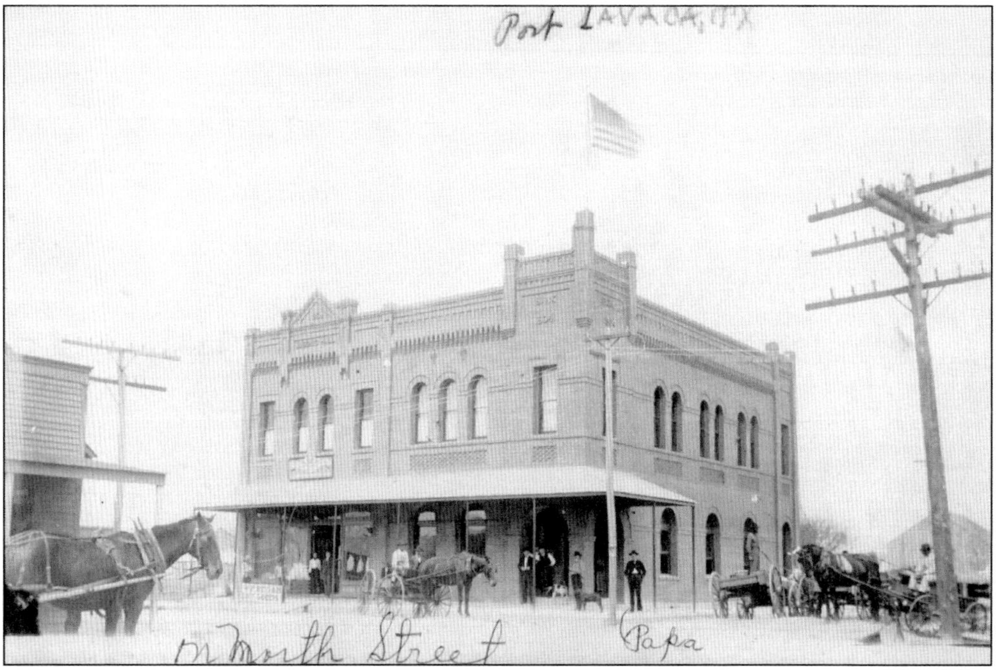

When the First National Bank first opened, W.C. Noble was the cashier. After the bank consolidated with the First State Bank in 1923, the building became the post office, which it remained until 1949. This first building was on North Street (now Main Street). W.P. Regan Dry Goods is on the first floor on the left side of the building, with the Masonic Hall above it.

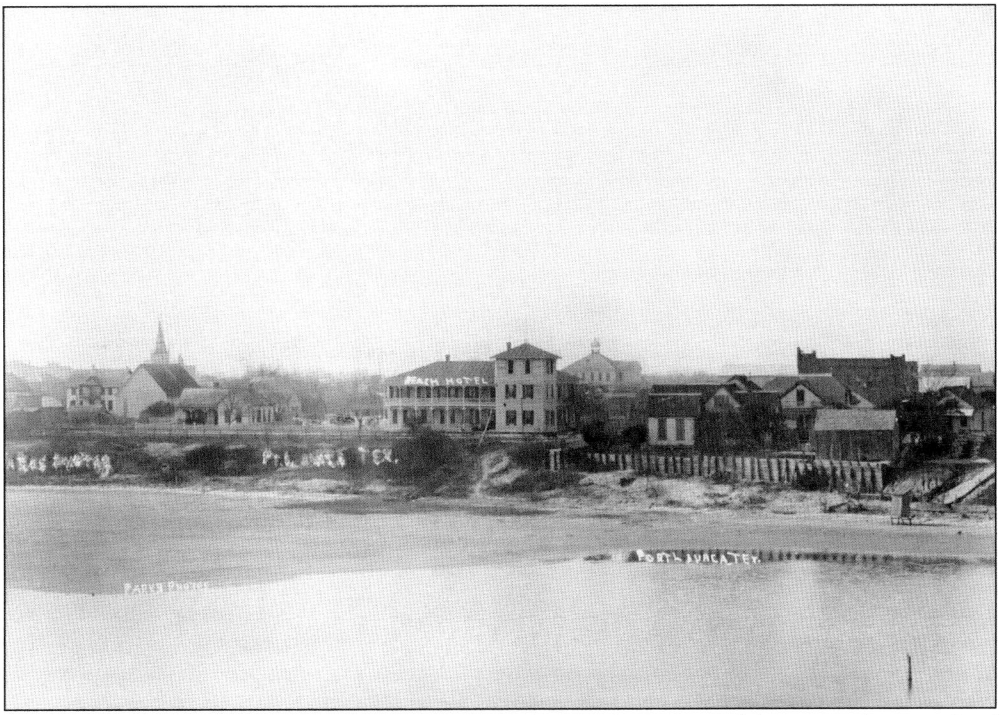

The Beach Hotel, also known as the Lavaca Hotel, is in the center of this 1910 photograph of the bay front at Port Lavaca.

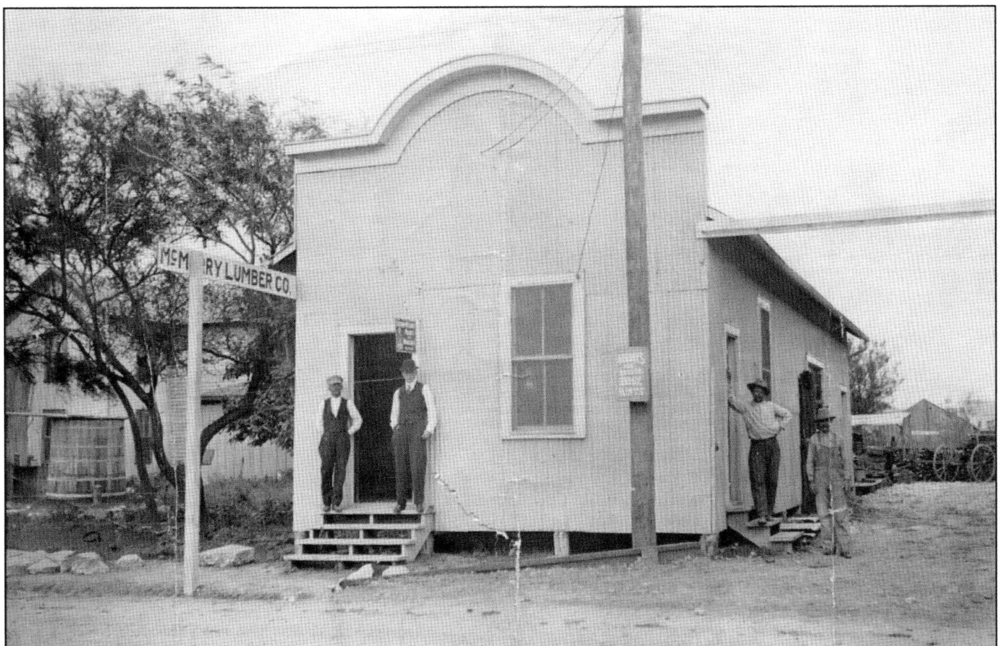

The McMurry Lumber Company office on Virginia Street in Port Lavaca is seen here. In front of it are, from left to right, Acy B. Jackson, Cornelius Stierling, Chas. H. Reichardt, and Tom Kelly. Stierling was mayor of Port Lavaca from April 16, 1928, to July 1, 1929.

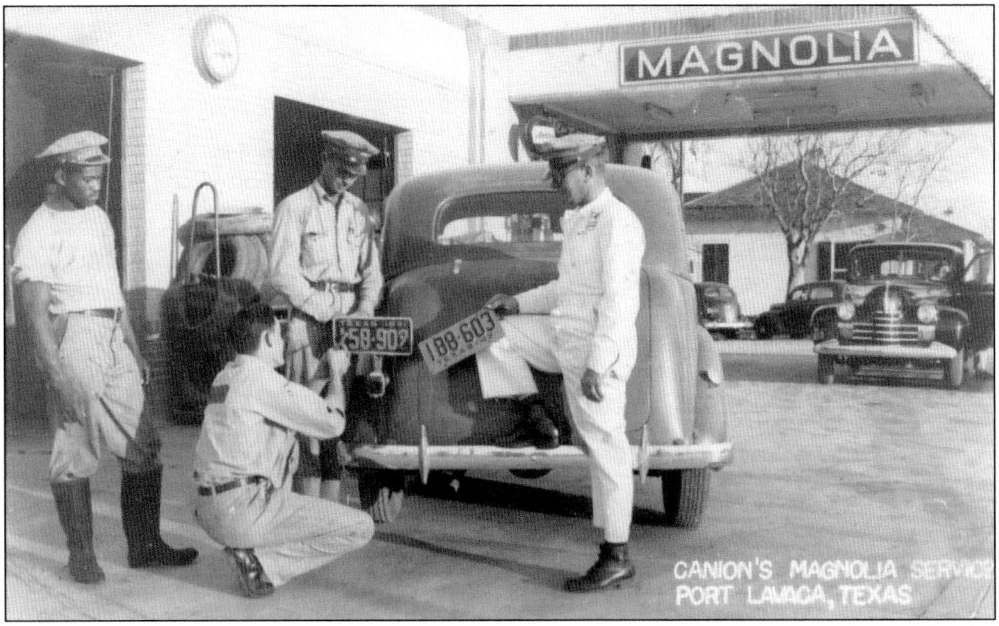

The Magnolia service station was run by Marsh Fields Canion in 1942. It was owned by the Magnolia Petroleum Company and was on the corner of Main and Commerce Streets. By the time World War II began, Canion had moved on to work for the Port Lavaca post office.

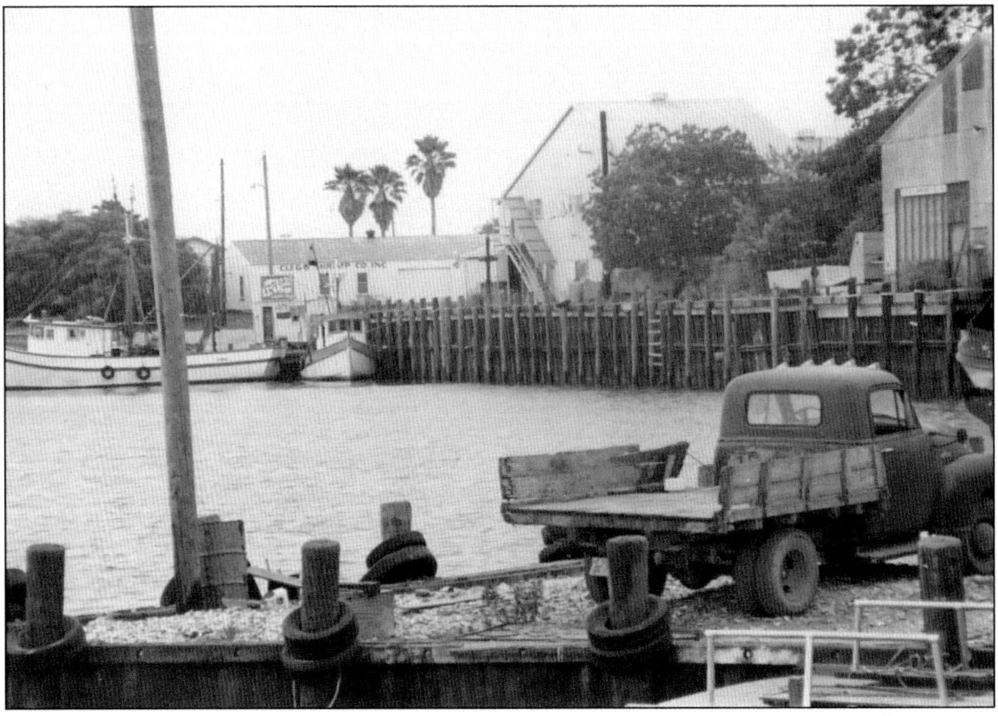

The Clegg Shrimp Co. and Anton's Shrimp House were located on the water's edge in Port Lavaca harbor.

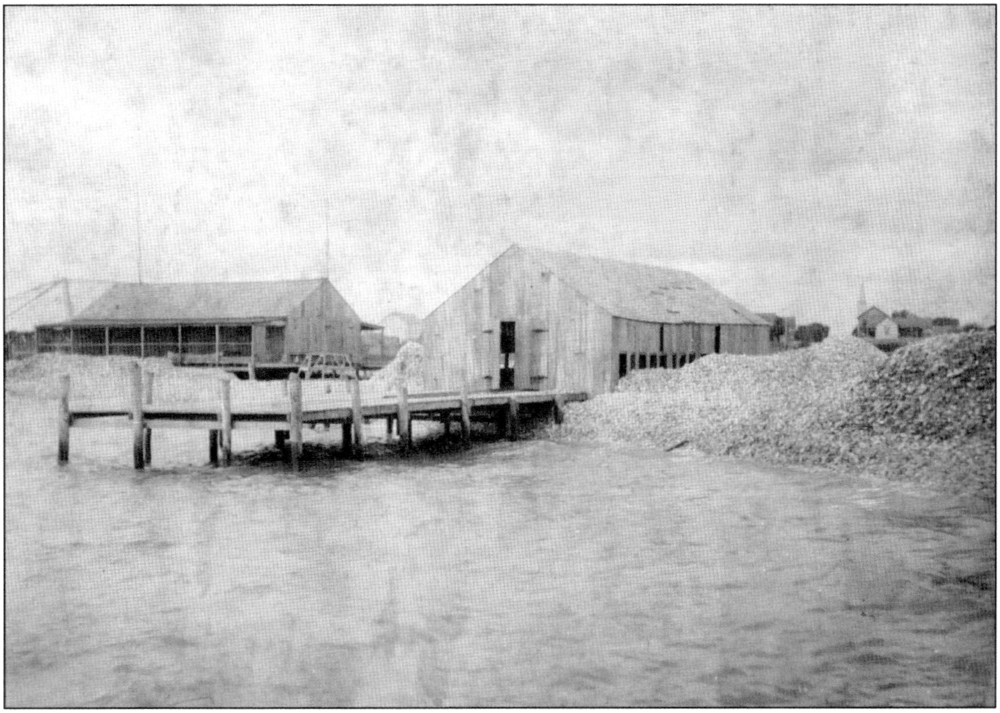

Oysters were an important commodity in the early 20th century. Here are just two of the many oyster houses near the bay.

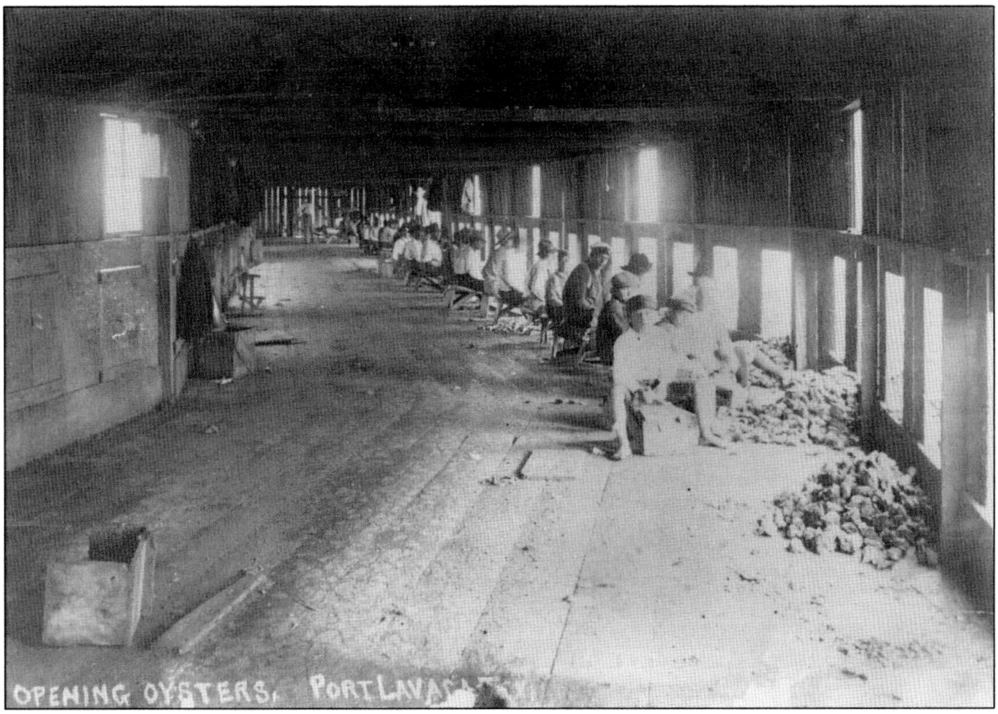

Shucking oysters was backbreaking work. Each man worked at a window on a low stool and threw the shells of the shucked oysters out of the window of this early oyster house.

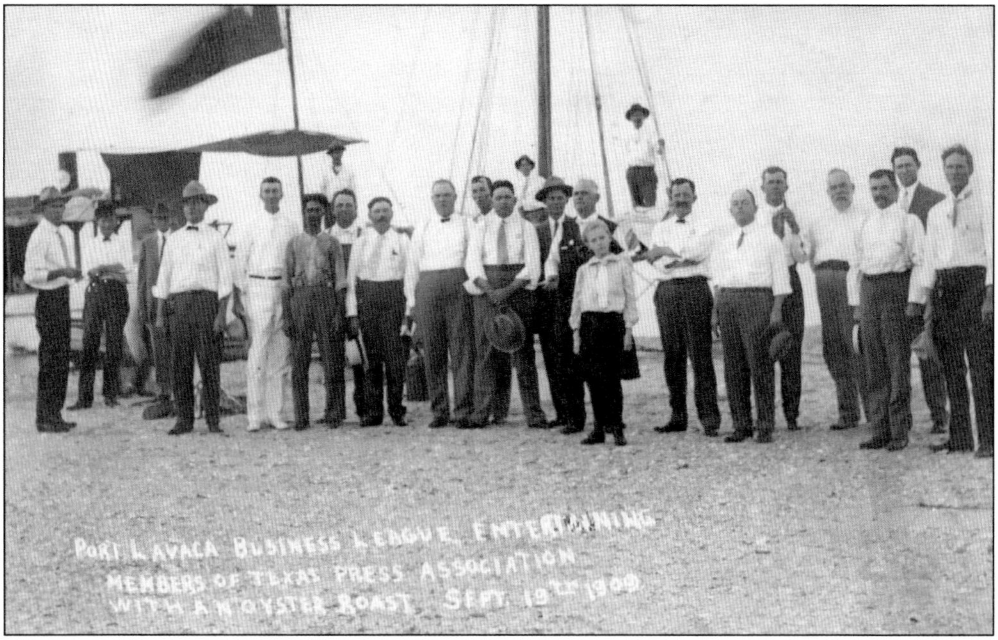

On September 19, 1909, the Port Lavaca Business League hosted this oyster roast at the edge of Lavaca Bay for members of the Texas Press Association.

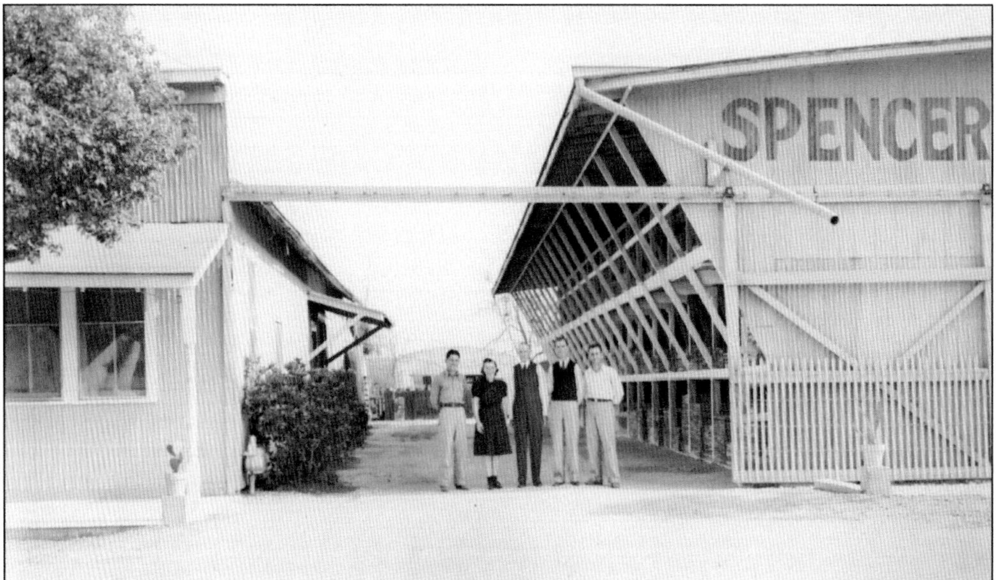

The lumber yard in Port O'Connor was begun in 1909 and managed by J.A. Armstrong. The yard was destroyed in the storm of 1919. All identifiable stock was moved to a lumberyard at Seadrift to be sold. In 1932, the Seadrift lumberyard was consolidated with the McMurry lumberyard at Port Lavaca. The combined business was successful and alternated with the railroad in being the most prosperous business in town. Here, Burnice G. Miller, Homoiselle Stierling, Cornelius Victor Stierling, Arthur Braden, and Woodrow Dierlam stand in front of the Spencer-Sauer Lumber Company in January 1939.

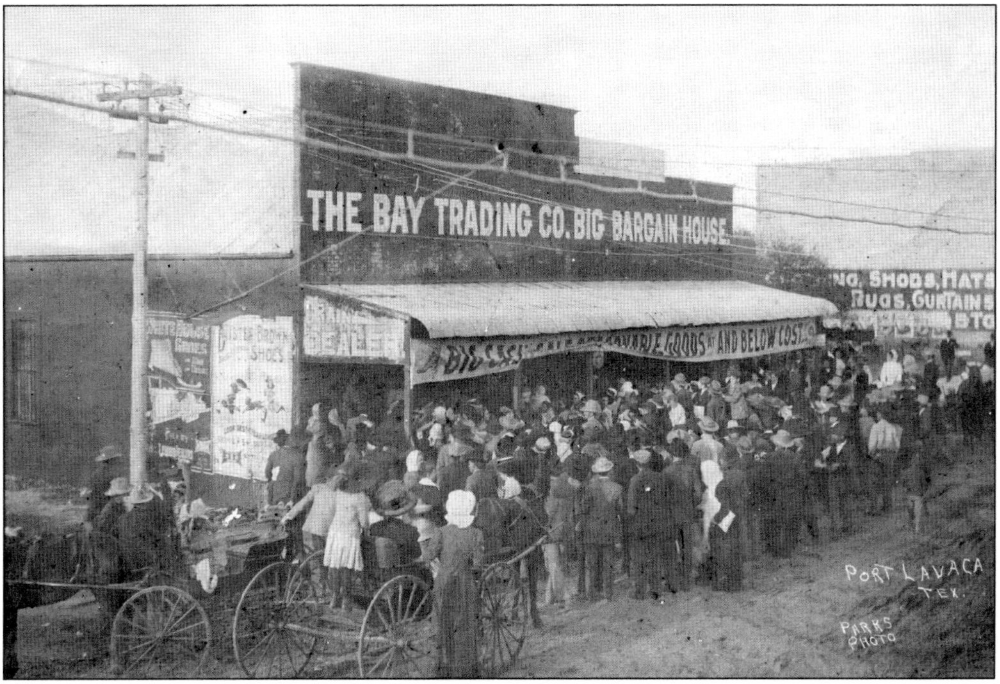

A large crowd gathers in front of The Bay Trading Company in this early postcard. Its building was owned by Charles U. Yancy and was sold to Tunnel Absolom McKamey, who opened the Trading Company. In 1917, Ed Melcher and his partner Eugene Branch moved their merchandising company into the building and Melcher bought it in 1847. Melcher ran Melcher's Hardware, which is still owned by his descendents today.

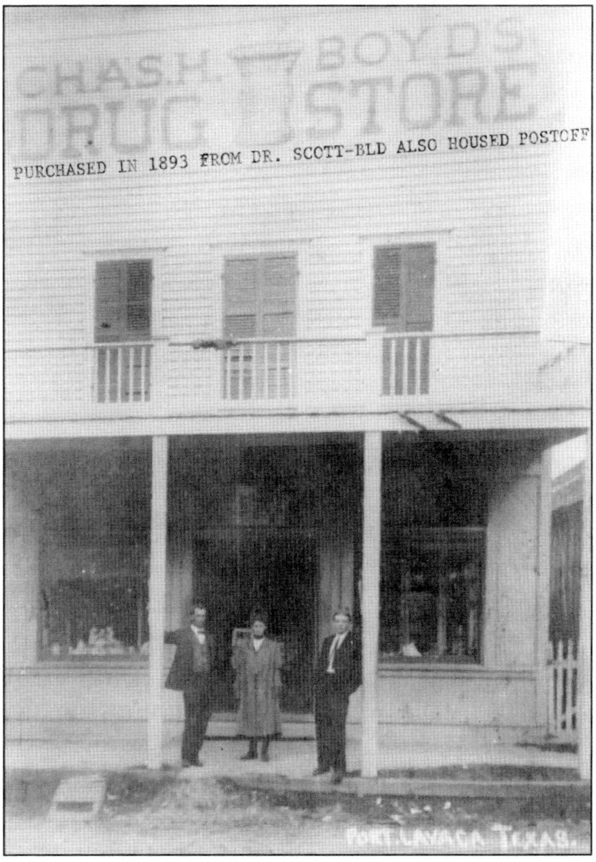

Chas. H. Boyd's Drug Store, seen here, was purchased in 1893 from Dr. Scott. Located in downtown Port Lavaca, it once housed the post office as well.

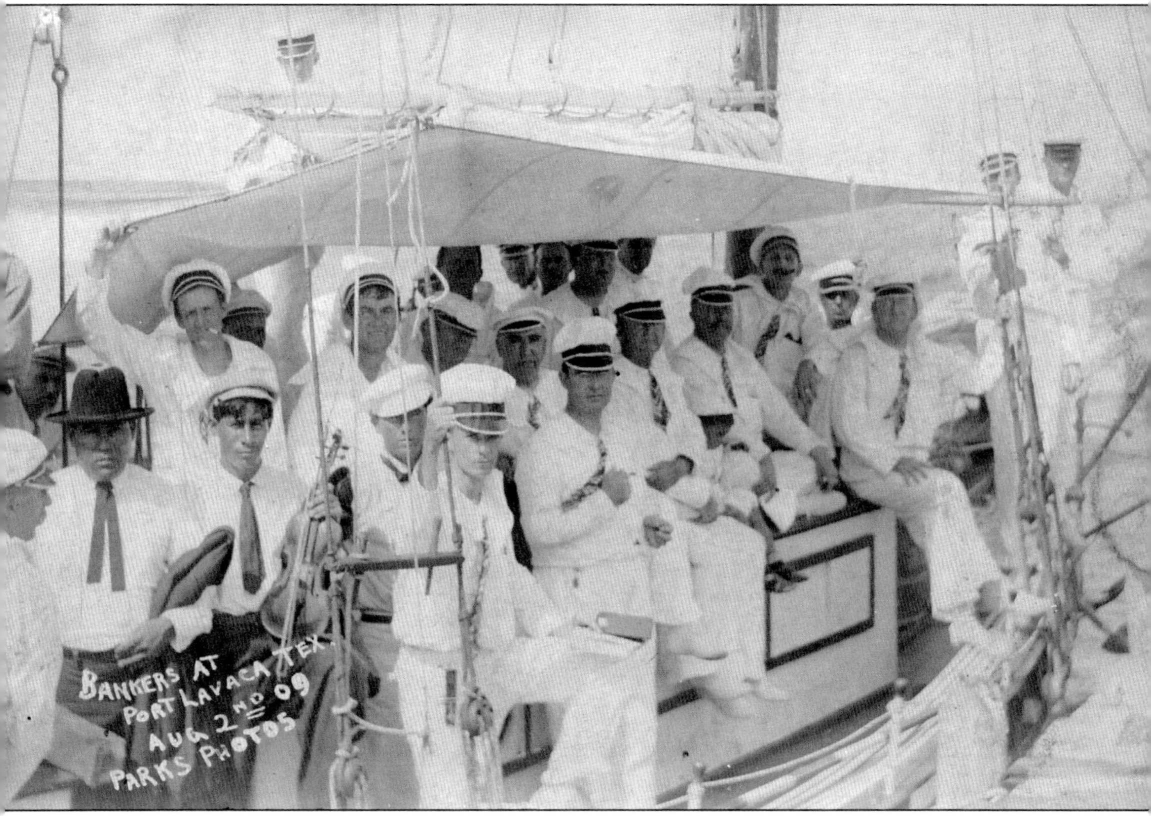

Bankers from Port Lavaca relax during a sailboat outing on August 2, 1901.

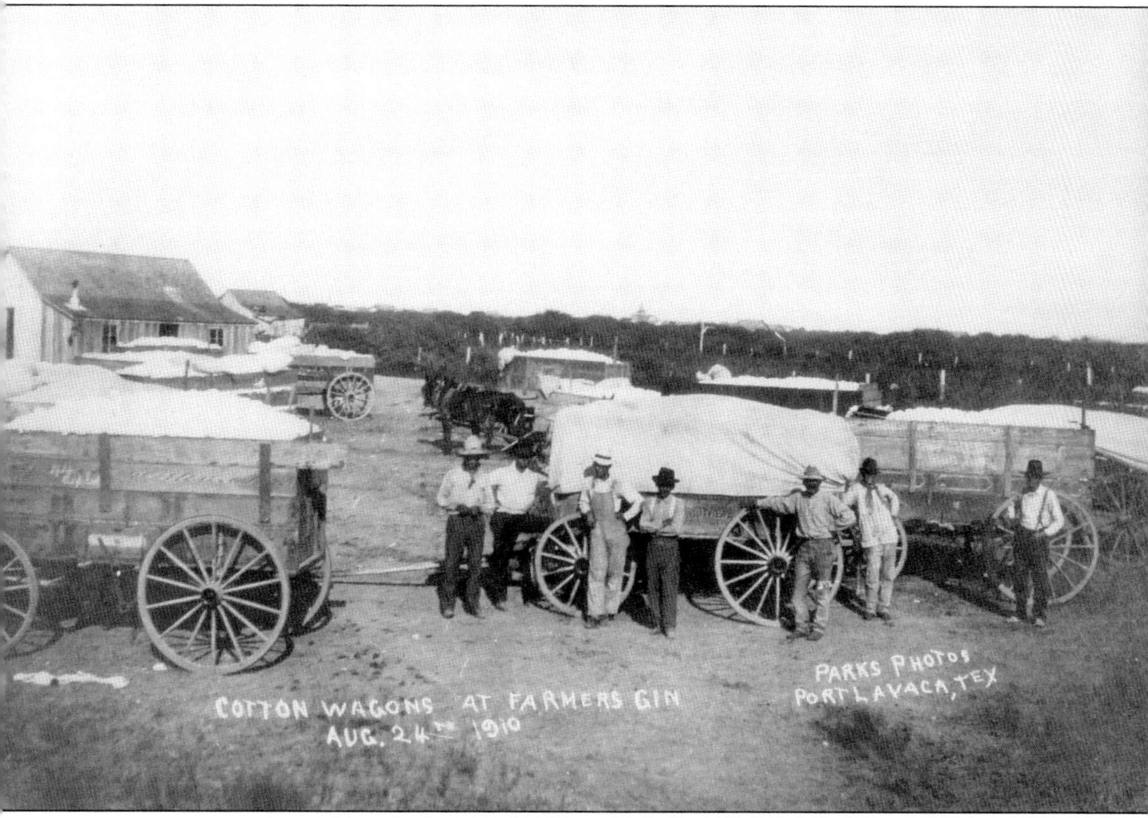

Cotton farmers stand with their harvest at the Farmer's Gin on August 24, 1910.

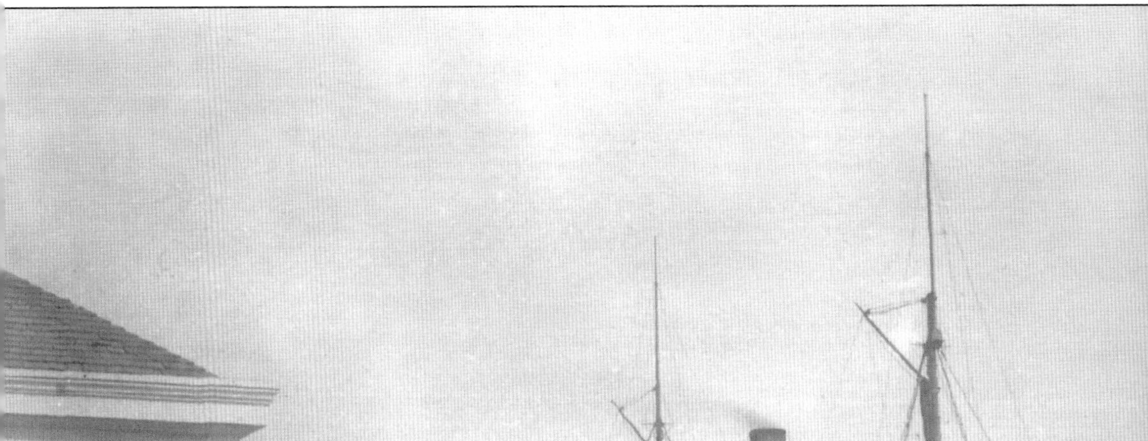

Indianola was one of the top ports in Texas. In 1869 and 1870, it was even larger than Galveston. If it had not been devastated by hurricanes, it might well have become the largest port. The Morgan Steamship Line moved to Indianola in 1849. Founder Charles Morgan brought the train to his wharf for easier loading and unloading from his steamships.

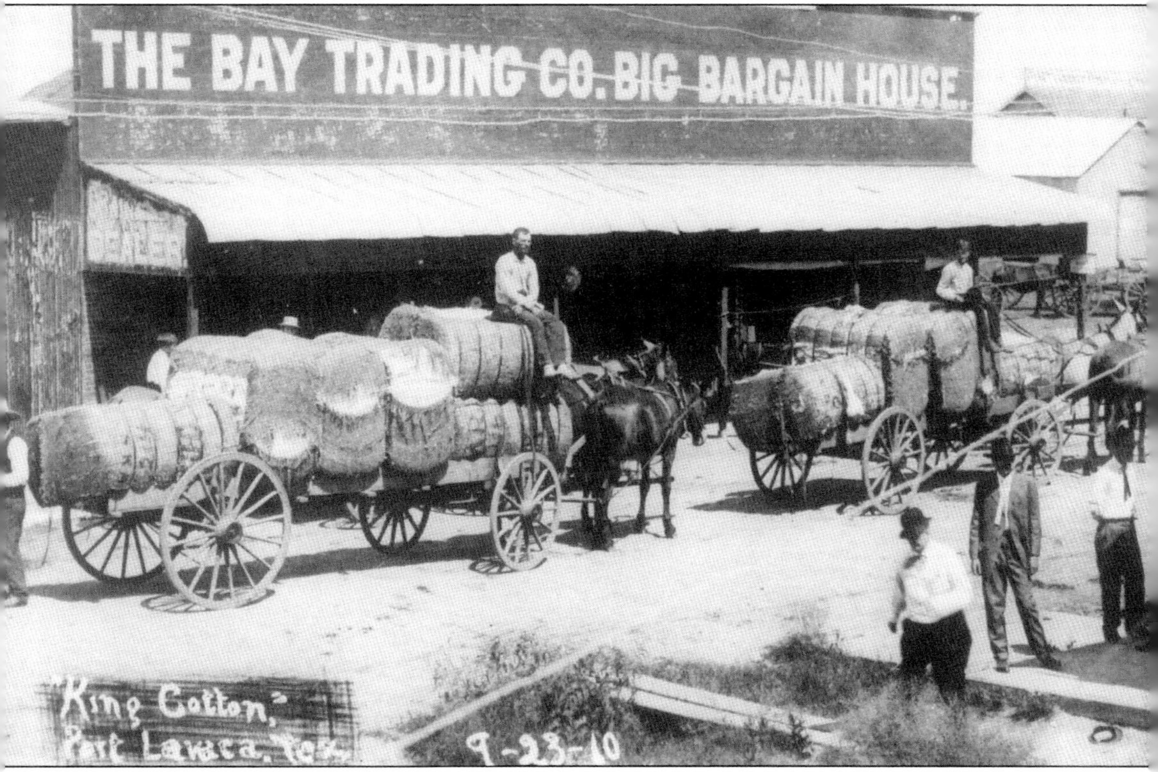

Bales of hay sit on carts in front of the Bay Trading Company, ready for sale or transport, on September 23, 1910.

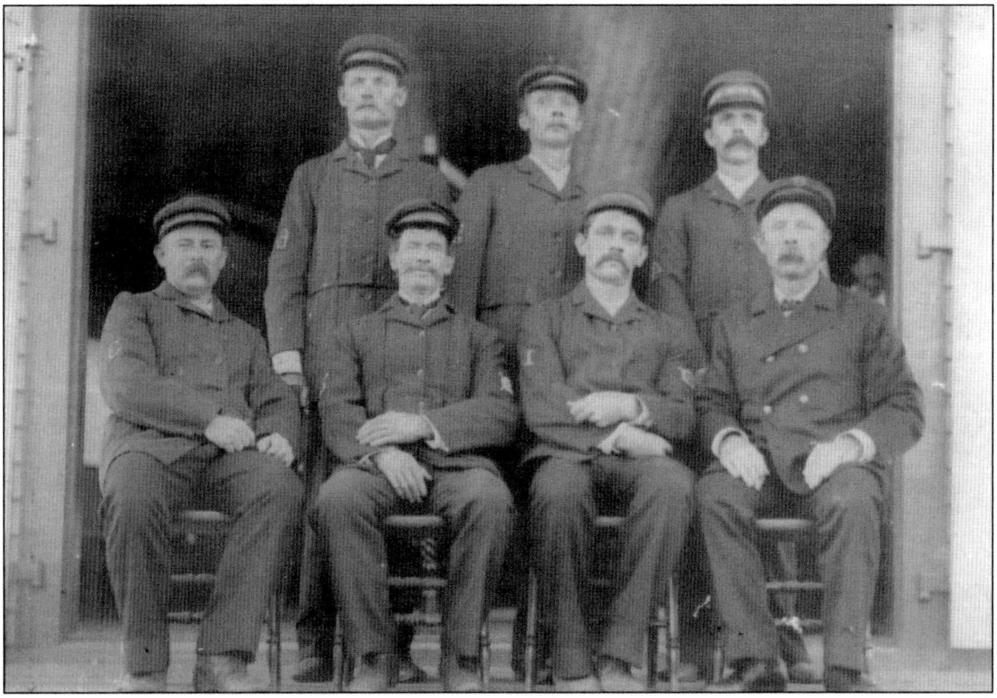

Members of the Coast Guard posed for this photograph. The Coast Guard station was originally called the Life Boat Station at Saluria or the Life Saving Station. Later it became part of the Coast Guard and was on Matagorda Island until 1961, when it was destroyed by Hurricane Carla. A new building in Port O'Connor replaced it.

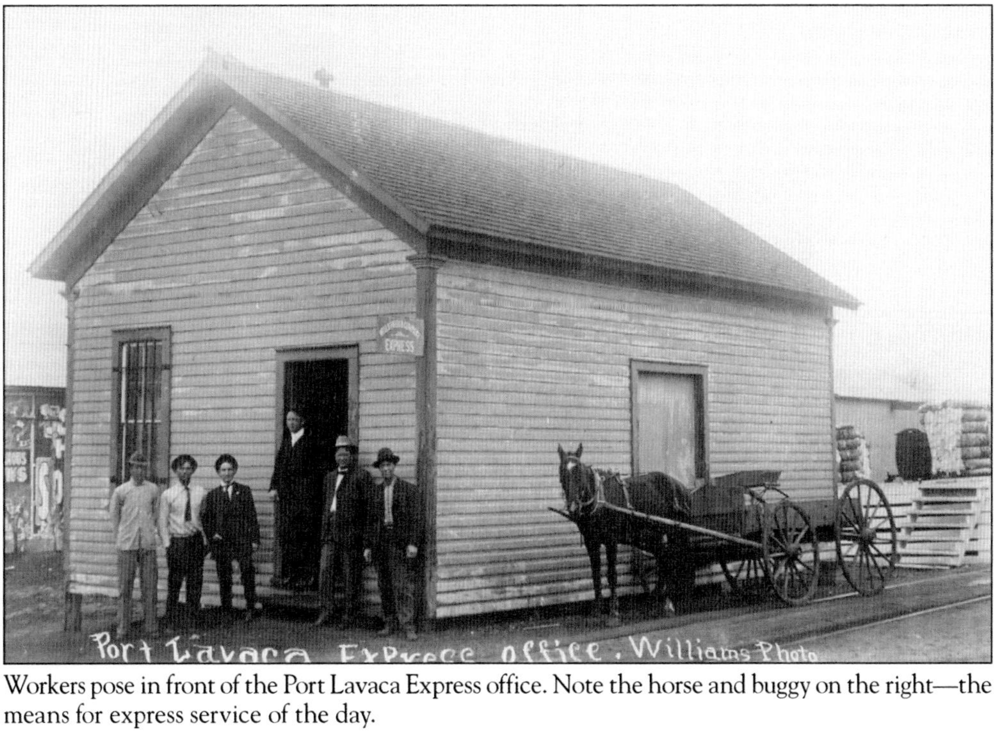

Workers pose in front of the Port Lavaca Express office. Note the horse and buggy on the right—the means for express service of the day.

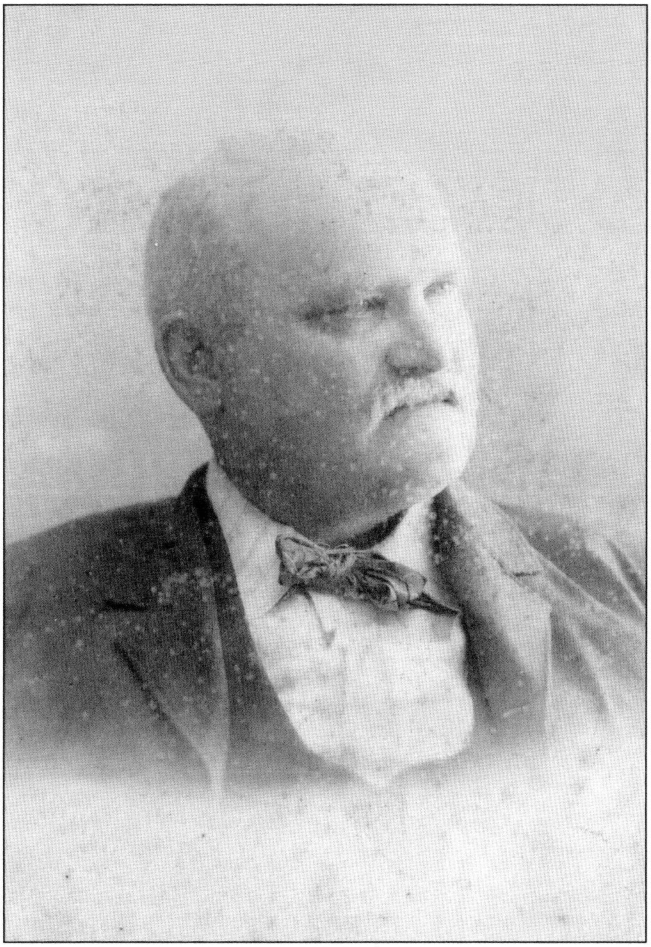

At right is Capt. Dan Simpson, who was appointed by Gov. L.S. Ross as the captain of pilots for the Port of Pass Cavallo in 1889. Pictured below are some early Alsatian immigrants.

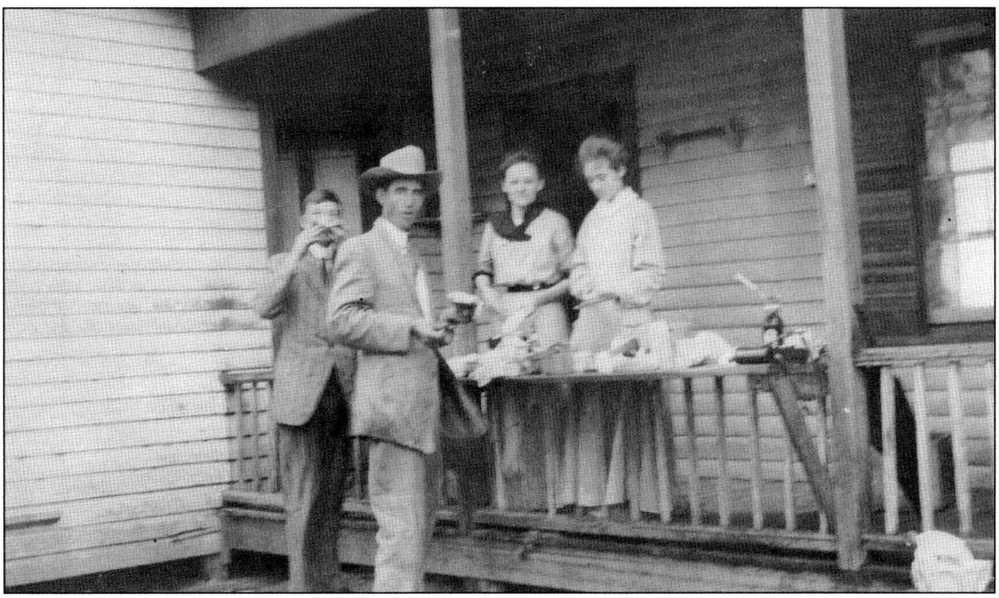

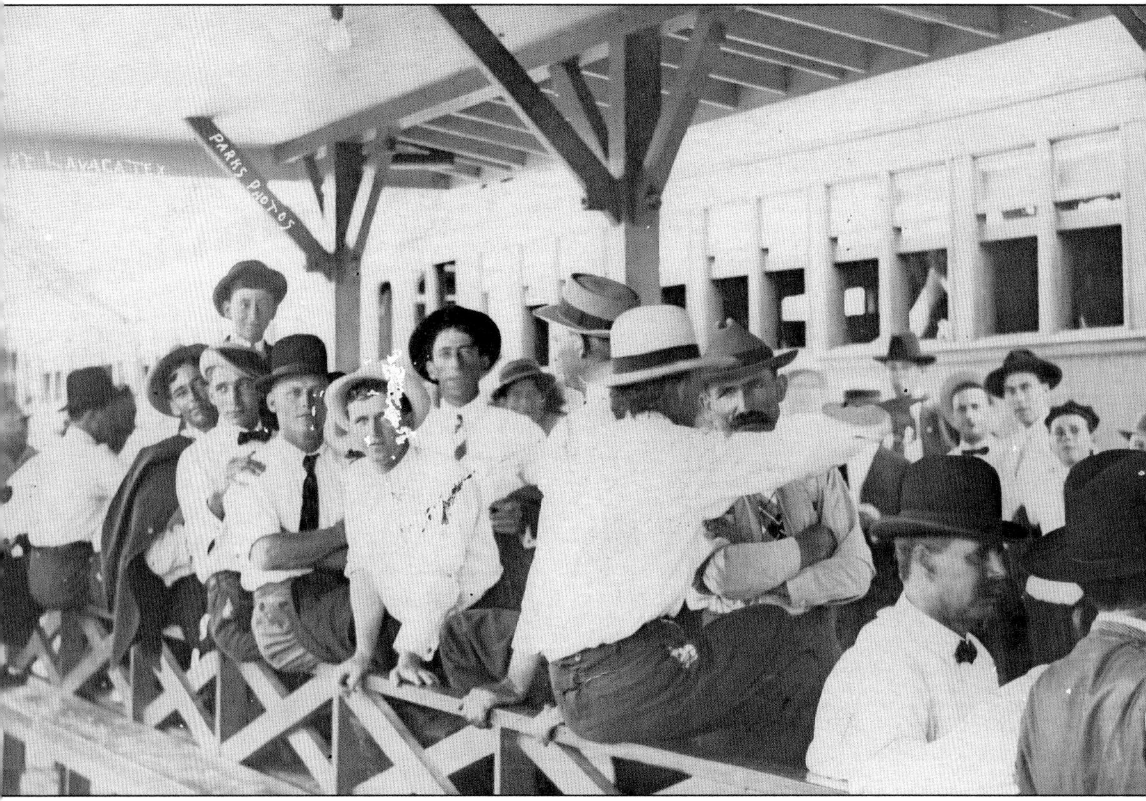

In this Percy Parks photograph, a large group of men congregate at the train depot around 1910. The train in front of them with all of the windows is waiting to take on passengers.

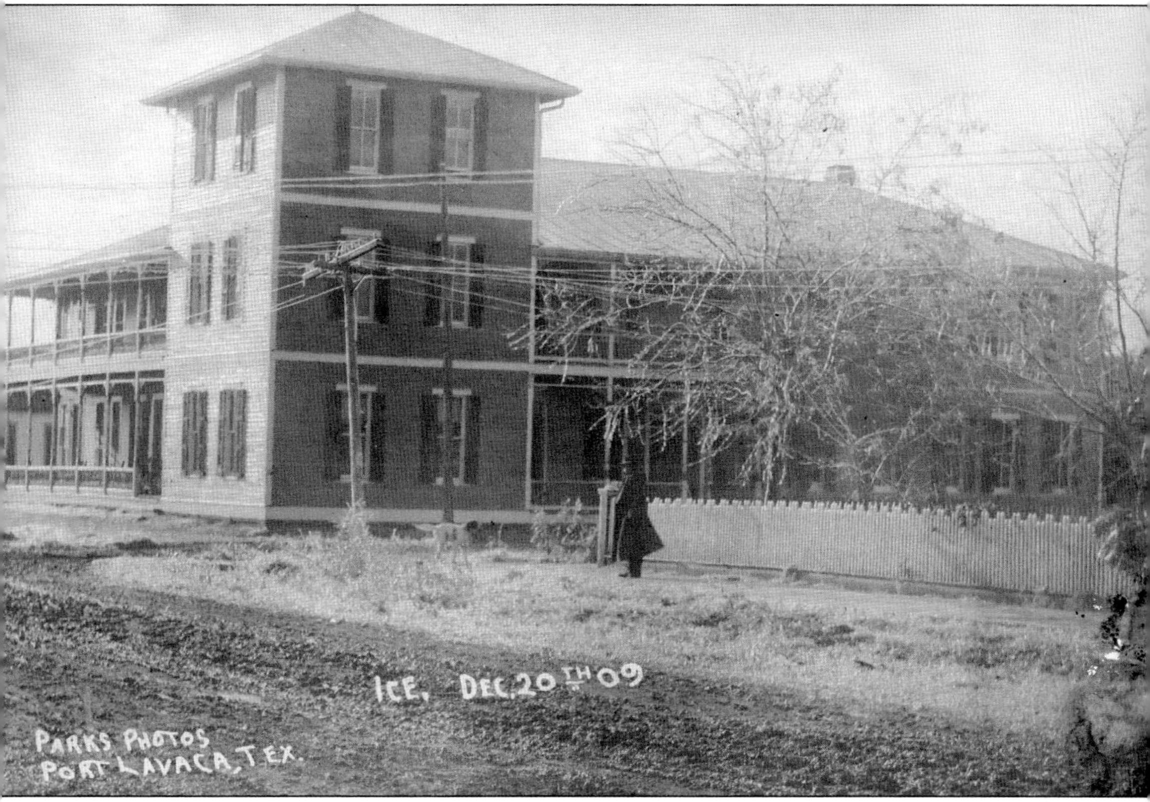

On December 20, 1909, Percy Parks documented one of the few ice storms to happen along the bay. The Beach Hotel, the trees, and the man with his dog are all surrounded by a heavy coating of ice.

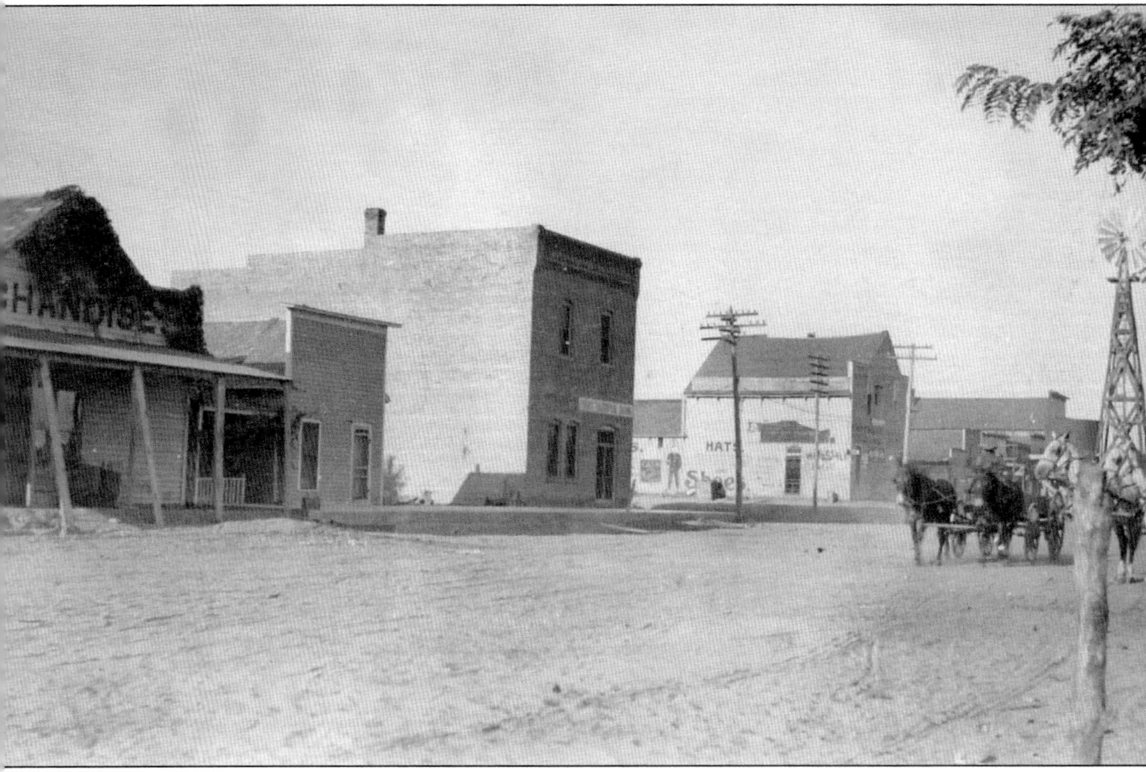

The First National Bank sits on the corner of a dirt road in Old Town Port Lavaca.

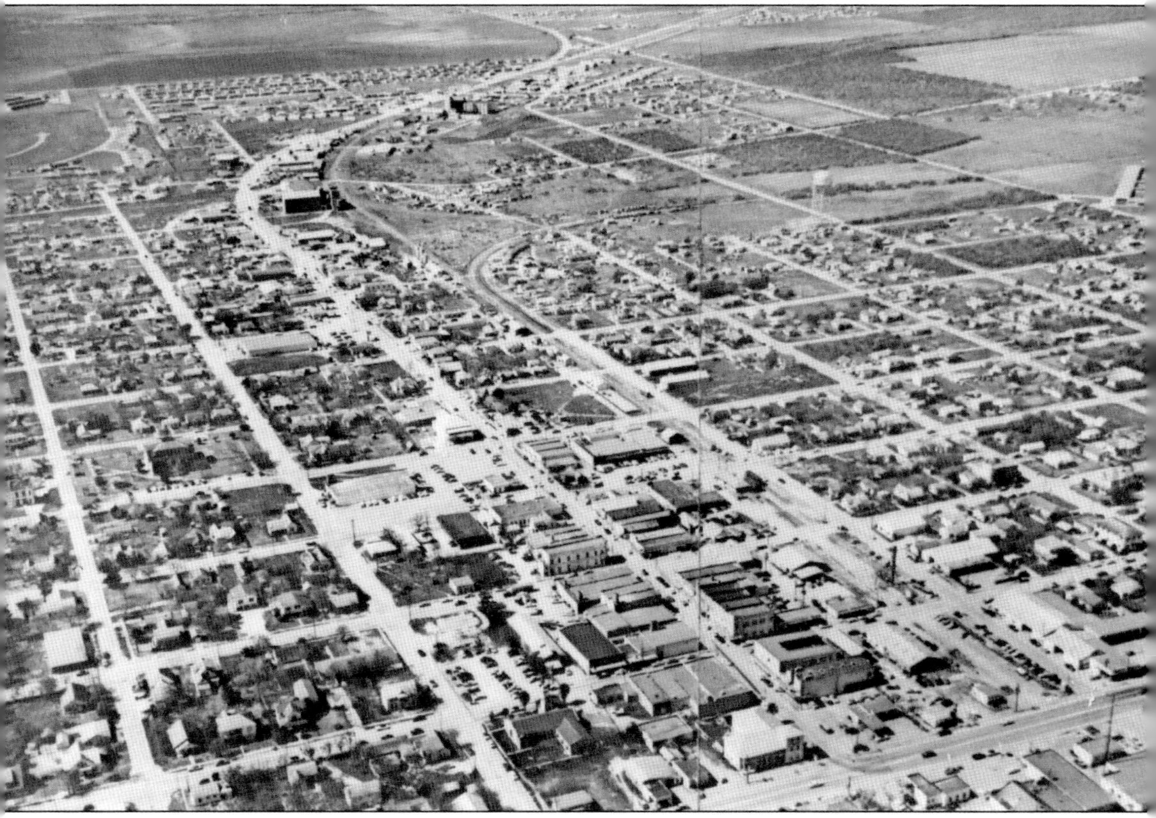

This bird's-eye view of Port Lavaca looks north around 1950.

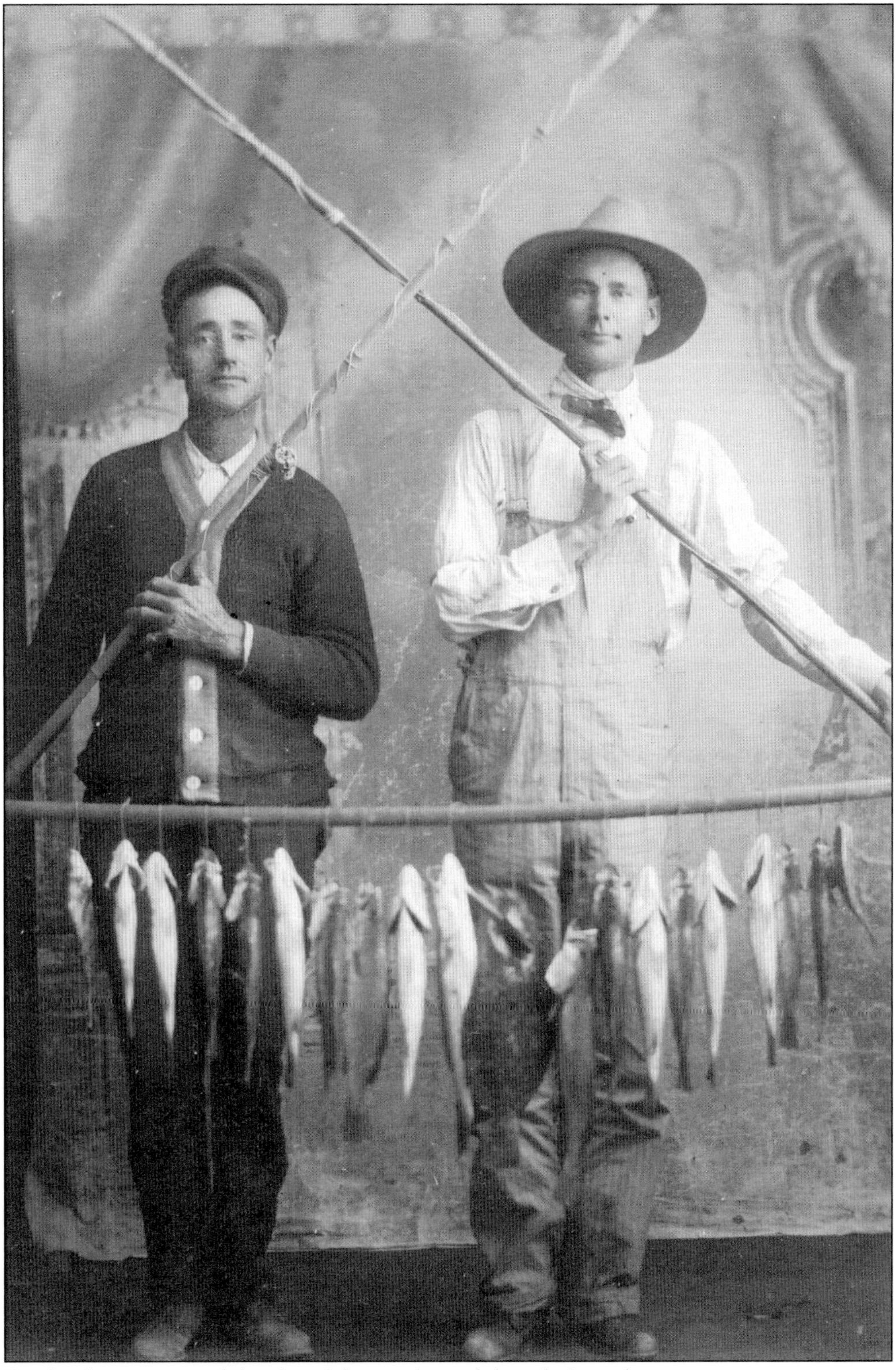

Two local men pose with bamboo fishing poles and their day's catch.

Four

Community and Tourism

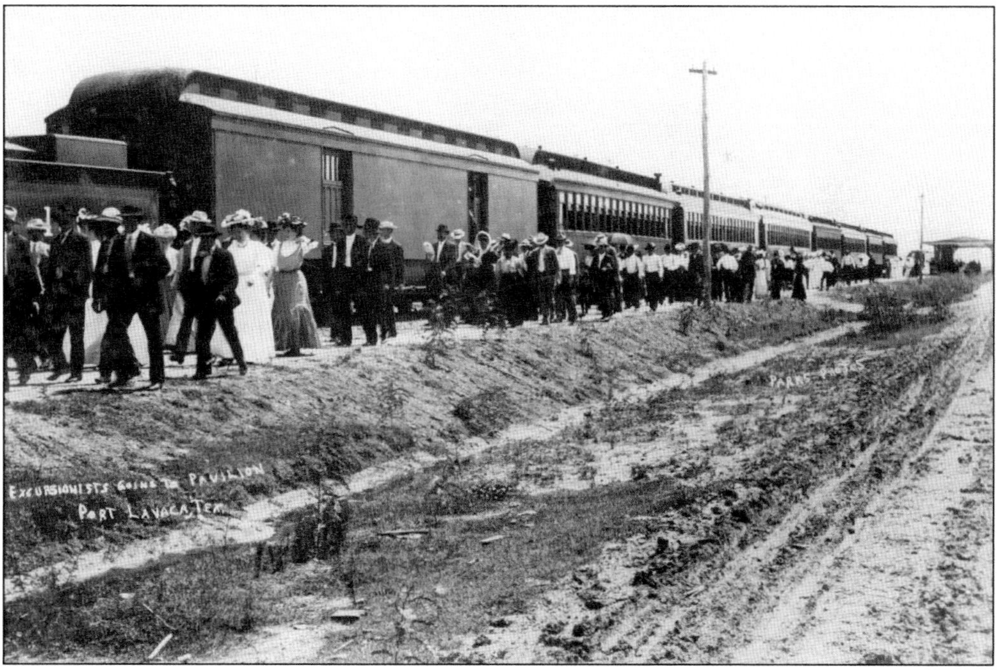

Weekend excursionists disembark to dance, dine, and party at the Port Lavaca Pavilion in the early 1900s. The San Antonio Mexican Gulf Railroad line opened in 1857, connecting Port Lavaca with Victoria. The Indianola railroad joined this line north of Lavaca at Clark's Station.

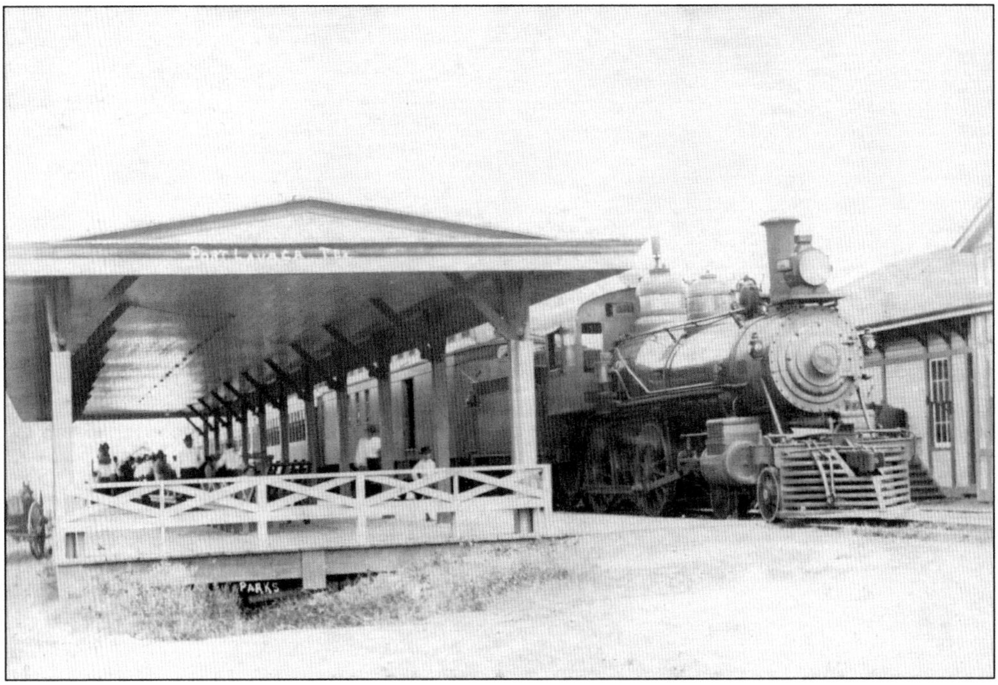

In the late 1800s and early 1900s, excursionists would ride to Port Lavaca onboard "Old Salty" and arrive at the depot, seen here, on Railroad Street. Train service continued from 1887 to 1935. The train was given its nickname by a brakeman who said coming to Port Lavaca was a "salty" job.

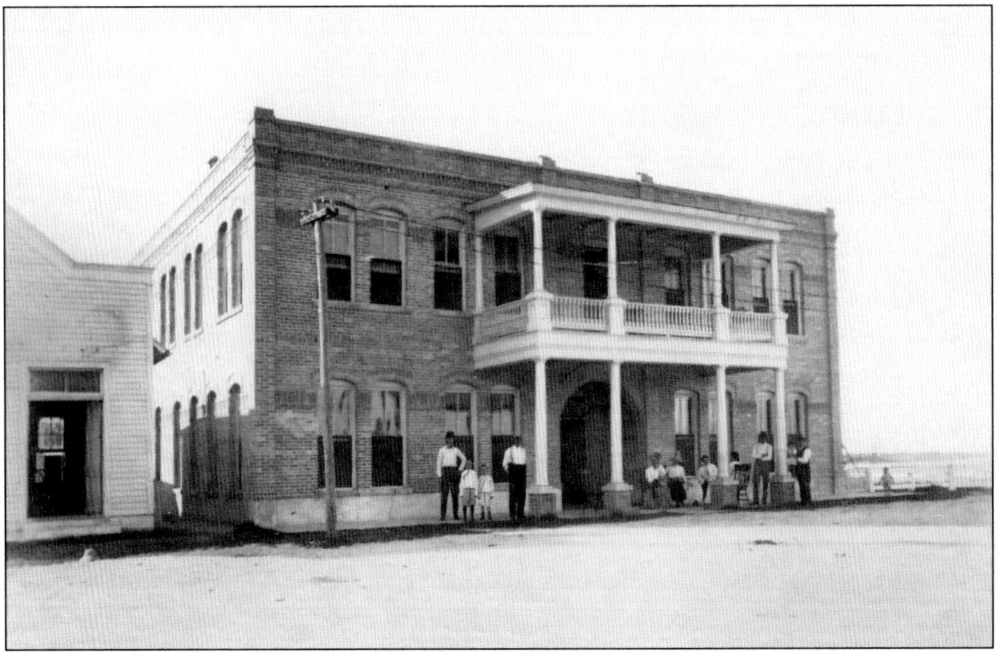

In 1907, the Navidad Hotel was built on the bay front, just off Commerce Street. Built by William Berry, the hotel provided rooms for tourists, hunters, and fishermen. In the 1950s, the hotel was purchased by Vera Kolbo and became known as the Seagull Hotel. This building still stands today.

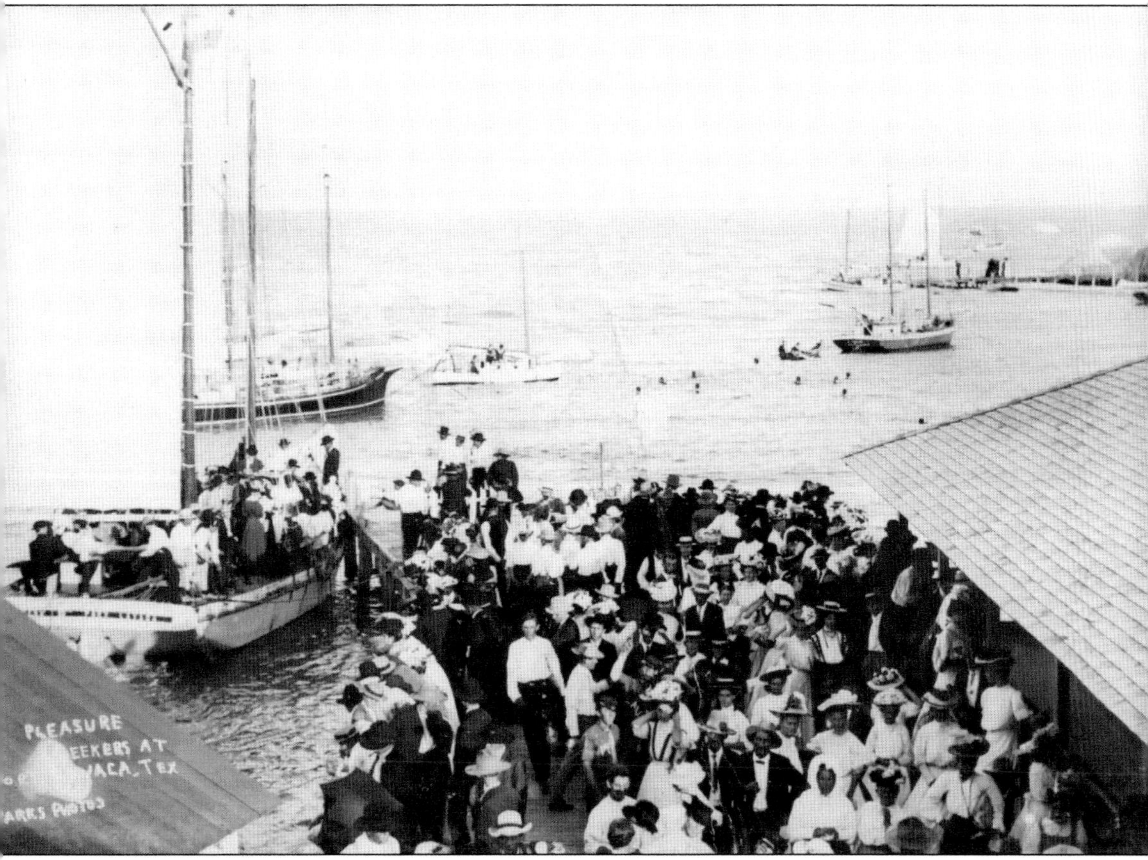

A large group of tourists wait to board boats for a day of sailing on Lavaca Bay.

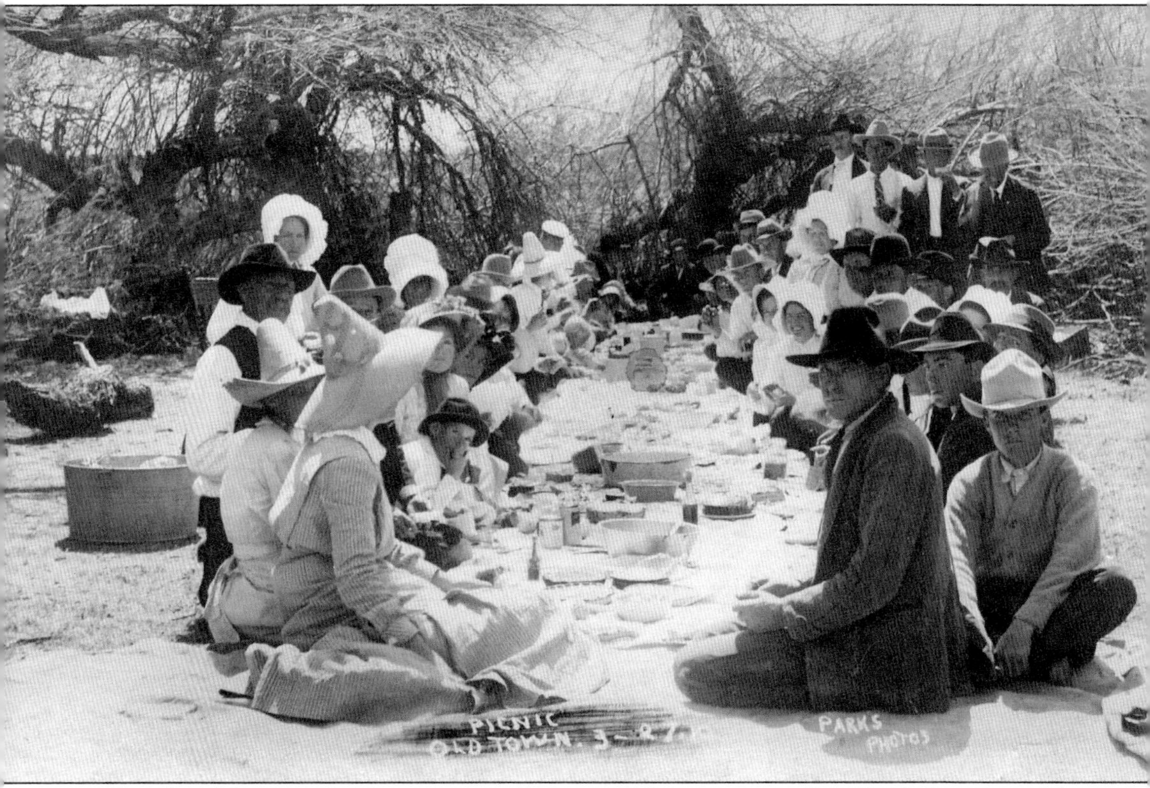

Friends and family gather for a picnic in 1910 near Old Town, originally called Indian Point. They are sitting near where Prince Solms-Braunfels brought in shiploads of German immigrants, who later developed New Braunfels and Fredericksburg.

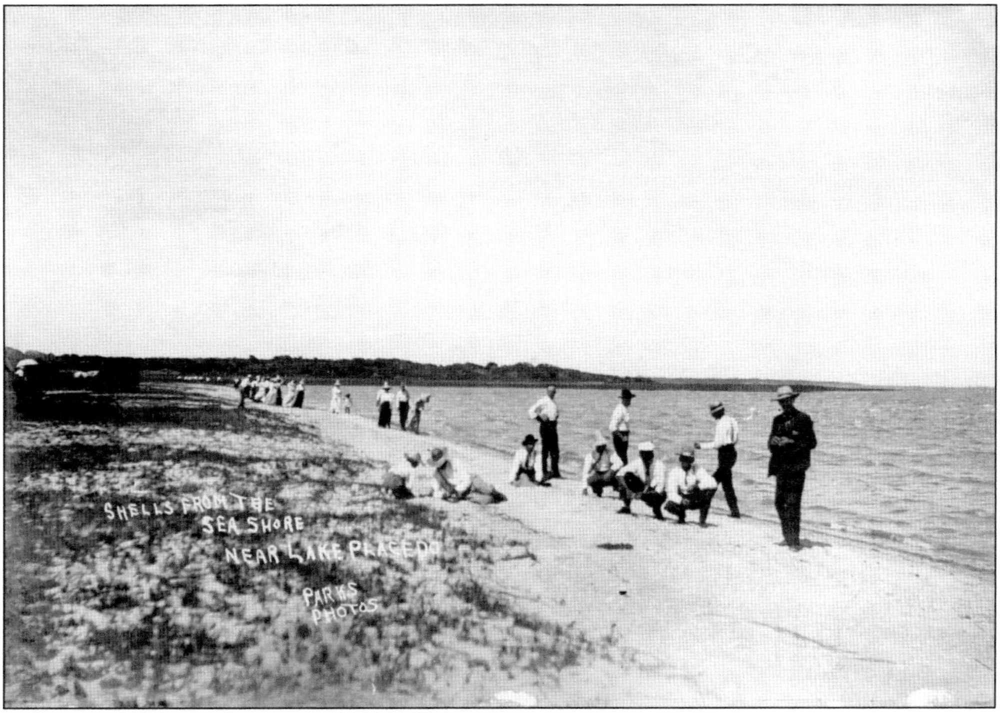

The young men above collect seashells, while the sunbathers below wade into Lake Placedo. Note the full attire and fashionable hats in both images.

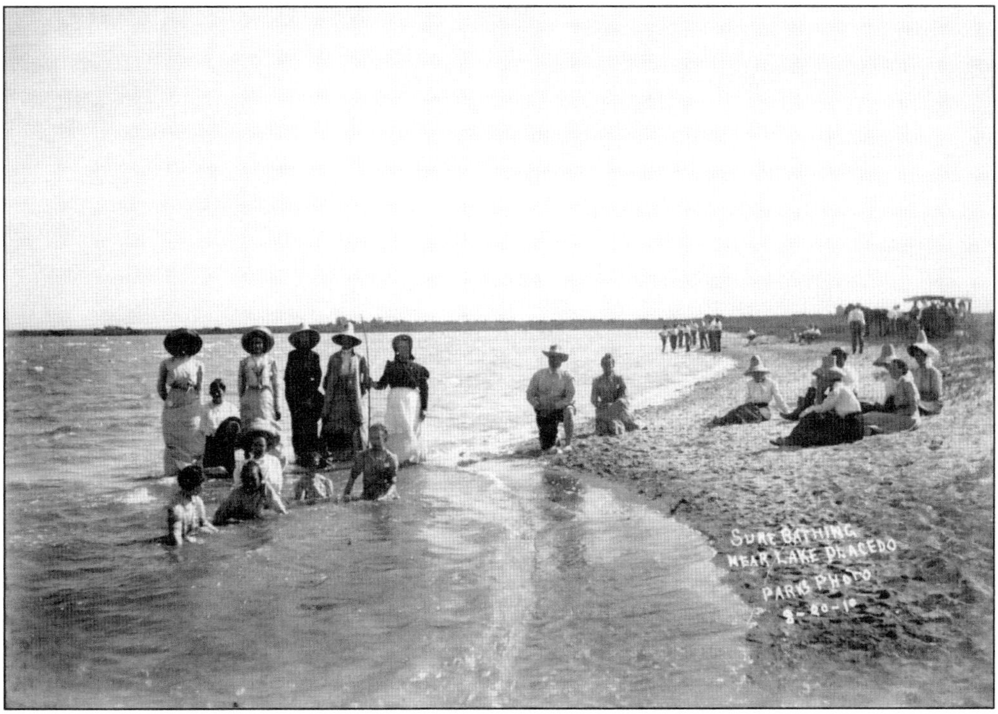

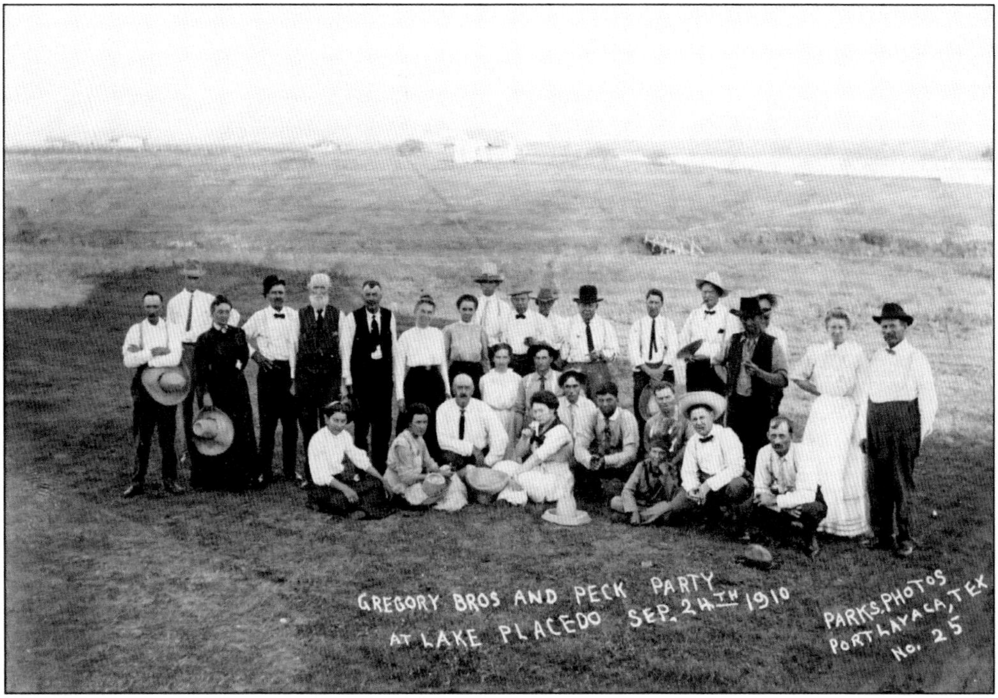

This group poses for a photograph at the Gregory Brothers and Peck party picnic on September 24, 1910.

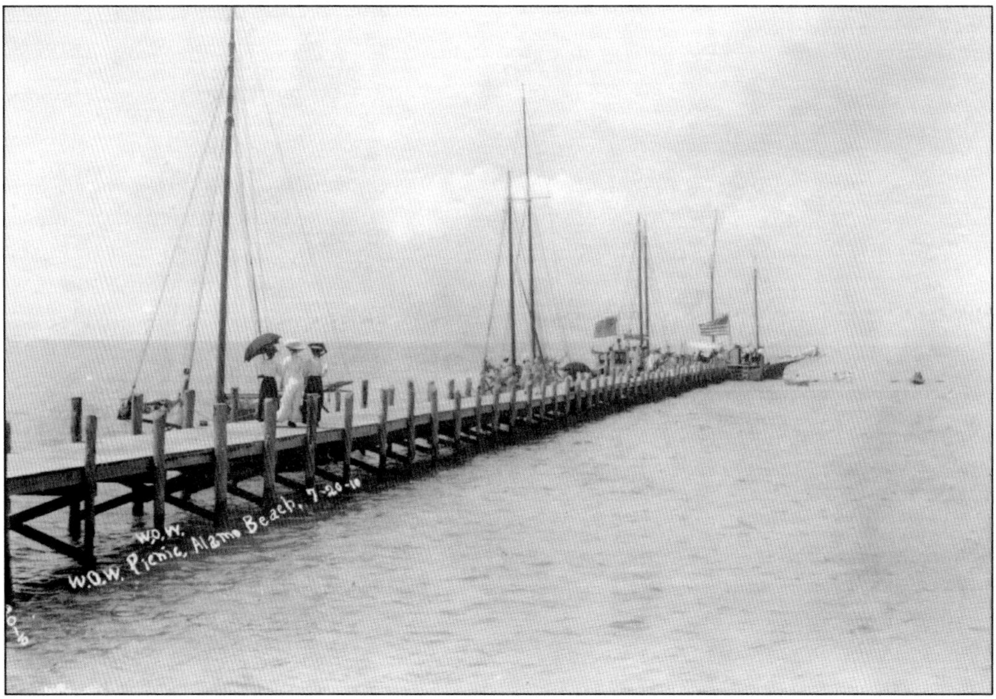

Members of the Woodmen of the World organization stroll down the pier to board the boats back to Port Lavaca after picnicking at Alamo Beach on July 20, 1910.

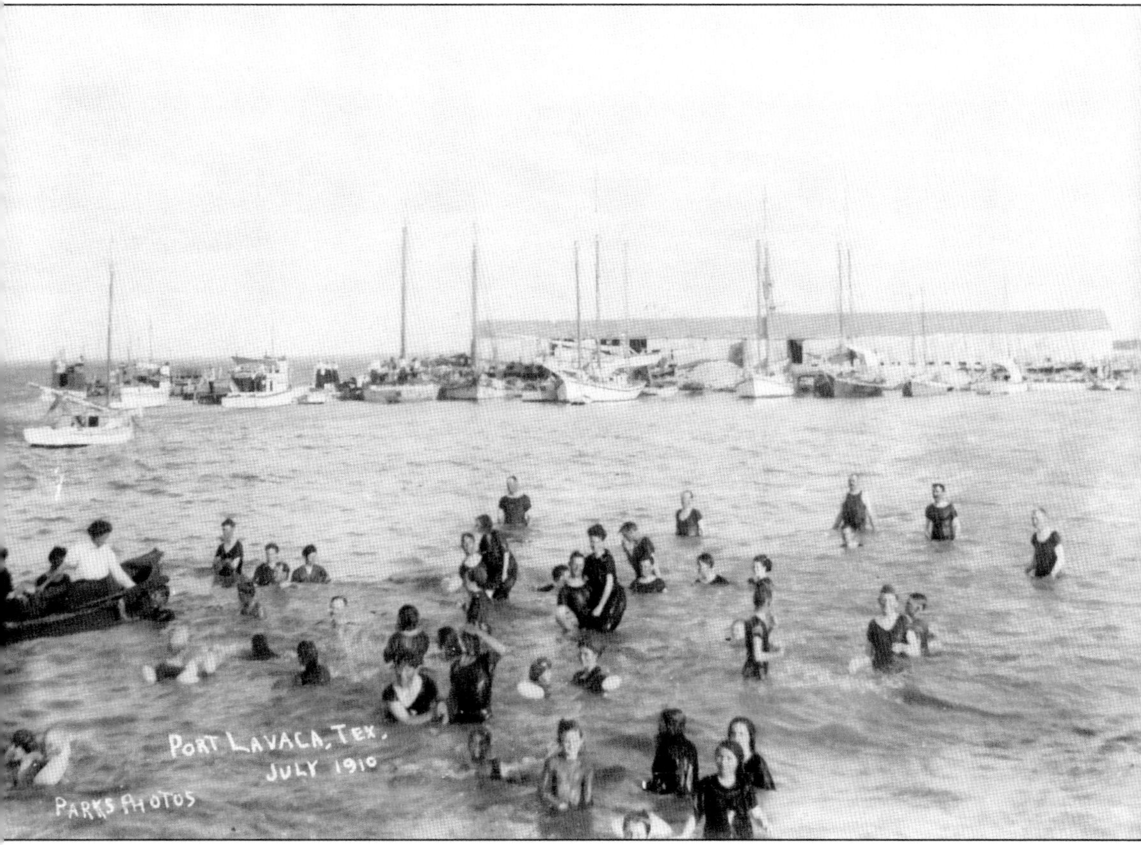

Tourists cool down in Lavaca Bay in July 1910.

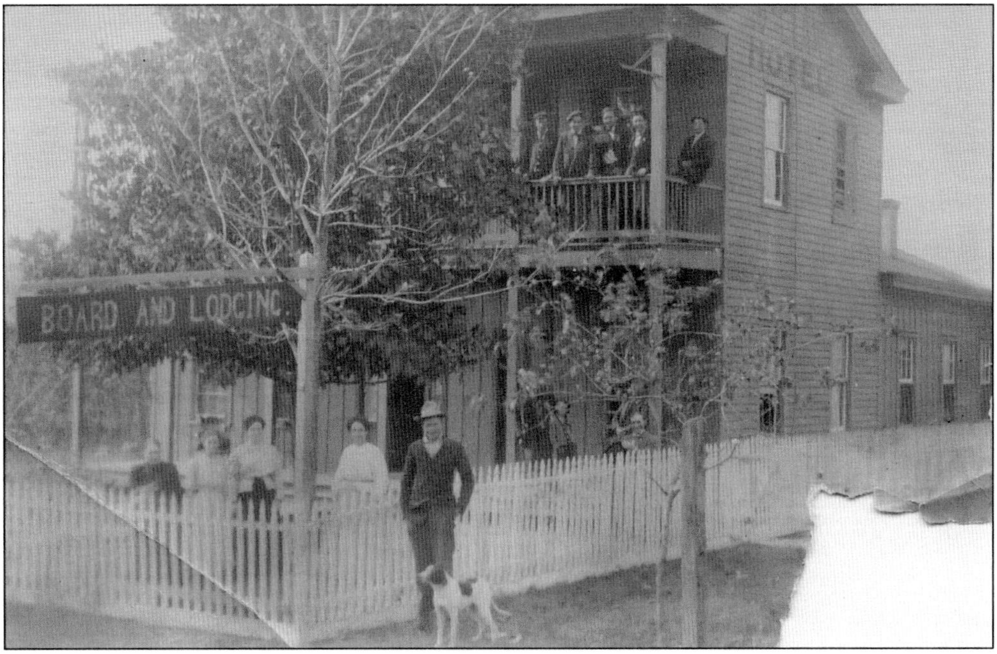

The Beach Hotel, also known as the Lavaca Hotel, was built by Charles U. Yancy in 1904. It is one of two historic hotels that still remain in Port Lavaca.

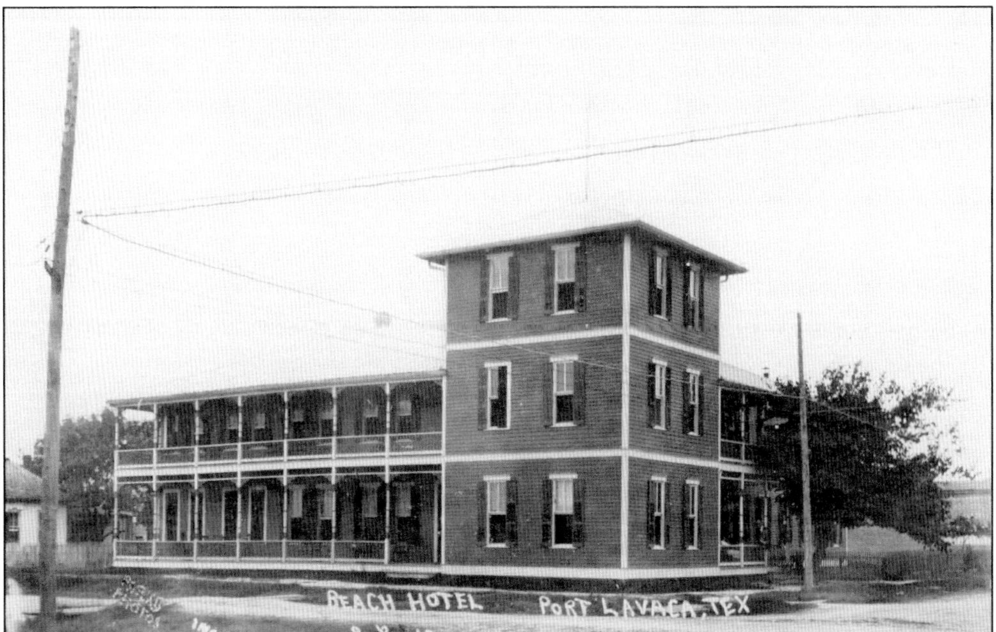

This Ino Studio photograph from August 8, 1910, shows the Beach Hotel, on the corner of Main and Commerce Streets. The Beach Hotel still stands, as does the Navidad Hotel, later known as the Seagull Hotel, on East Railroad Street.

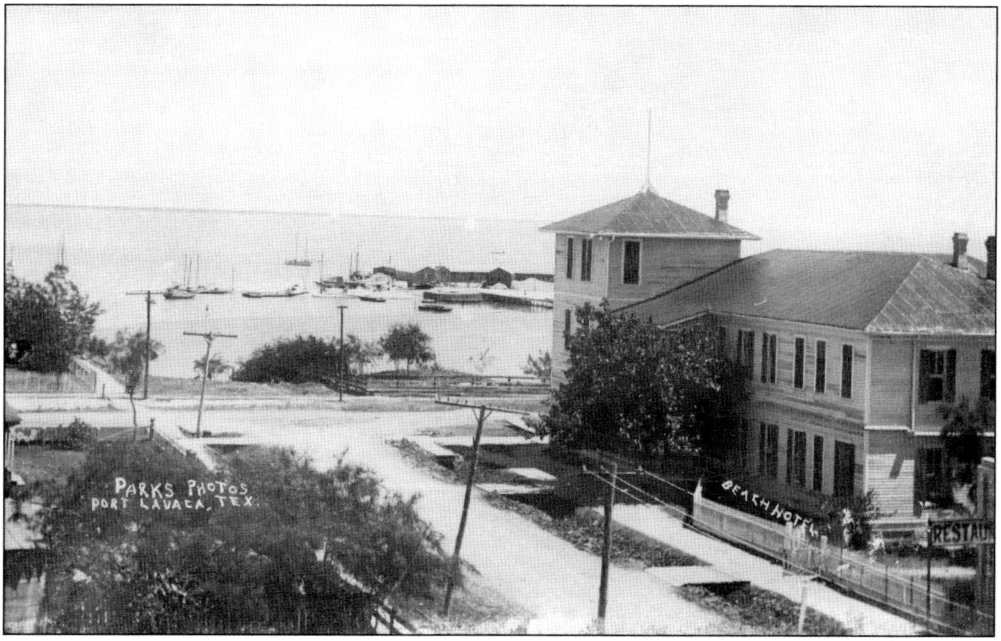

Fish and oyster houses sat in the bay in front of the Beach Hotel, at the corner of Main and Commerce Streets.

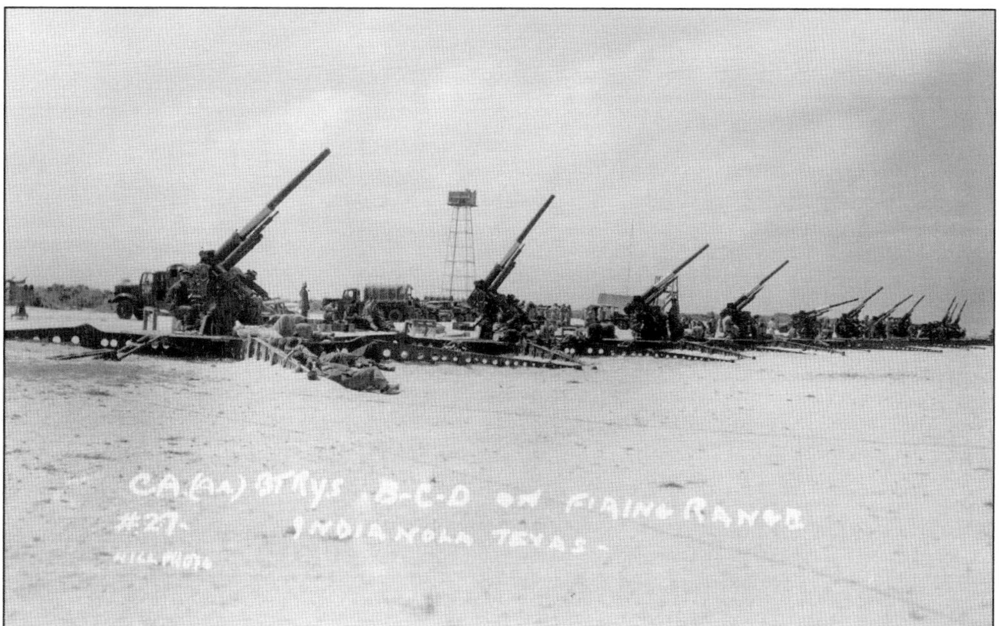

During World War II, Camp Indianola was a training area for American military personnel. Soldiers from Camp Hulen were transported to the beach area to train in the use of anti-aircraft guns, as seen in this photograph, taken by Hill Photos.

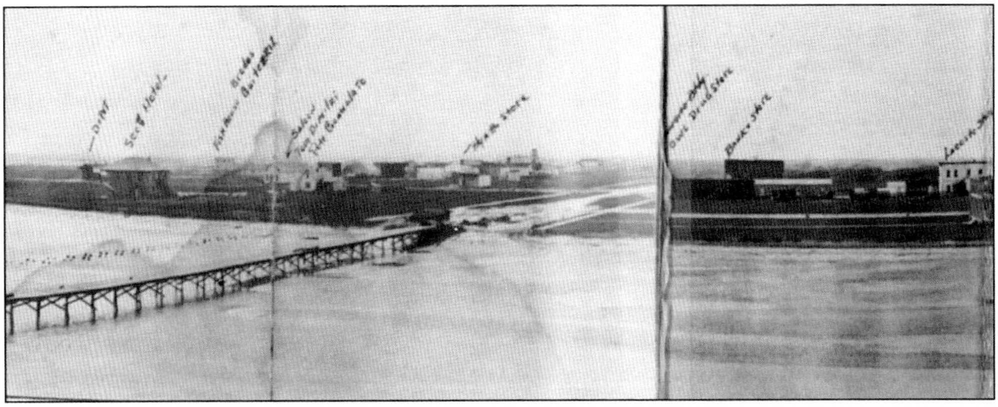

The rare panoramic photographs on these two pages show Port O'Conner, which was laid out in 1909 on what had been the settlement of Alligator Head. It was named in honor of the man who sold the land for the town, Thomas M. O'Connor, and developed by the Calhoun County Cattle Company. In 1910, the beautiful pavilion below was built out over the water, bringing visitors from all over Texas. A branch of the railroad was built from Seadrift to Port O'Connor

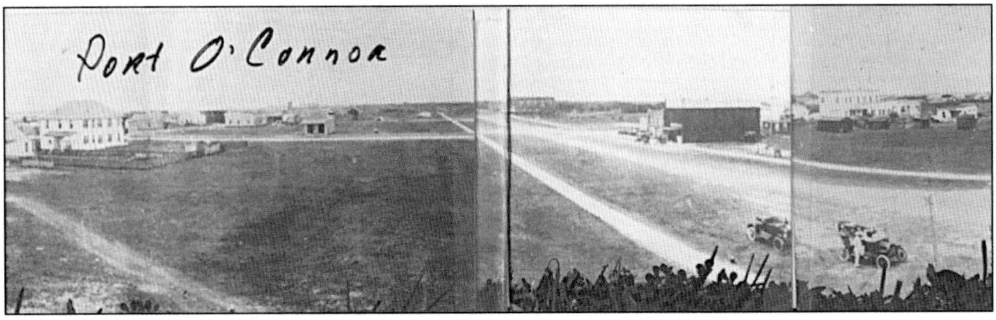

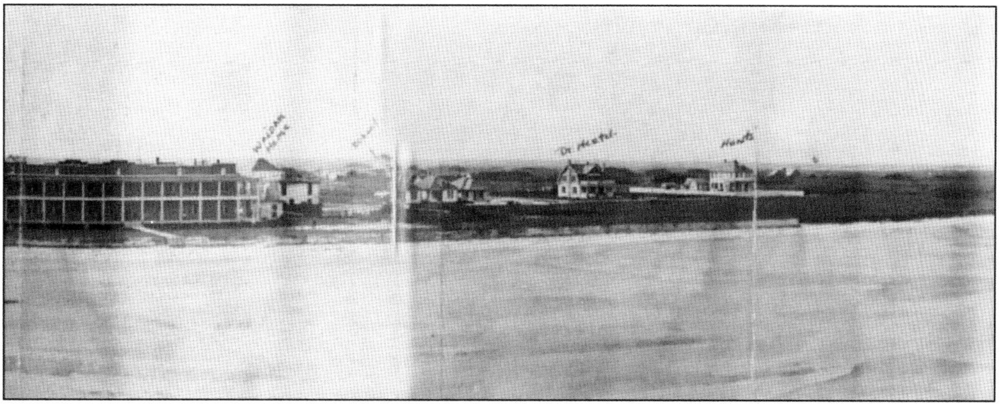

and hotels were built. In 1919, a hurricane did a great deal of damage to the town, destroying the large La Salle Hotel as well as the pavilion. By 1927, the shrimp industry started to become very important to the town, and a new school was built, along with an ice factory, stores, and churches. The intracoastal waterway was completed through the area in 1939.

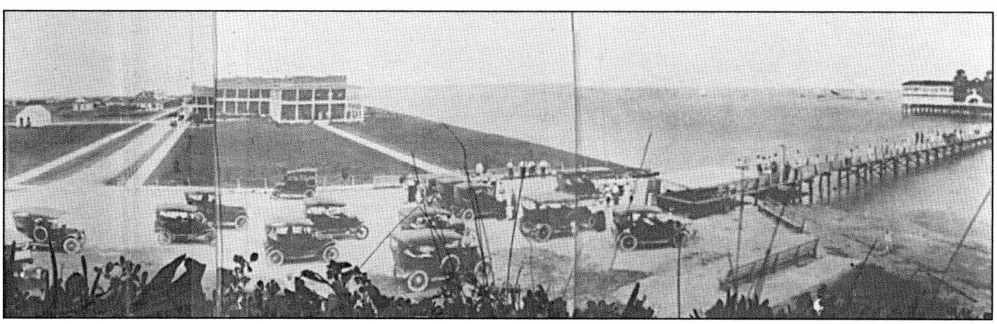

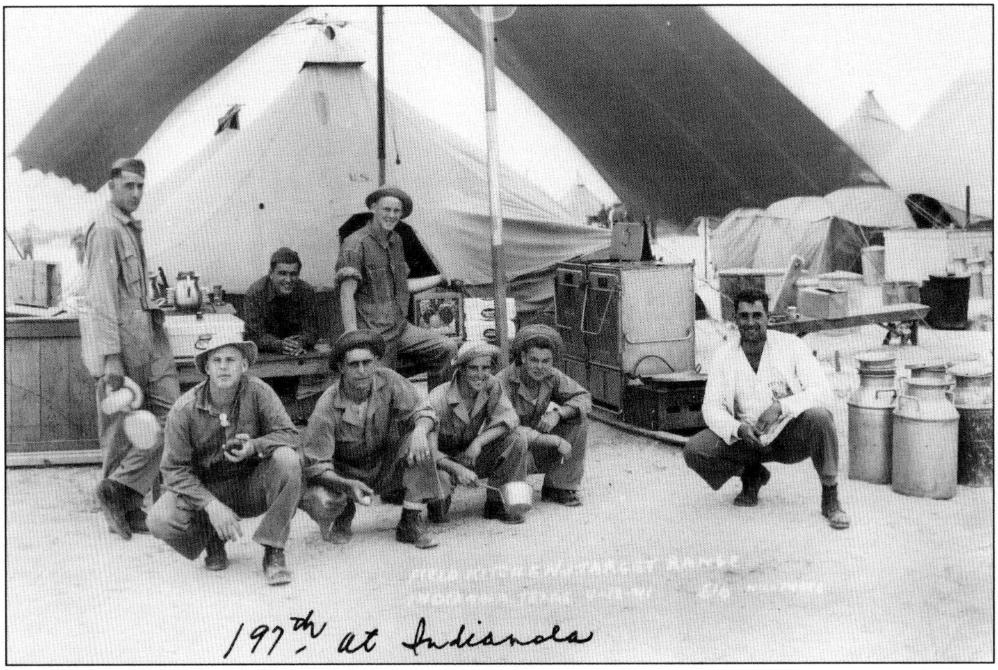

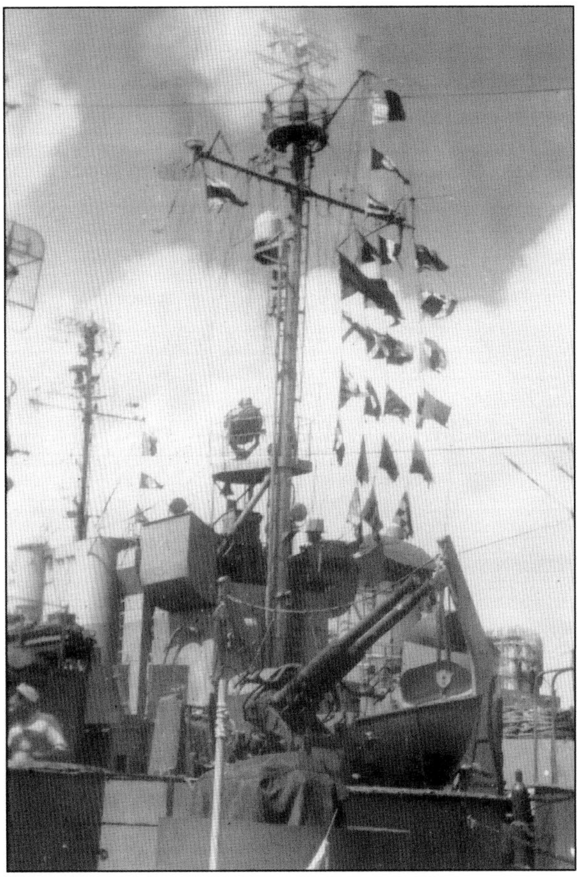

The military took over control of Matagorda Island and Indianola during World War II. These men pose for a photograph in front of the field kitchen set up at the bombing range. Craters are still visible today from practice runs when the federal government used Matagorda Island as a bombing range. Matagorda Island was essential to the control of Texas and the Gulf of Mexico during the Civil War and World War II.

On July 4, 1944, Navy ships came into Port Lavaca harbor to celebrate the reopening of the causeway after it was damaged in a 1942 hurricane. The causeway was used to transport troops from Camp Hulen to the Indianola Gunnery Range.

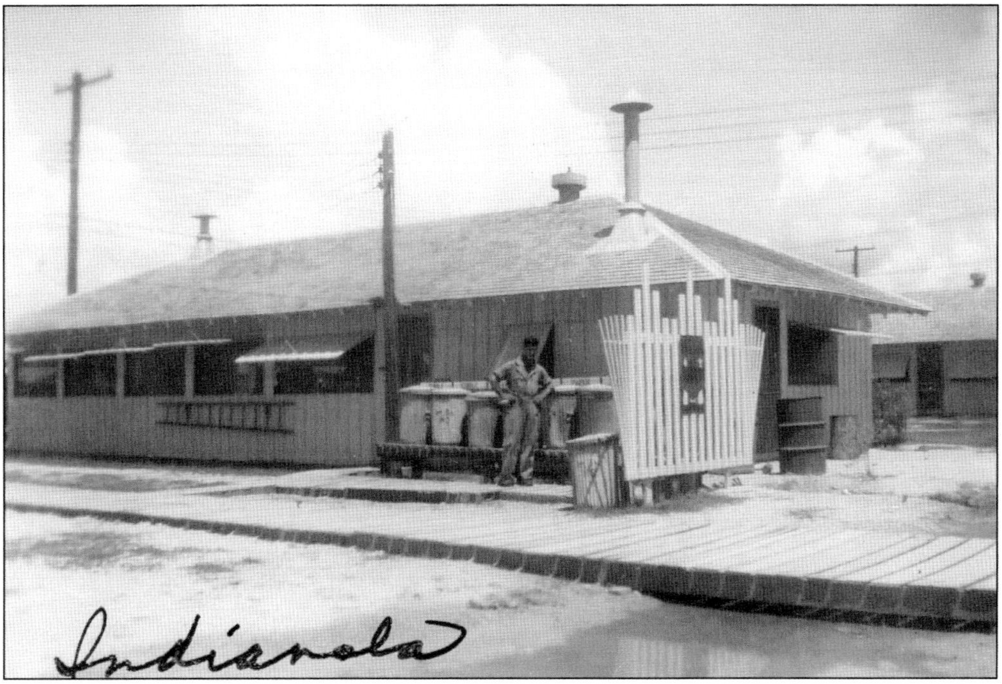

A young soldier stands near the mess hall at the training camp at Indianola in 1941.

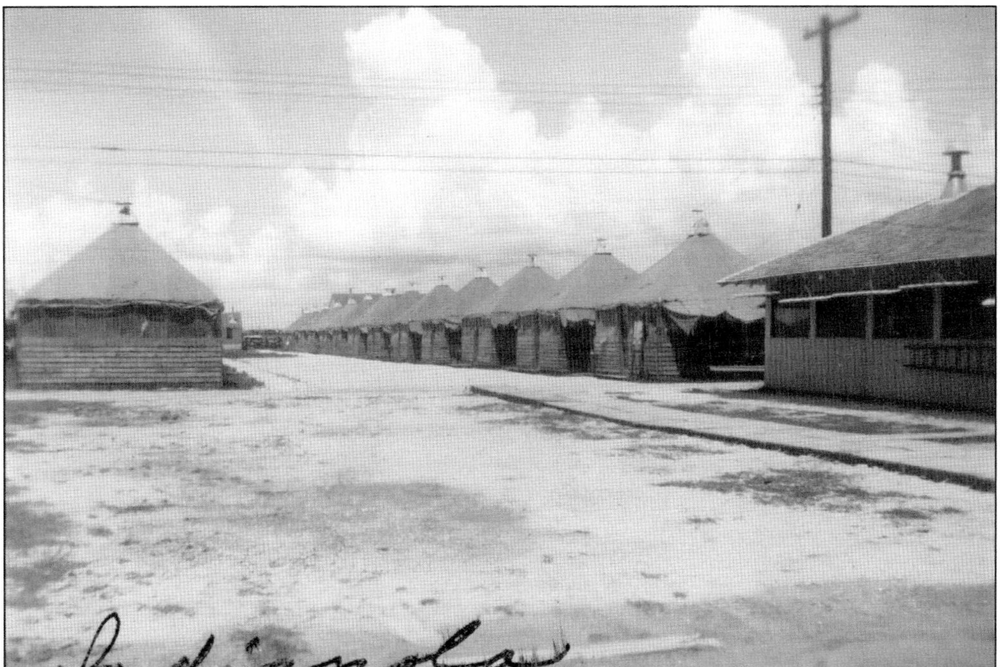

This 1941 image shows the tents that lined the sand street at Camp Indianola. At this time it was the headquarters of the 197th Battery.

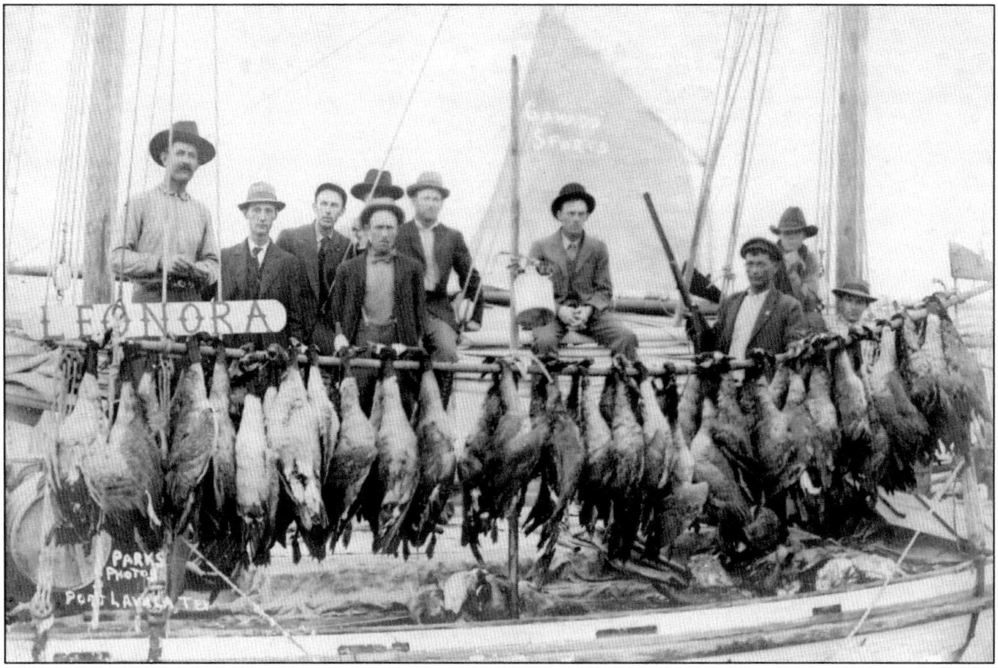

The migration of game birds to Calhoun County has always attracted hunters to the coastal winter feeding grounds of geese, sandhill cranes, and numerous varieties of ducks. Here, the Ganado Sports Club shows off its daily catch aboard the boat *Leonora*, which also carried the mail and freight from Olivia to Port Lavaca before the causeway was built.

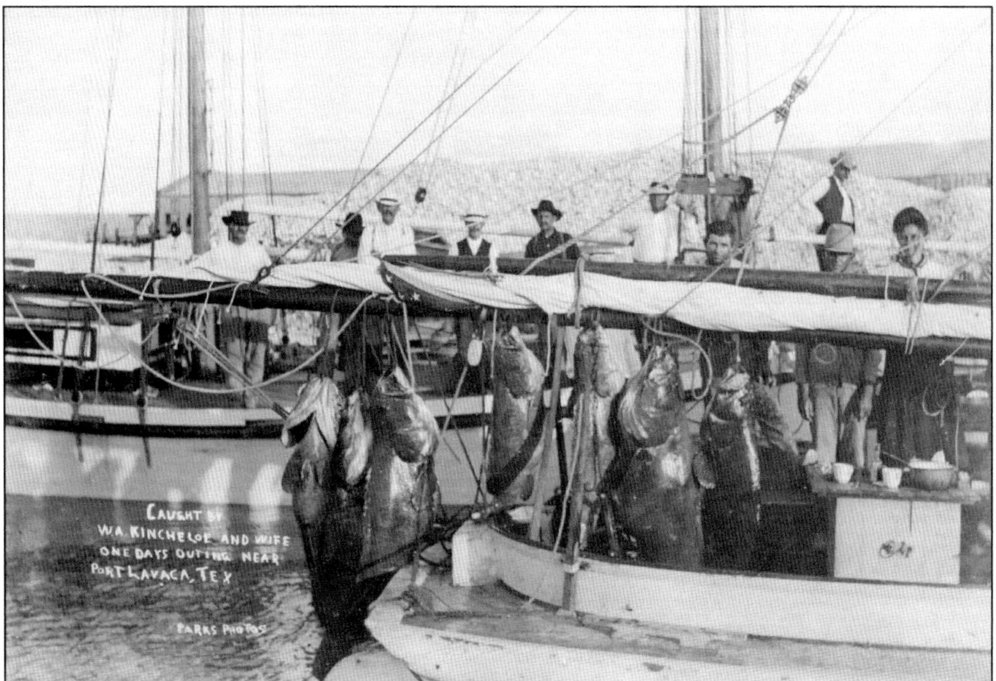

Calhoun County's waters lured anglers with all types of sport fish. The Atlantic goliath grouper seen here were a day's catch for Warren A. Kincheloe and his wife, Marilyne, around 1910.

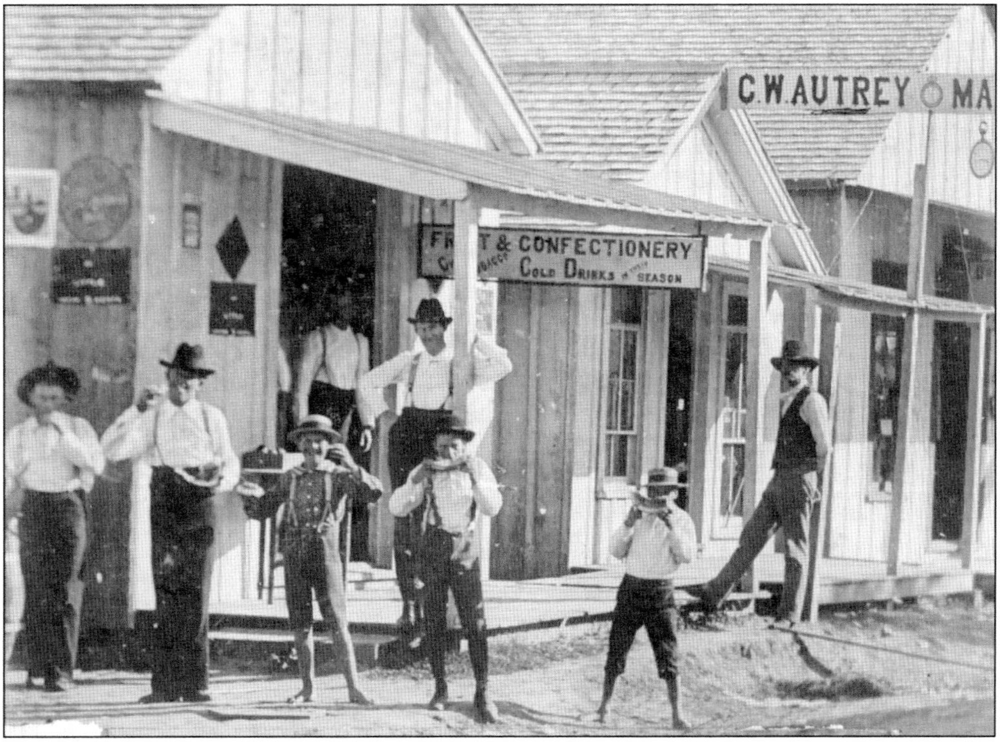

C.W. Autrey, Watchmaker, and the Fruit & Confectionery were just two of the businesses in Port Lavaca in the 1880s. Standing in the first row are, from left to right, Joe Deutsch, Will Henderson, Rowland Clement, Frank Boyd, Billy Wilson, and Jimmie Hatch leaning against the post. Winn Traylor stands nearest the door. The men inside the door are unidentified.

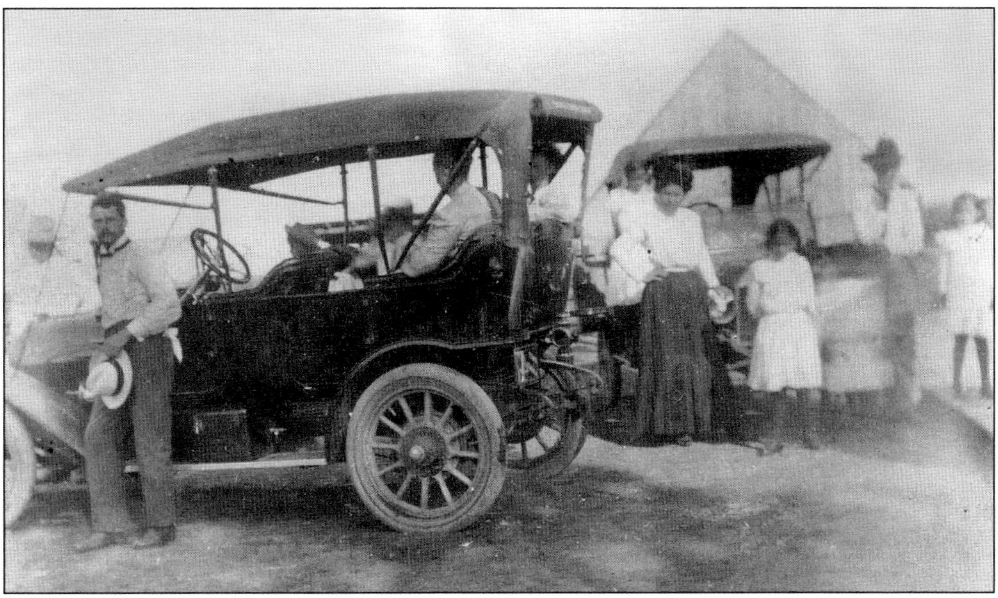

Families congregate around automobiles on North Street in the early 1900s, just after automobiles began to outnumber horse-drawn carriages. North Street was officially renamed Main Street in 1956 or 1957; however, locals called it Main Street well before the official name change.

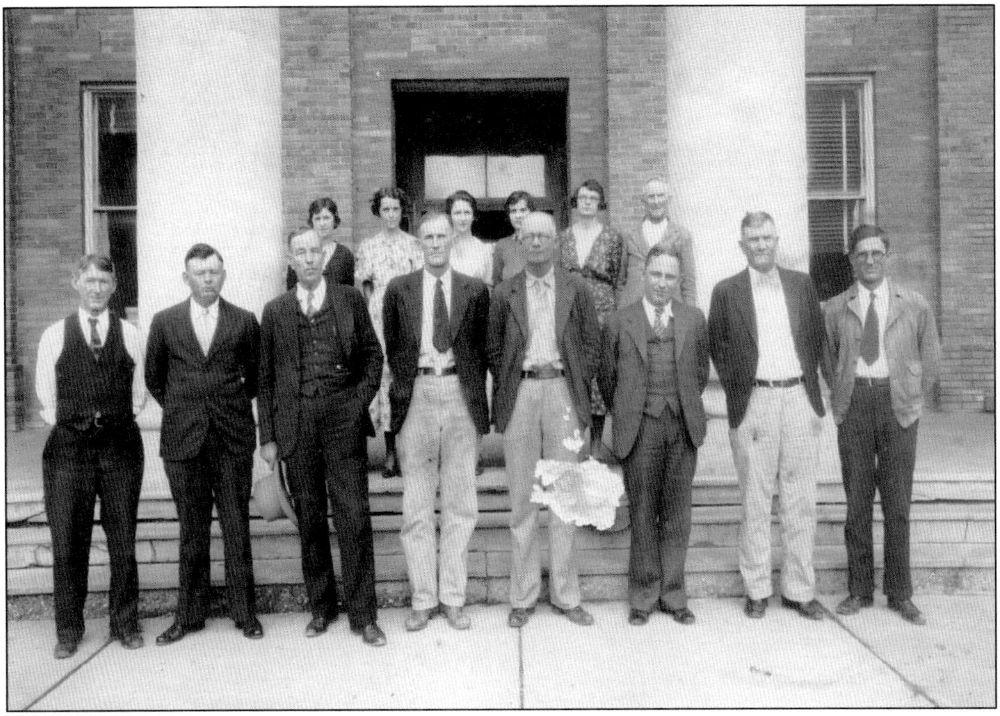

Calhoun County employees pose on the courthouse steps in 1931.

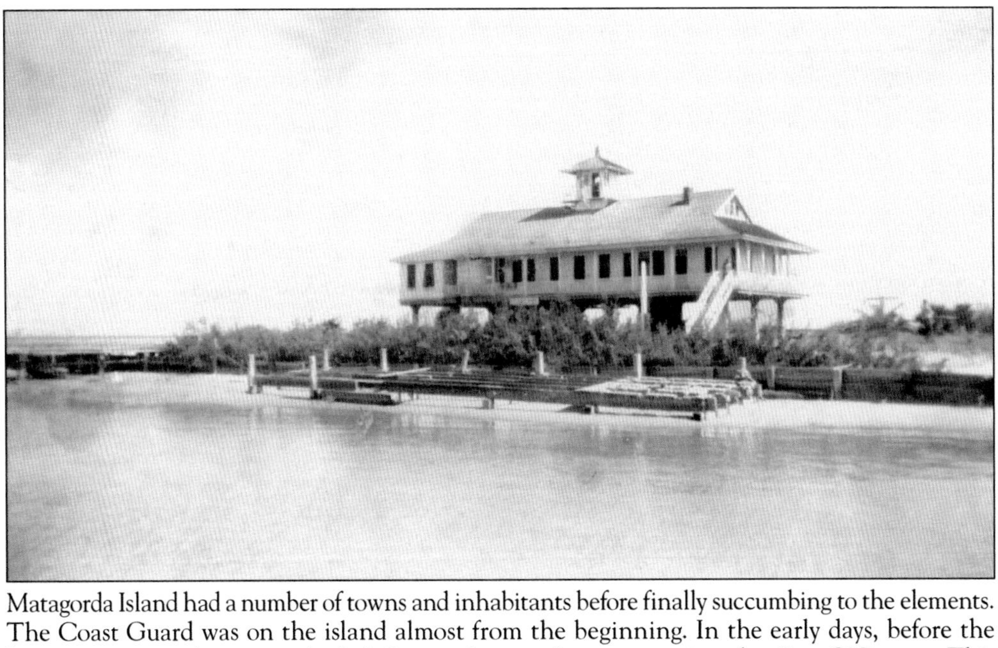

Matagorda Island had a number of towns and inhabitants before finally succumbing to the elements. The Coast Guard was on the island almost from the beginning. In the early days, before the hurricanes, it was known as the Life Saving Station. It is now stationed at Port O'Connor. This photograph of the old station was taken in August 1946. It was destroyed by Hurricane Carla on September 11, 1961.

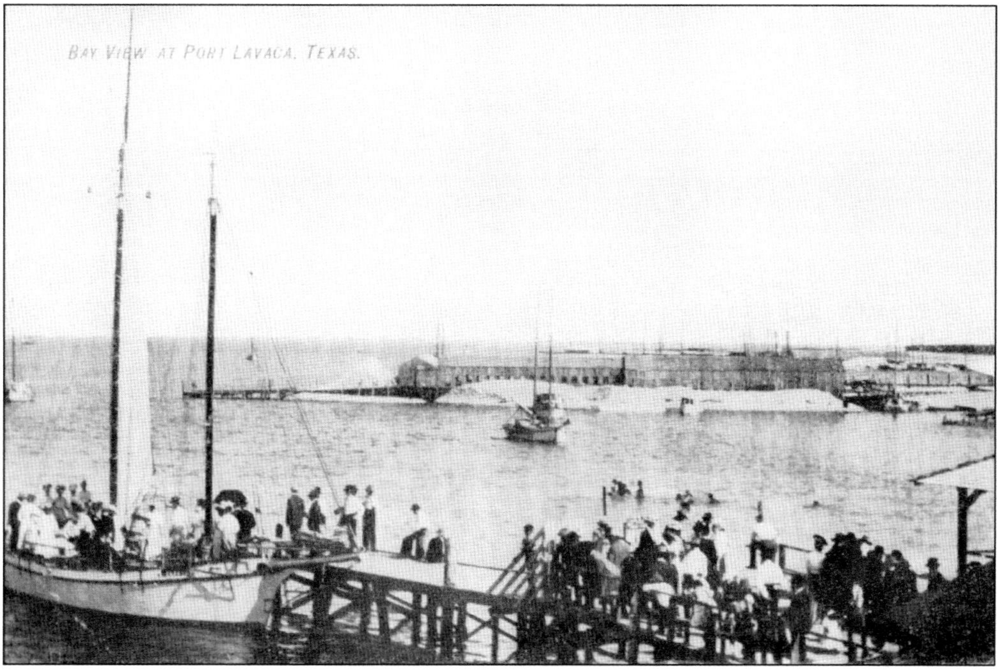

Oyster houses are visible in the background as tourists wait to board boats to tour Lavaca Bay.

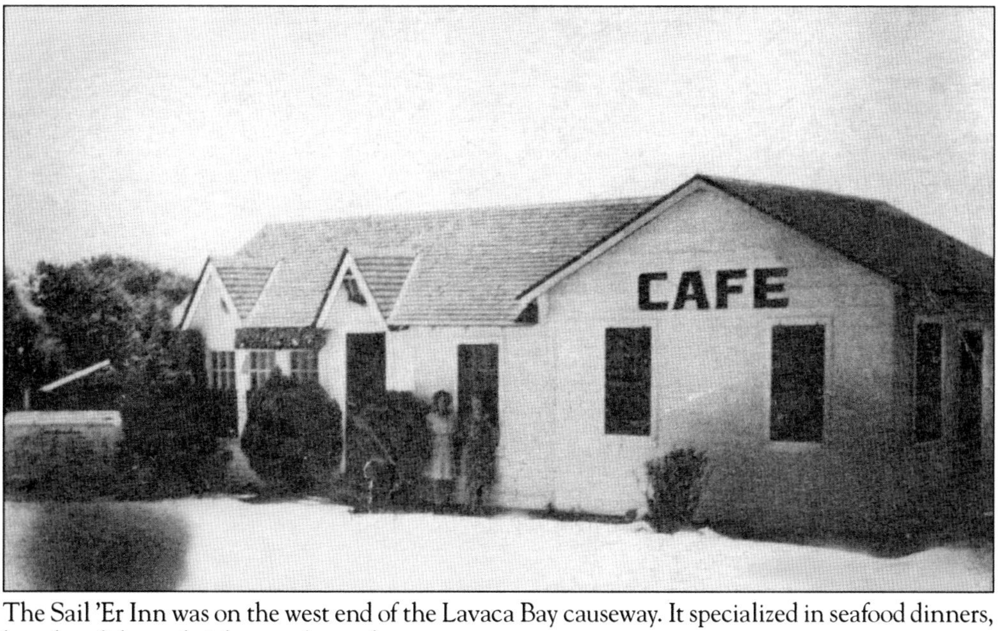

The Sail 'Er Inn was on the west end of the Lavaca Bay causeway. It specialized in seafood dinners, boneless fish sandwiches, and corndogs.

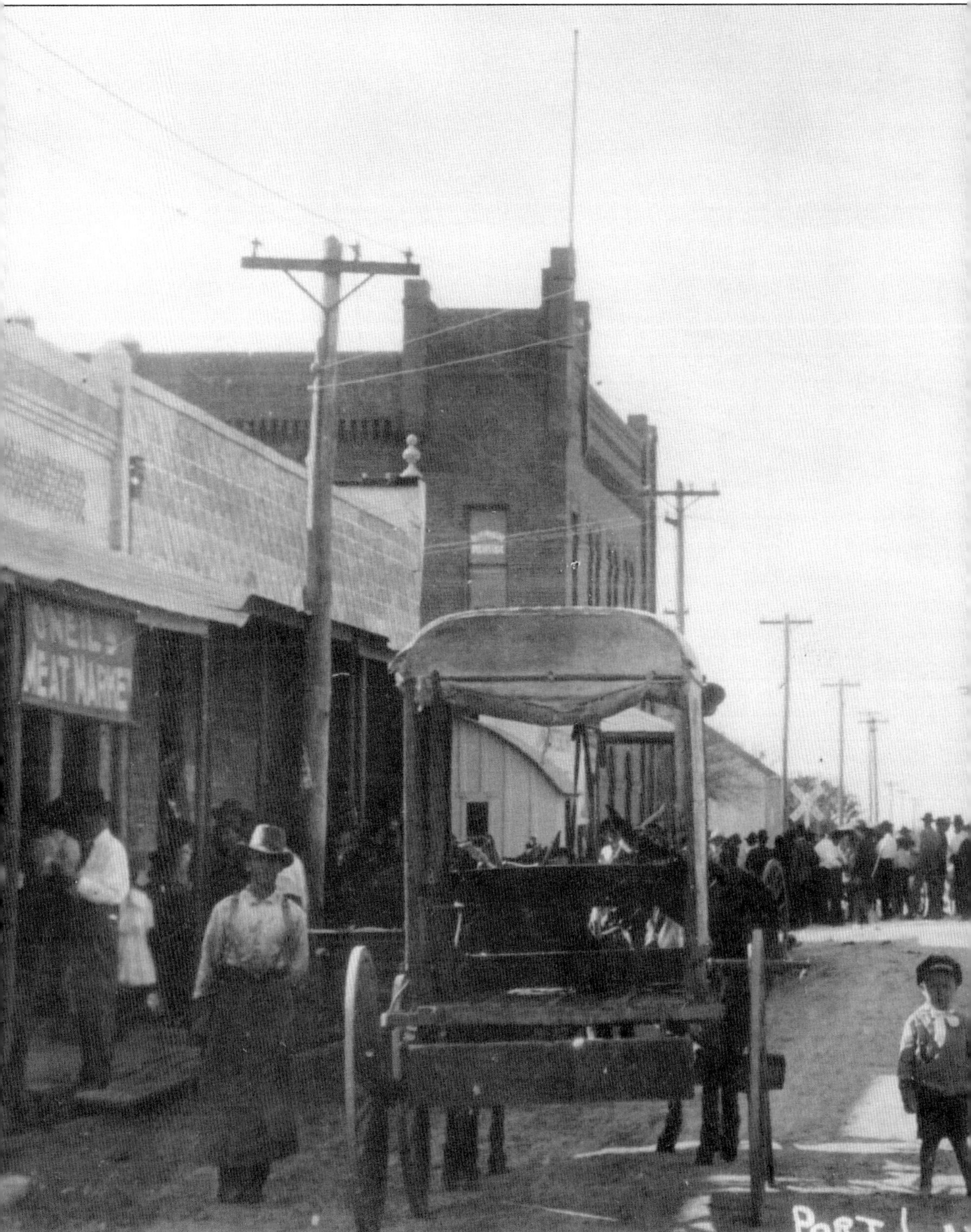

This downtown scene in Port Lavaca shows O'Neil's Meat Market on the left. On the right, in the center of the block, is the tower of the 1907 Cruce Building, which later became the home

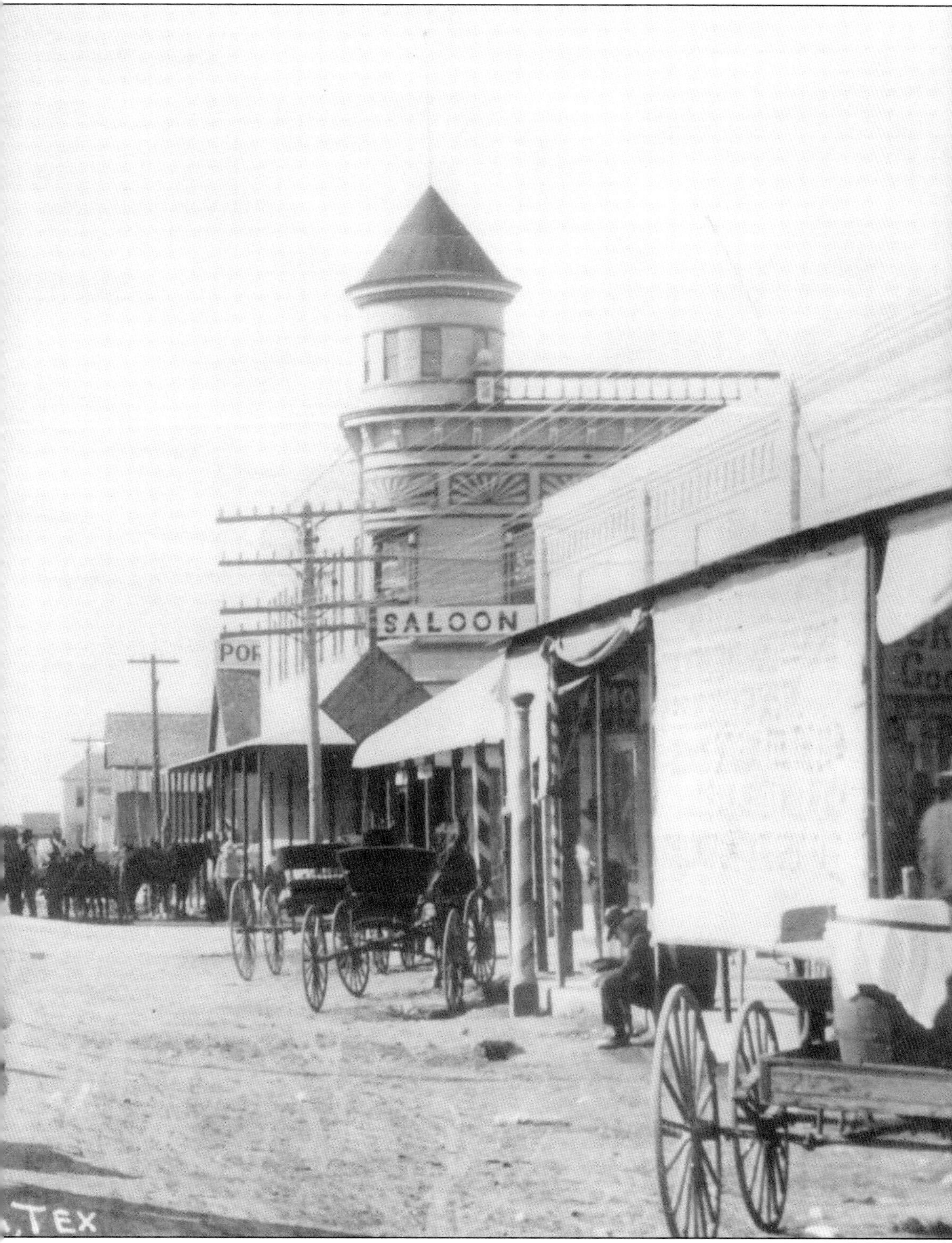

of the Sterling drugstore. Note the two small boys facing the camera.

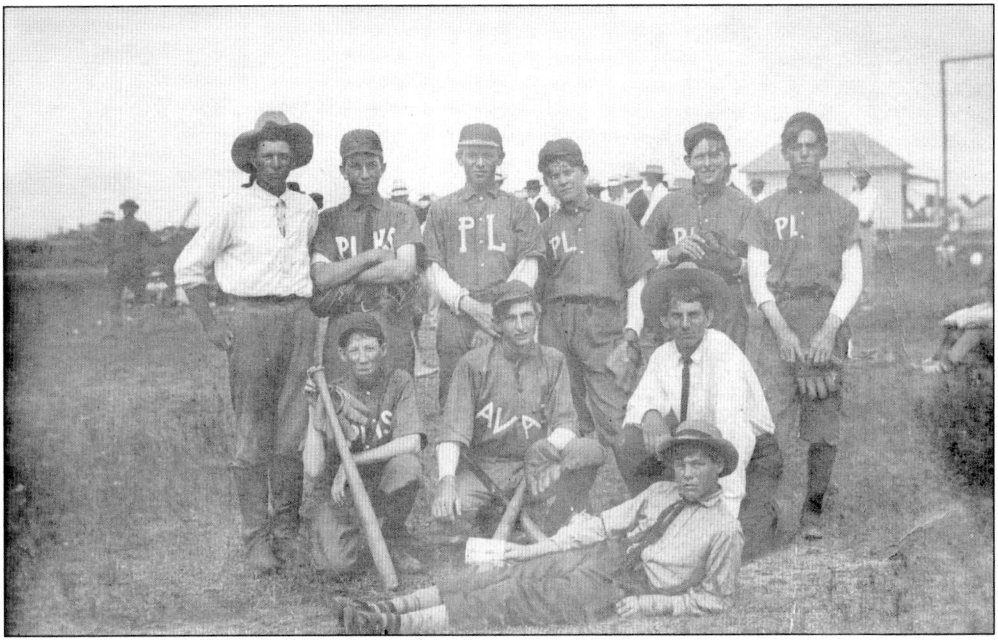

An early Port Lavaca baseball team poses for a team photograph around 1910.

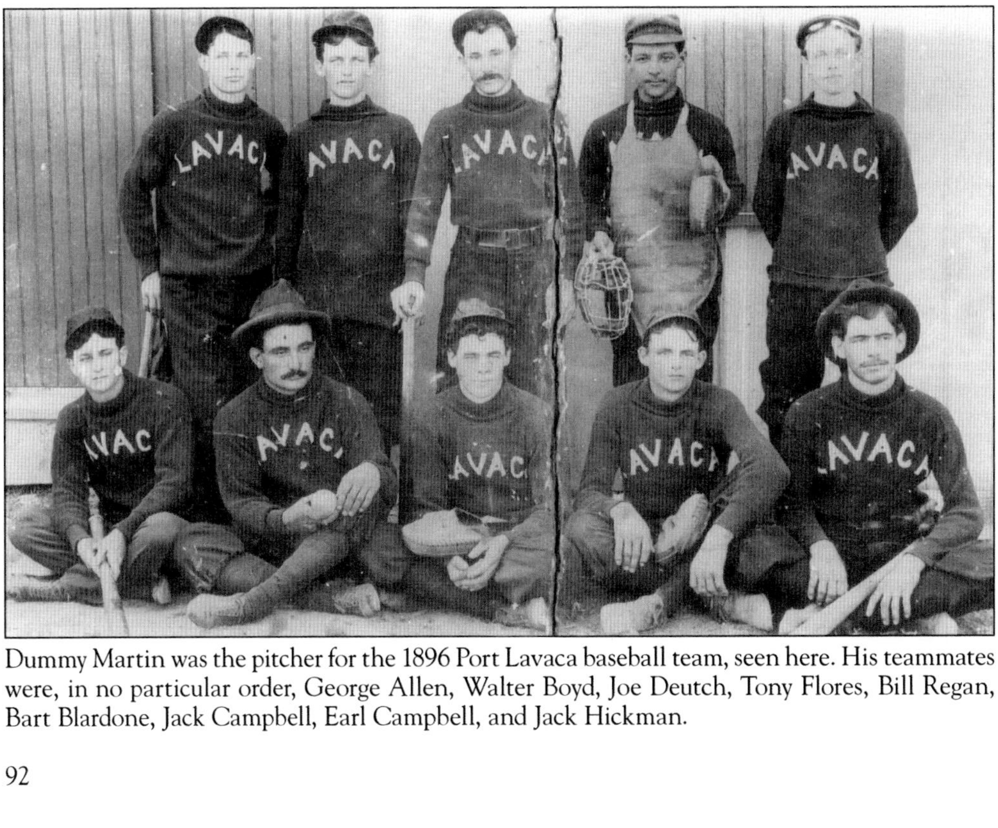

Dummy Martin was the pitcher for the 1896 Port Lavaca baseball team, seen here. His teammates were, in no particular order, George Allen, Walter Boyd, Joe Deutch, Tony Flores, Bill Regan, Bart Blardone, Jack Campbell, Earl Campbell, and Jack Hickman.

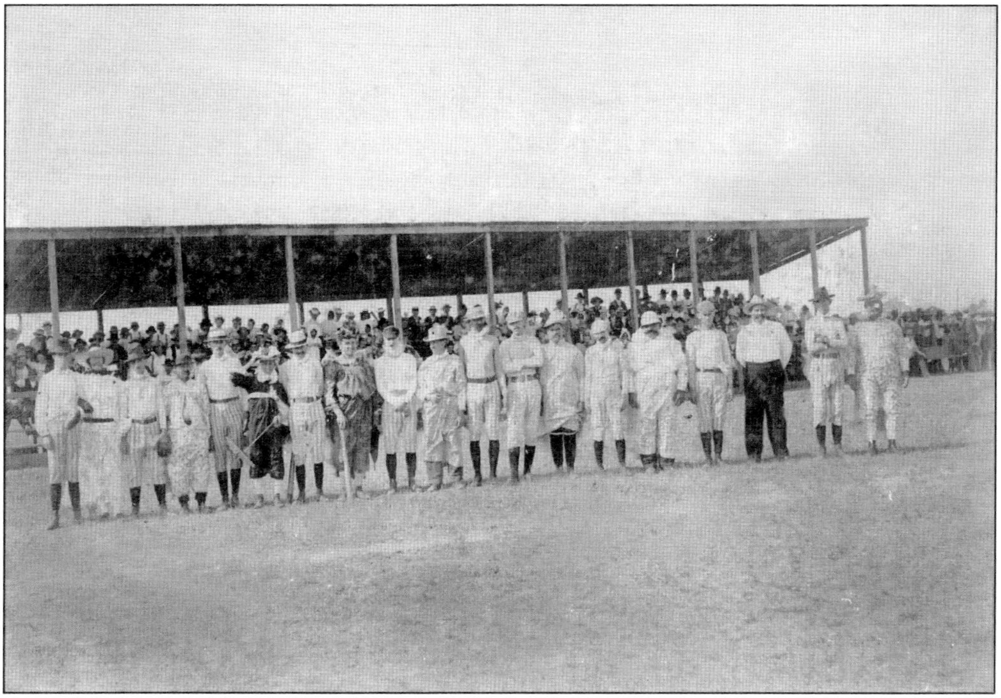

This is another vintage baseball scene at Port Lavaca. Note the full grandstands in the background. On July 14, 1897, the team played a fundraising game.

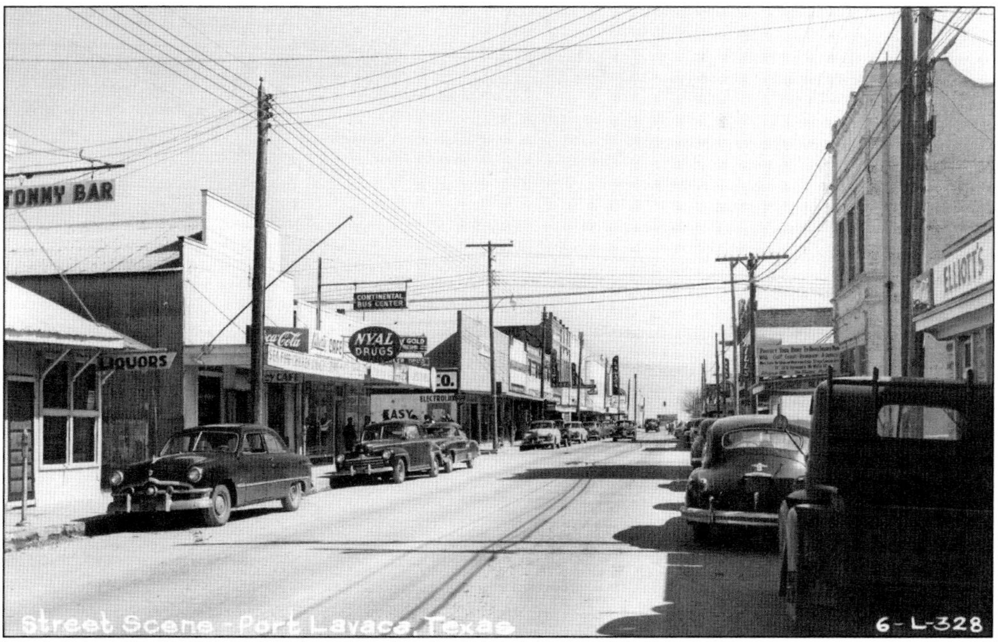

In the 1940s, Main Street was the heart of the community. A few of the businesses seen here are Tommy Bar, the Liberty Cafe, Nyal Drugs, Melcher's Hardware, Vela's Grocery, Horsheim Shoes, and the La Salle Restaurant.

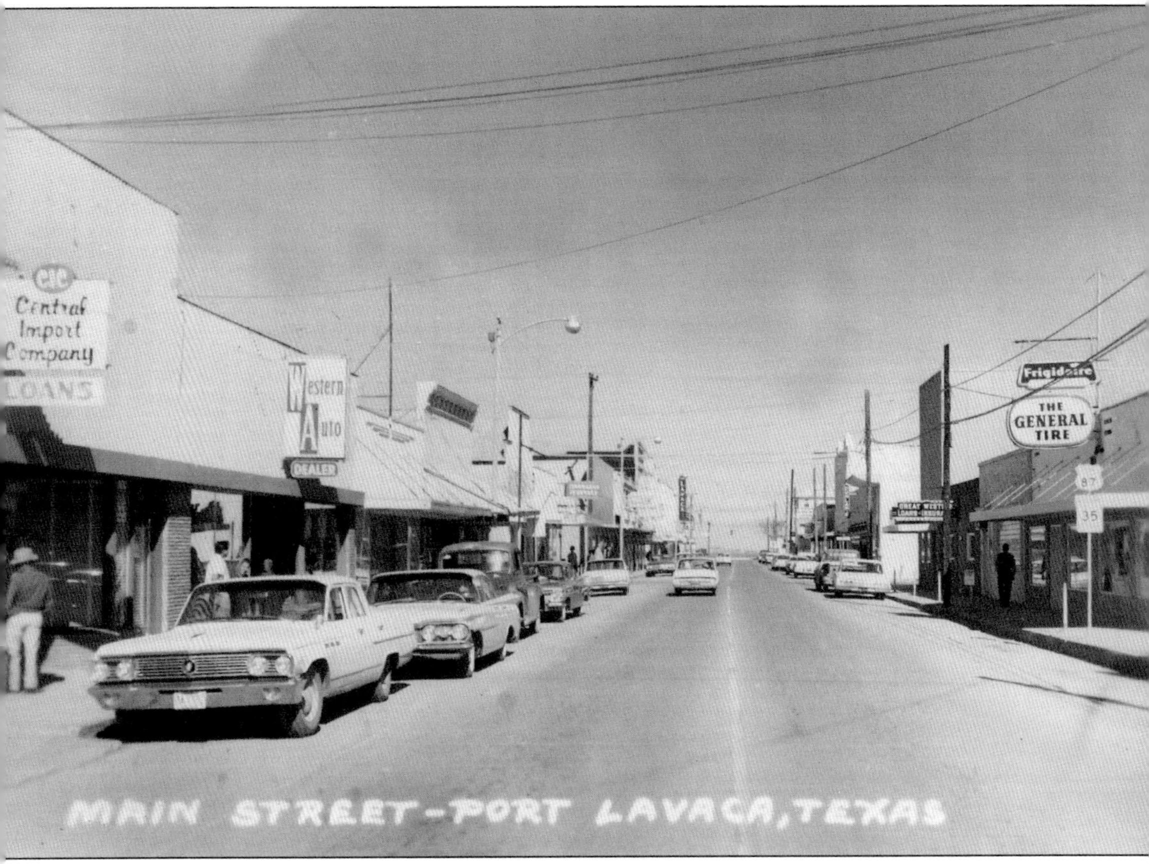

In the 1950s, Main Street in Port Lavaca was home to the Central Import Company, Western Auto, General Tire, Great Western Loans and Insurance, and the Lavaca Theater.

Born in 1873 in Port Lavaca, James D. O'Neil served as sheriff of Calhoun County from 1910 to 1920 and again from 1930 to 1942.

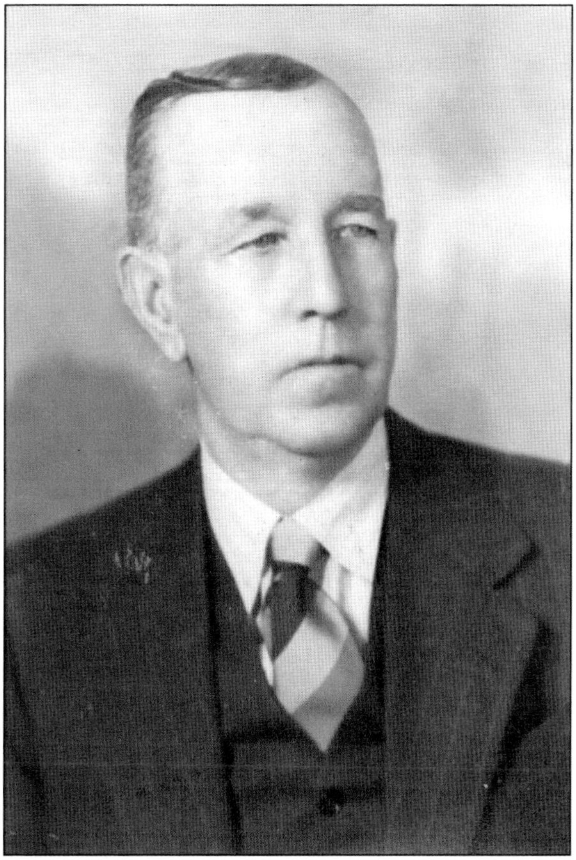

These two old oyster shacks in Port Lavaca appear to be abandoned, and the beach is strewn with oyster shells.

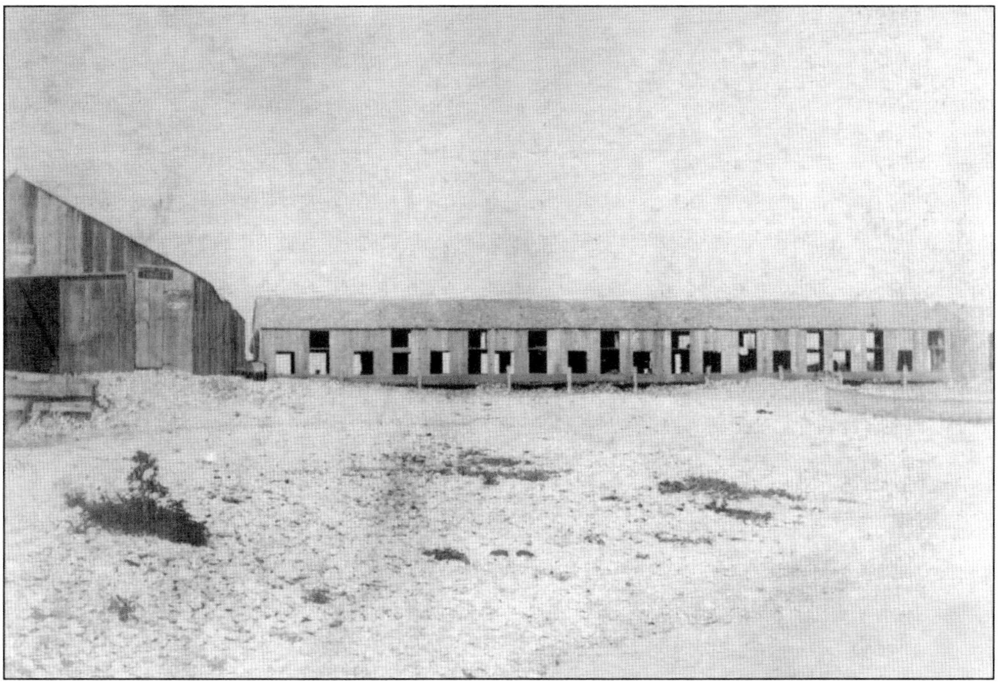

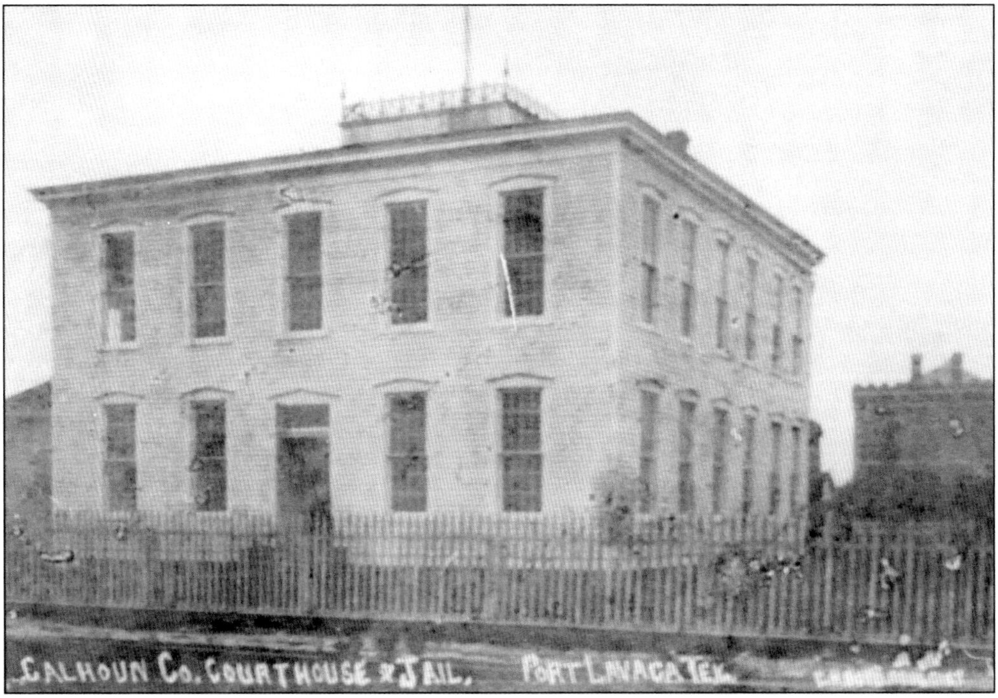

Although not the first Calhoun County courthouse, this was the first one built specifically for that purpose in Port Lavaca. E.L. Miller was the low bidder and was granted the contract to build the courthouse. The building was accepted as complete on September 1, 1887. An earlier courthouse was built in Indianola when it was the county seat.

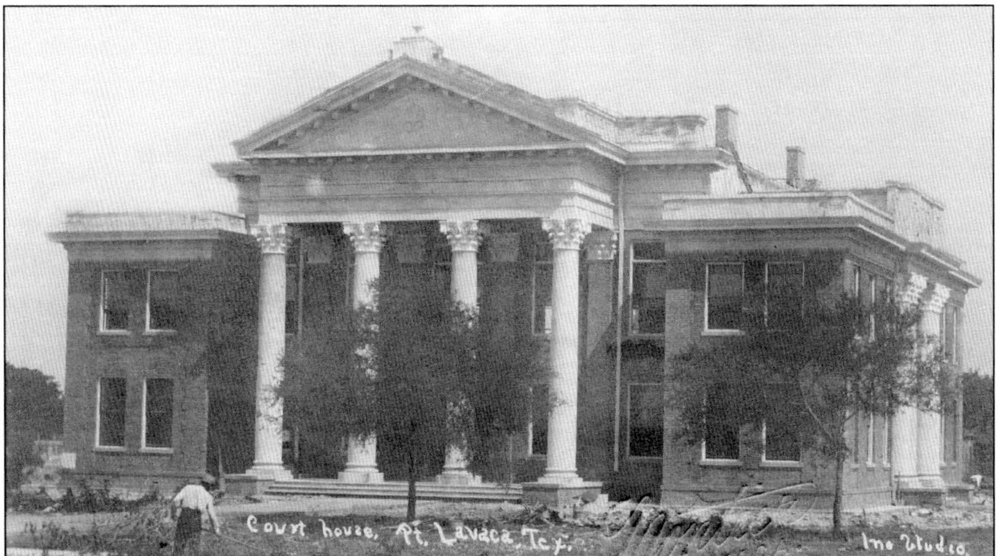

In 1911, a new courthouse made of brick and wood replaced the 1887 building. It was constructed by the Falls City Construction Company and designed by architects Chamberlain & Co. The new building cost $44,000.

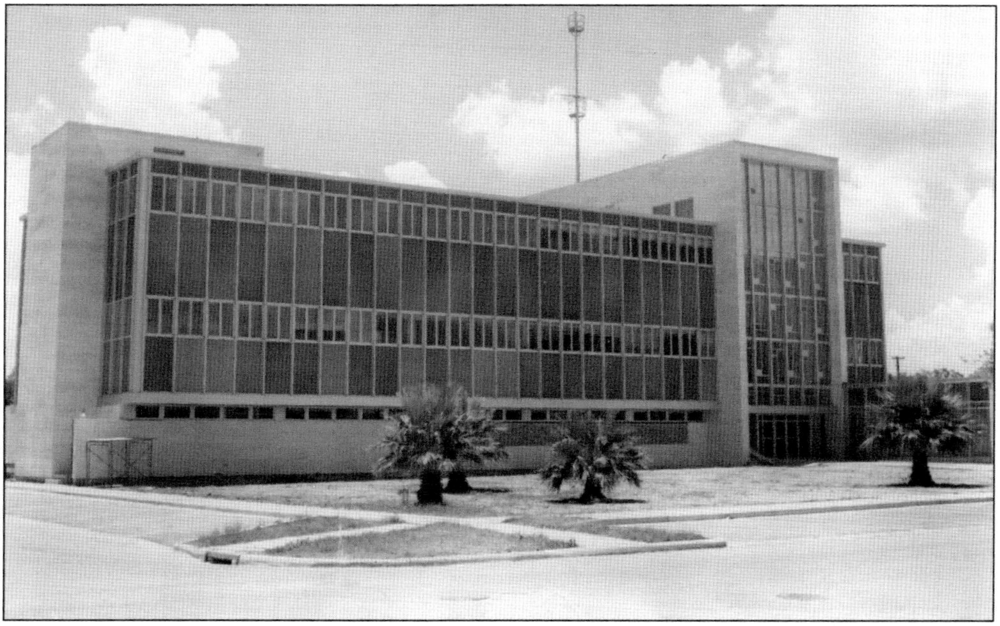

The third county courthouse in Port Lavaca was dedicated on July 3, 1959. Architects Rustay and Martin of Houston designed it; it was built by the D.W. Marshall Company of Victoria, Texas. In late 2004 and early 2005, the courthouse was closed for remodeling, which was ultimately completed in 2007.

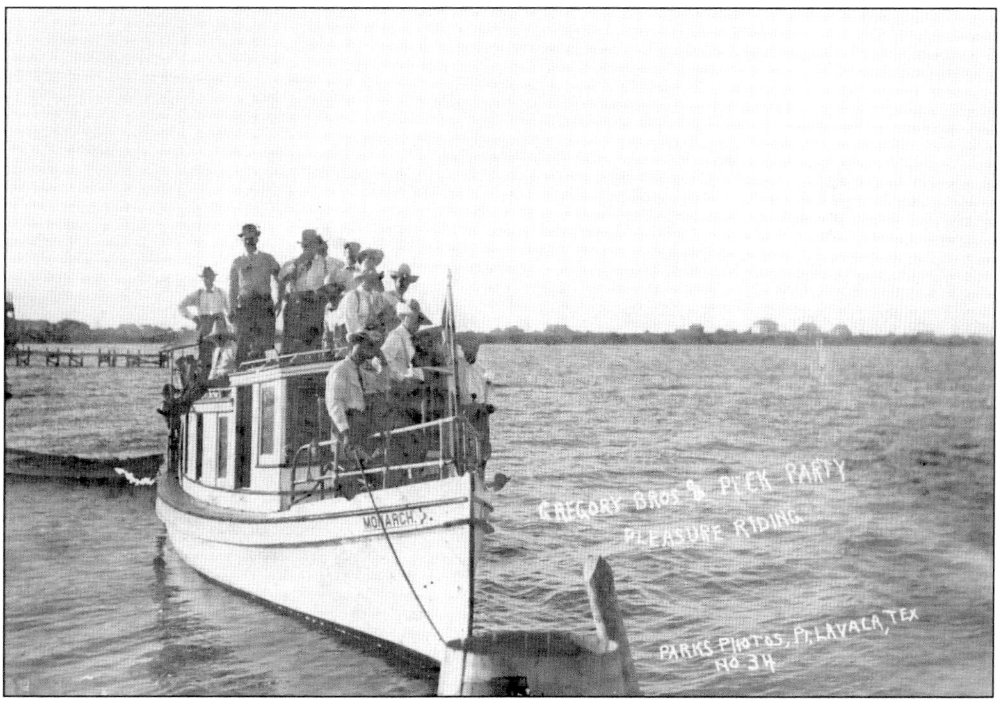

The Gregory Brothers and Peck party go out for a pleasure ride aboard the *Monarch* in Port Lavaca Bay.

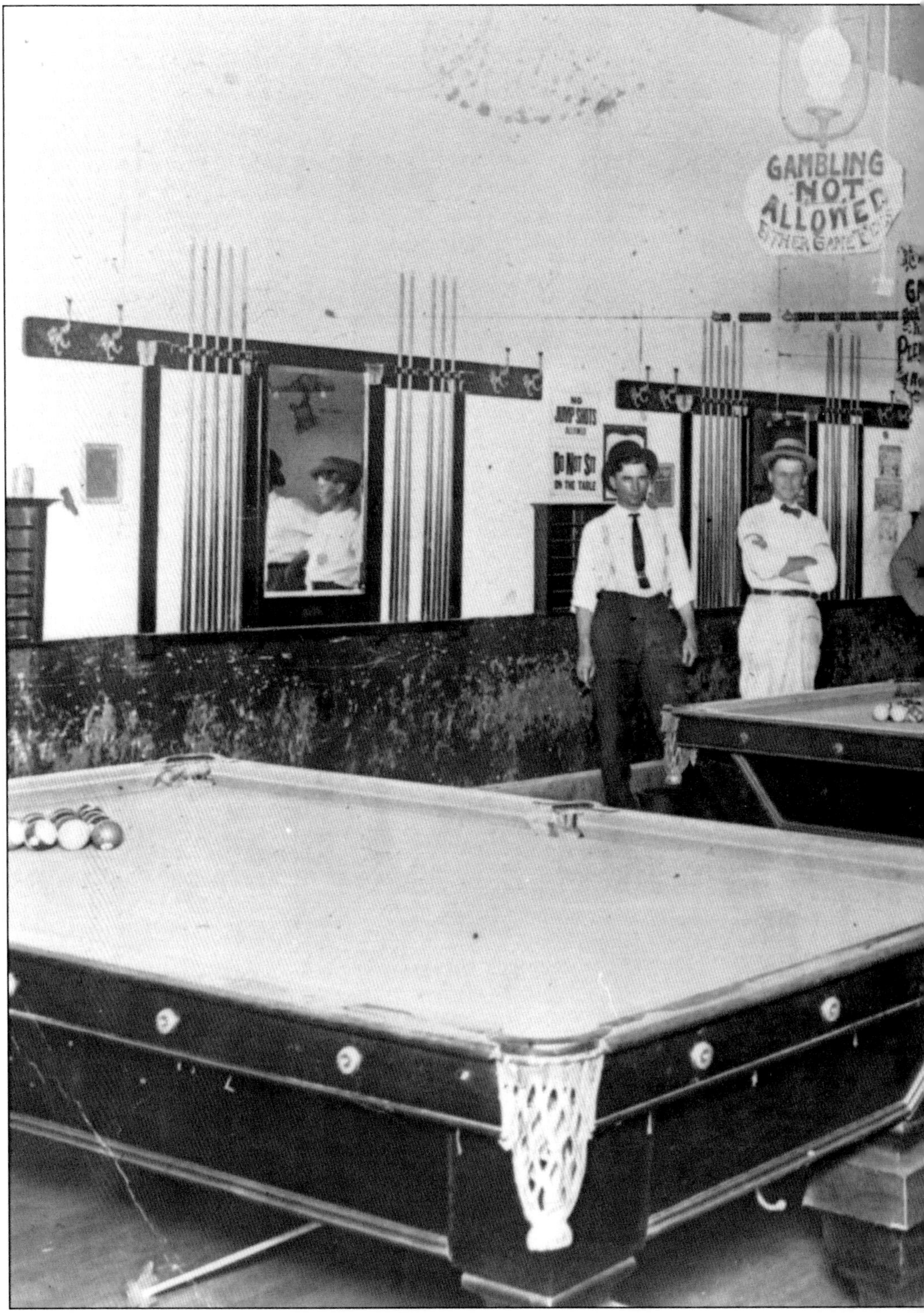

Stutzenbecker's pool hall, pictured here in 1912, was a gathering place for local men. Will and Harry Stutzenbecker are on the far left and far right, respectively. Dr. Fred Roemer and Gotlieb

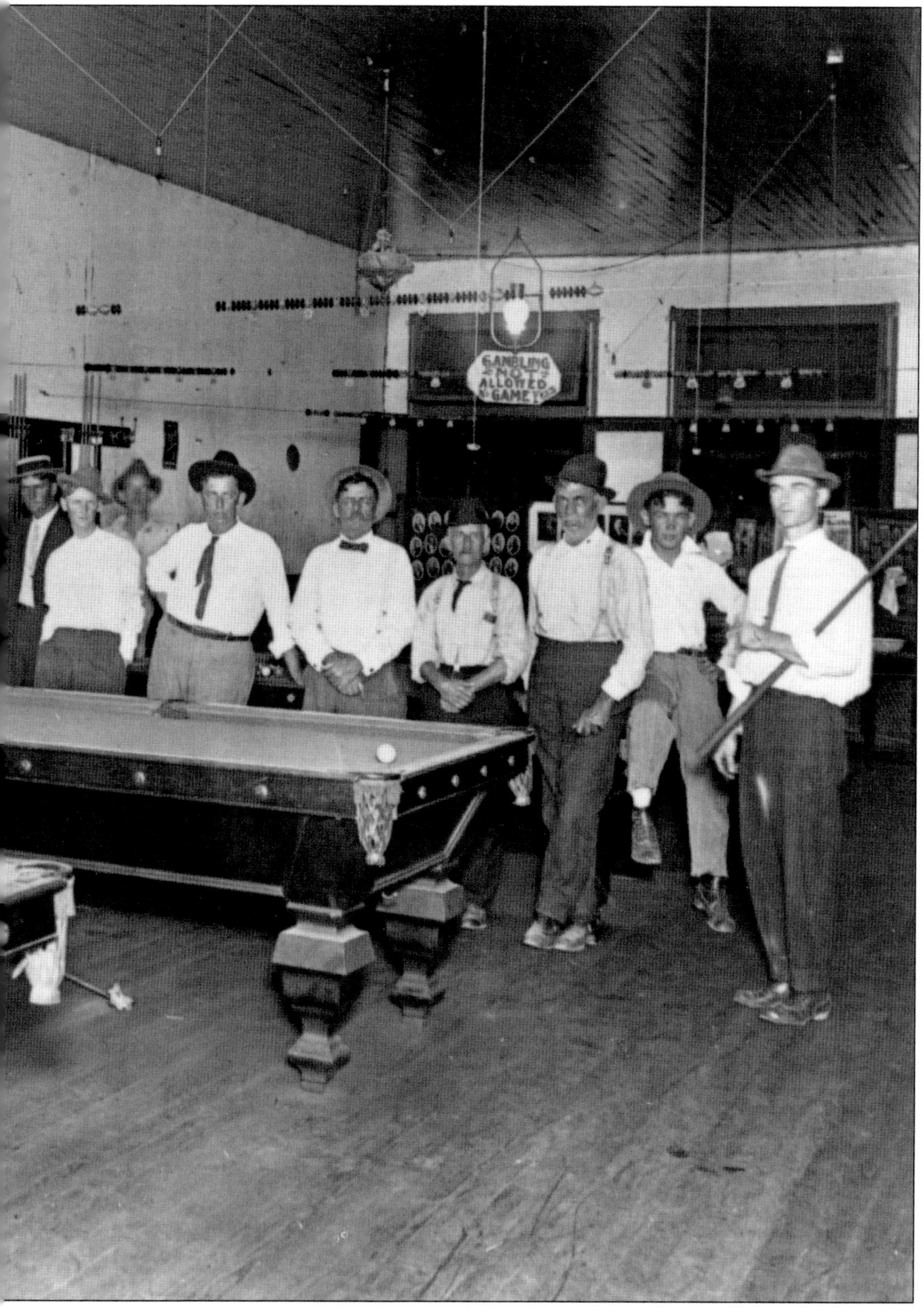

Charbula are also included in the photograph, but their position is not identified. The other men are unidentified.

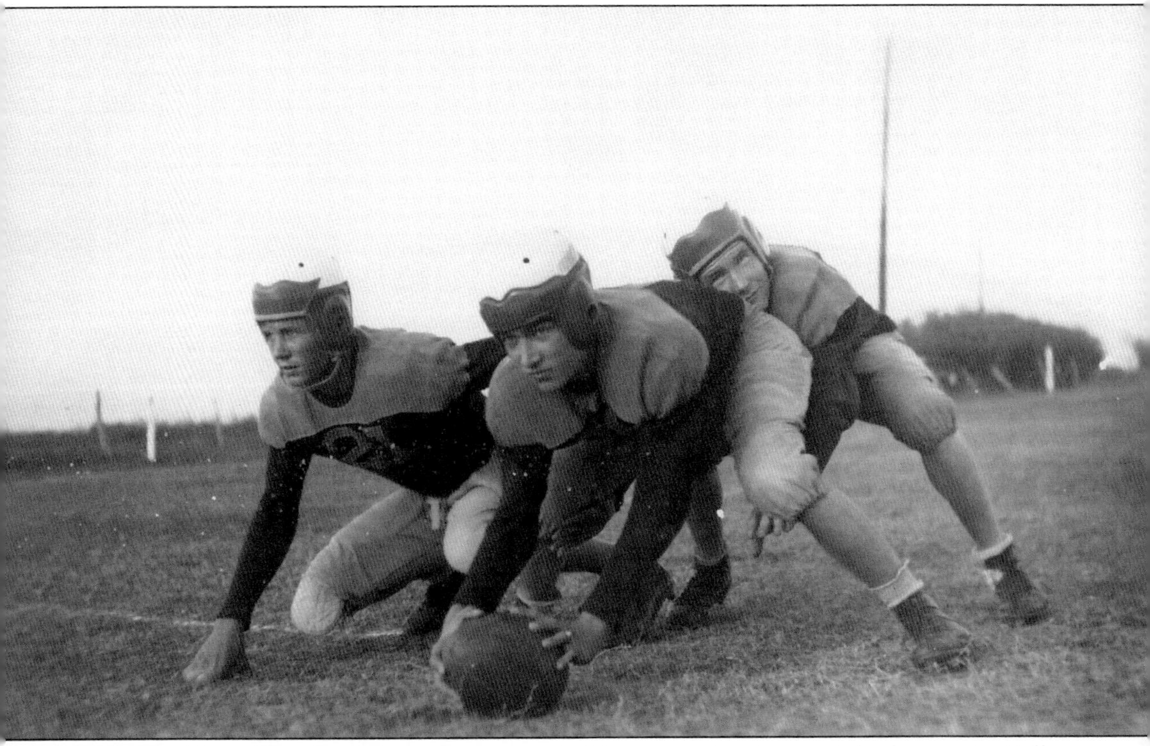

Football has always been the primary sport in Texas, and that is certainly the case in Calhoun County. These Port Lavaca High School football players are Lamar Marshall (far left), George Fred Rhodes (with football), and Wesley Newlin.

Port Lavaca High School football player Jack Miller is seen here in 1932.

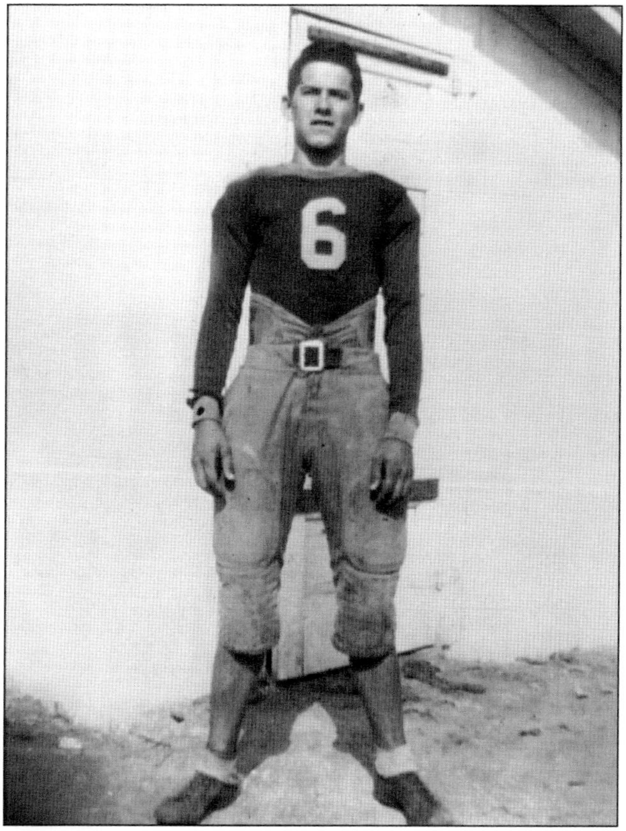

Below, the 1927–1928 Port Lavaca Sandcrabs pose for a team photograph, with Coach North standing behind them.

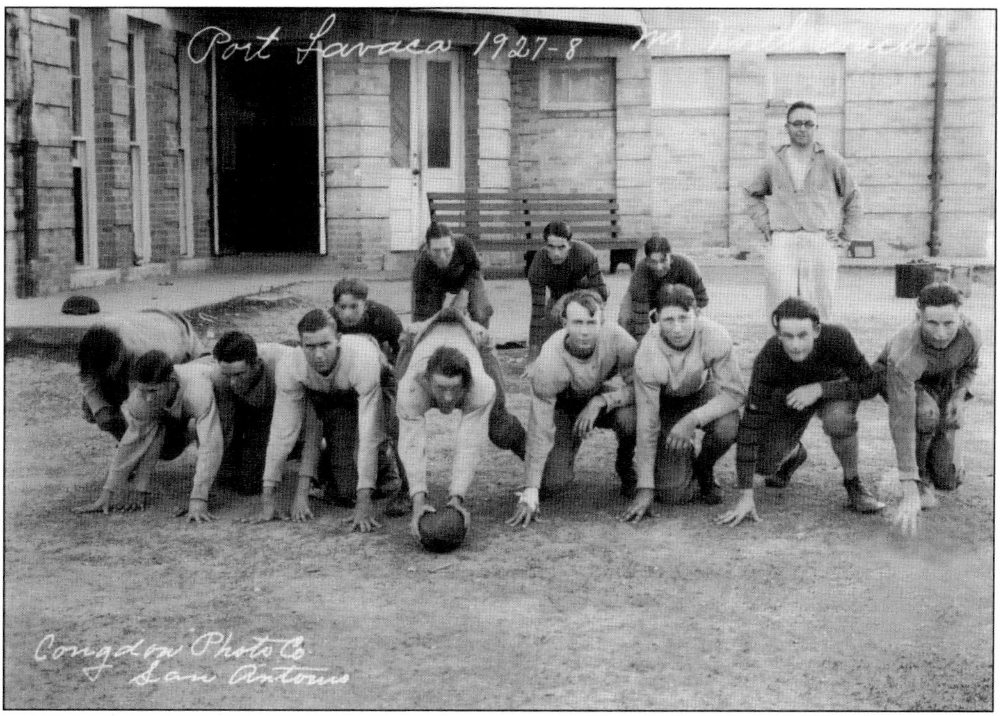

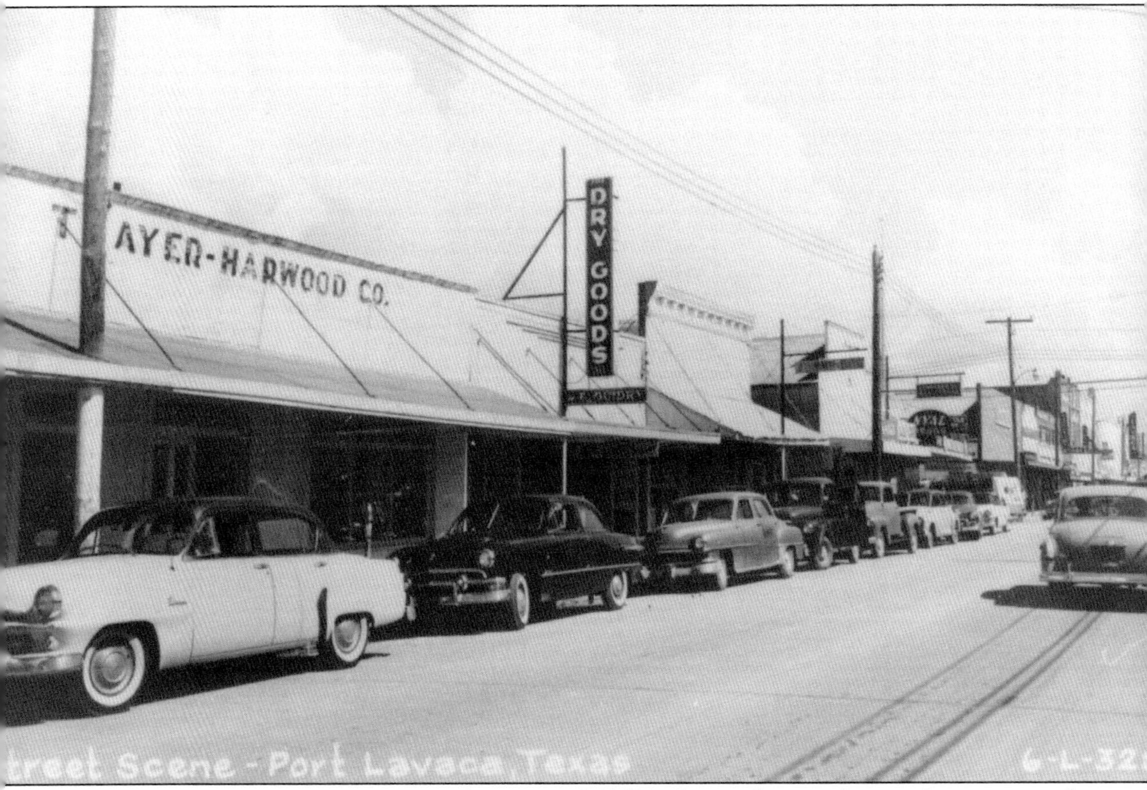

Main Street in Port Lavaca is seen here around 1950. It featured many thriving businesses at the time along with the latest automobiles.

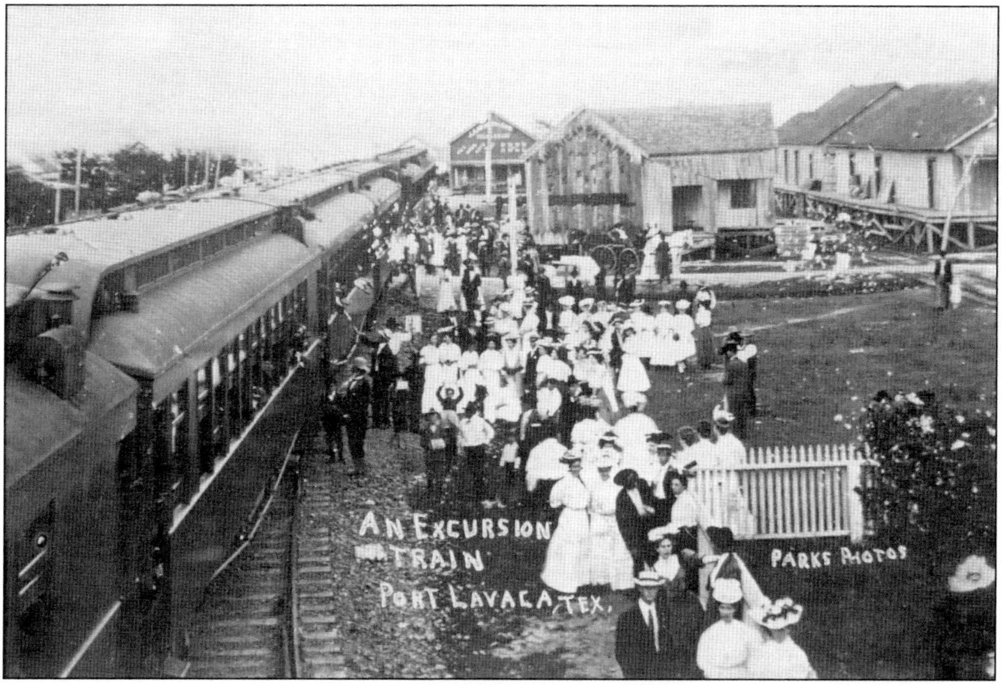

Above, excursionists disembark from the train near downtown Port Lavaca. The American Brewing Company (center) sold beer and ice. The company behind it sold wood and coal.

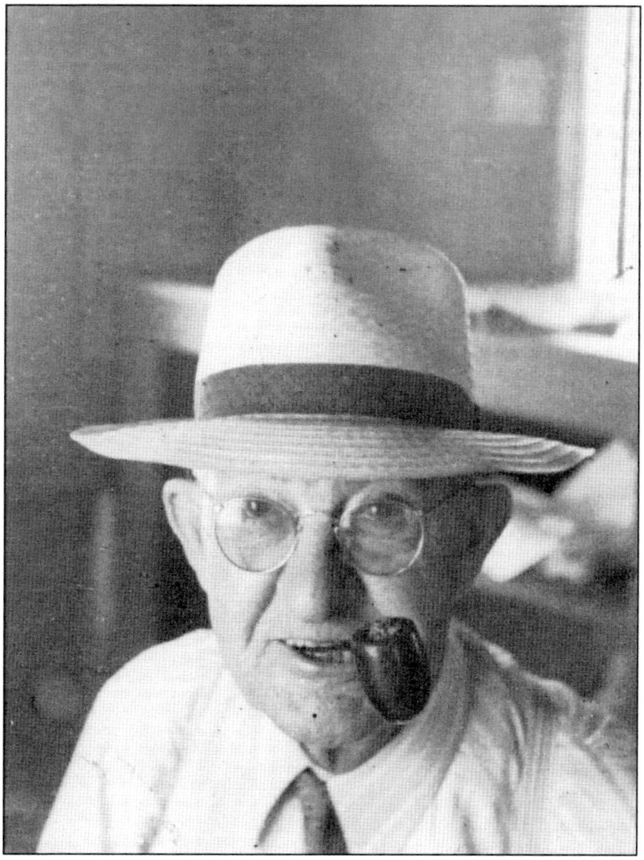

W.J. Thomas was the depot agent in Seadrift from 1910 to 1920. He passed away in 1969 at the age of 92.

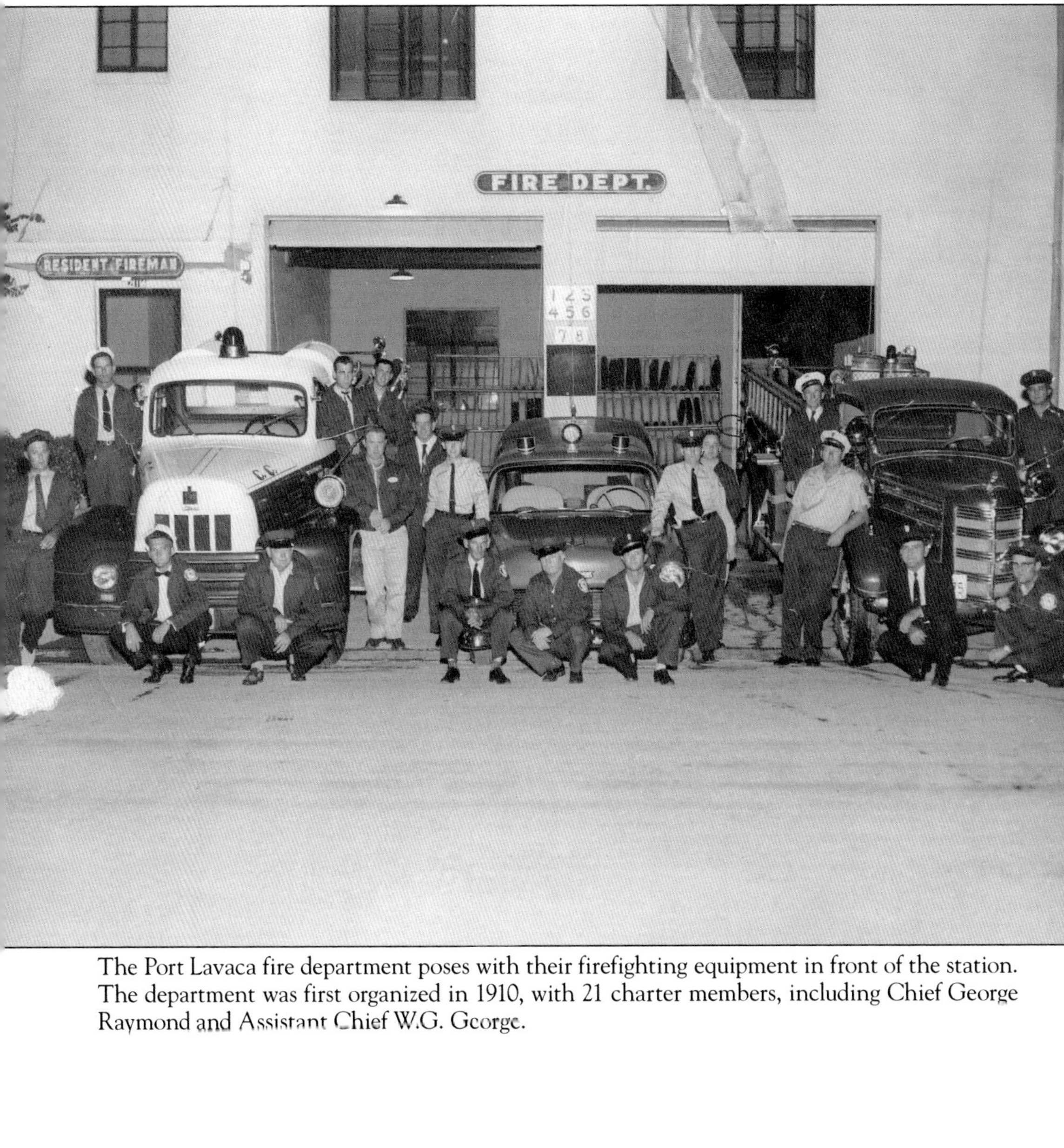

The Port Lavaca fire department poses with their firefighting equipment in front of the station. The department was first organized in 1910, with 21 charter members, including Chief George Raymond and Assistant Chief W.G. George.

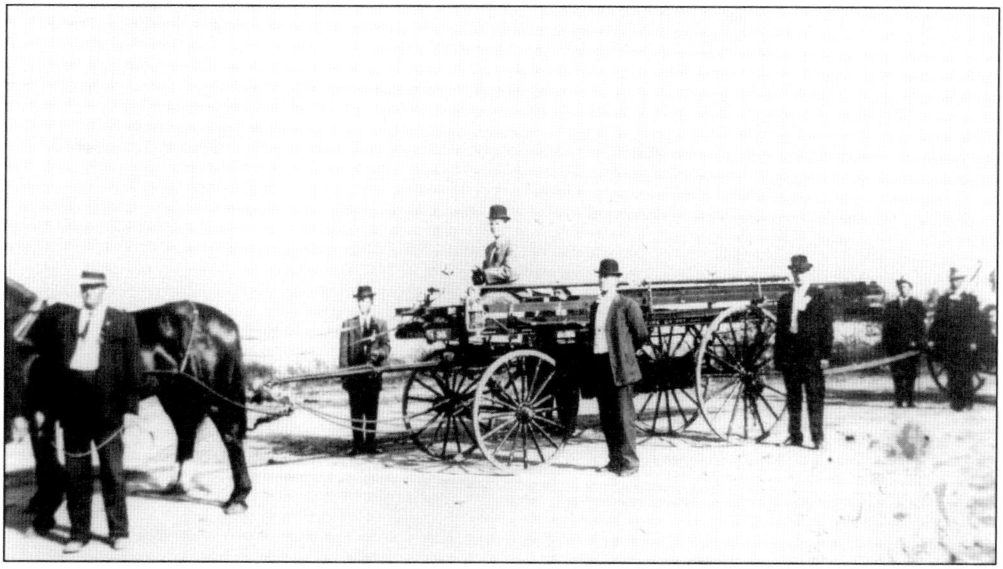

An early Port Lavaca hook and ladder company is seen here.

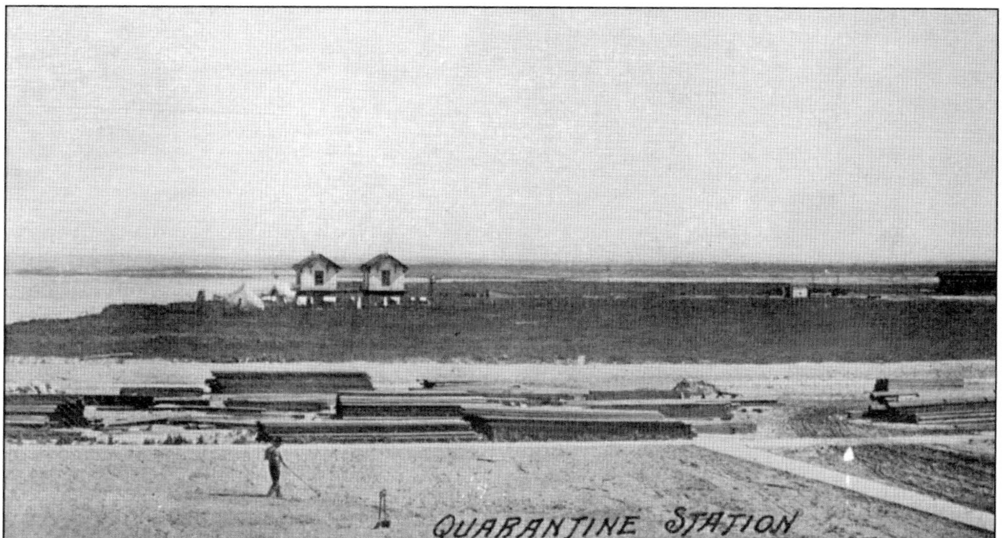

In 1906, George Holzheuser was in charge of the Port O'Connor Quarantine Station, seen here, and William Barr was a boatman. The station was located at Alligator Head, the future site of Port O'Connor. Barr's son Arthur was the last keeper of the Matagorda Island lighthouse.

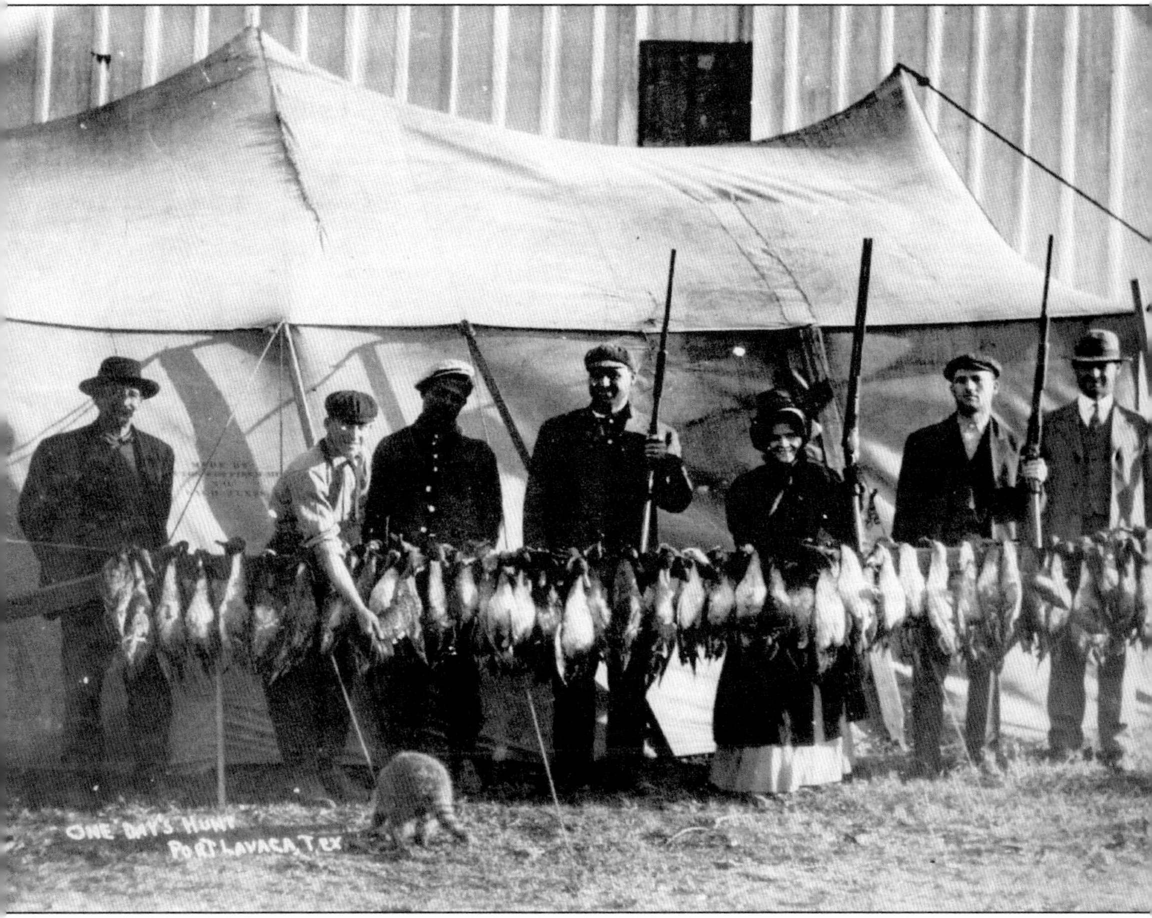

At the turn of the 20th century, waterfowl hunting was at its height. Here William Henry Smith and Harry C. Smith show off the catch from a one-day hunt. William and Harry were both very active in local business. William worked for the First National Bank, became deputy county clerk, was involved with the Rachgens-Smith Lumber Company, and helped to form the Smith-Ulrich Dredging Company along with his brother Harry and his father William.

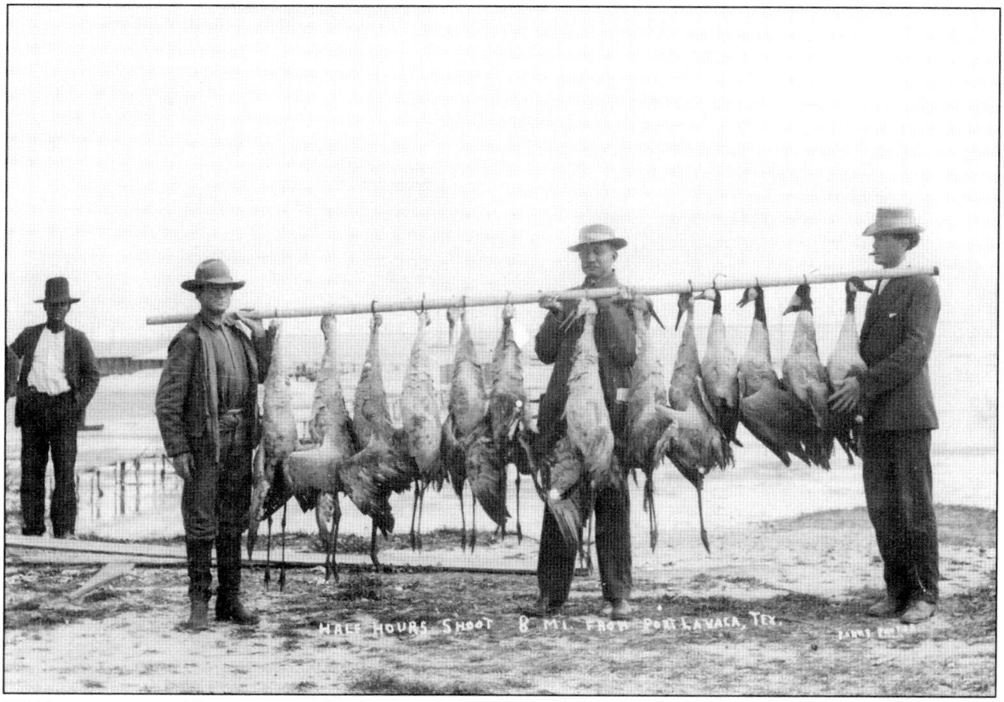

Wild game was sold commercially during this period, including large numbers of Canadian geese, cranes, and ducks. The take seen here was from just a half-hour of hunting, about eight miles from Port Lavaca.

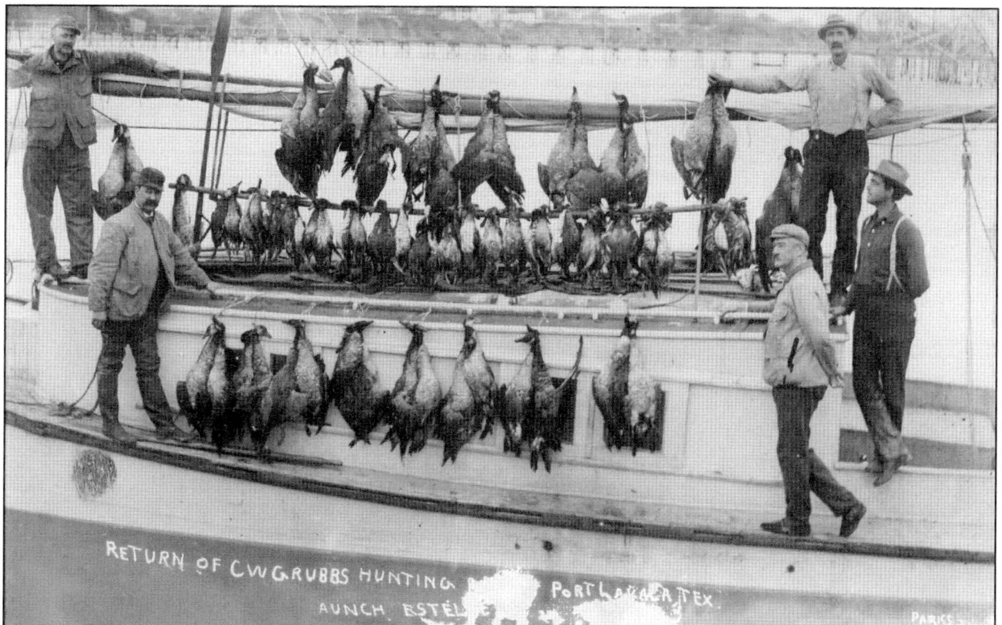

Famed hunter, decoy artist, and birdcall maker Charles Grubbs came to Calhoun County to hunt. He is seen here posing with fellow hunters aboard the *Estelle* after a hunt around 1910. He is believed to be at front right, in the light-colored jacket.

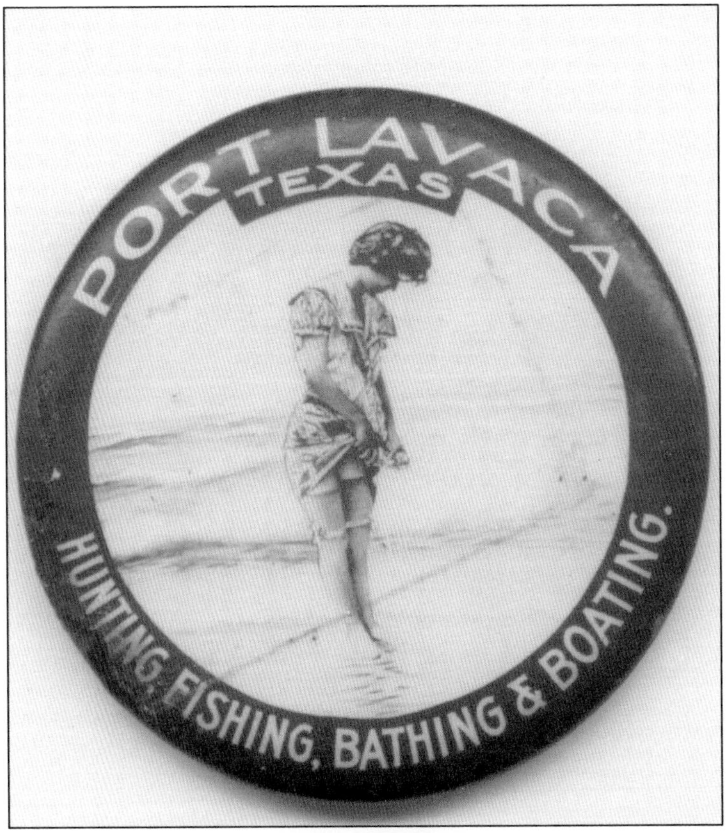

This vintage lapel pin touts the hunting, fishing, bathing, and boating of Port Lavaca—the outdoor activities that continue to draw thousands of visitors to the area every year.

This Yellow Cab Co. bus advertised "playtime all the year." Seen in 1928, it would have brought locals and tourists alike to the beachfront for popular activities like swimming, sunbathing, and shell collecting, as well as family outings and company picnics.

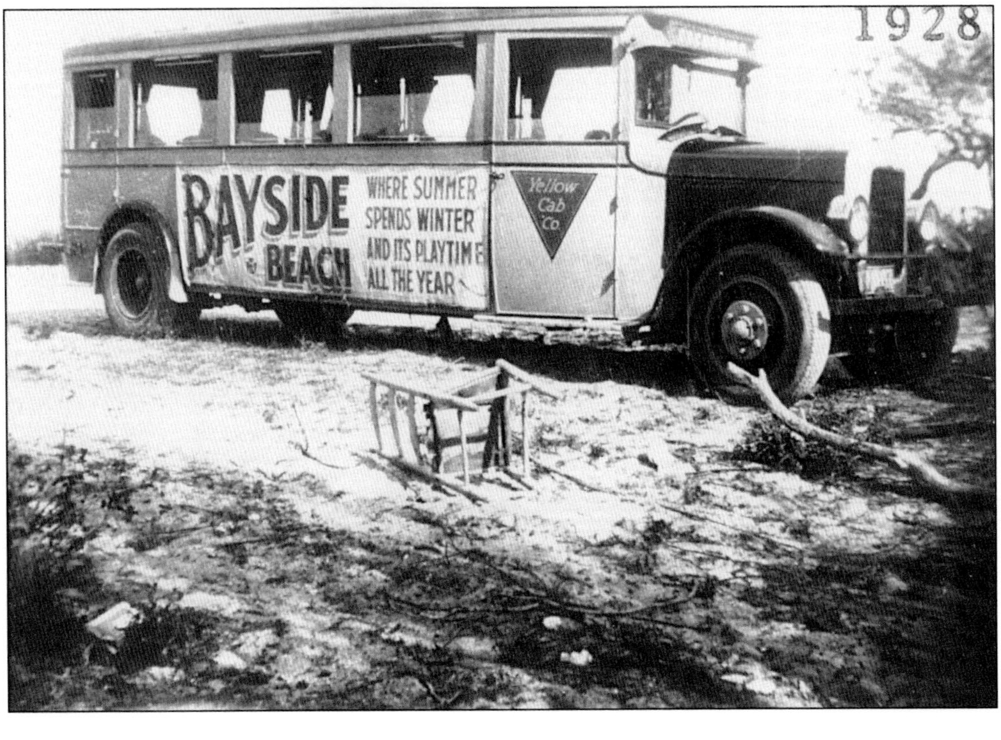

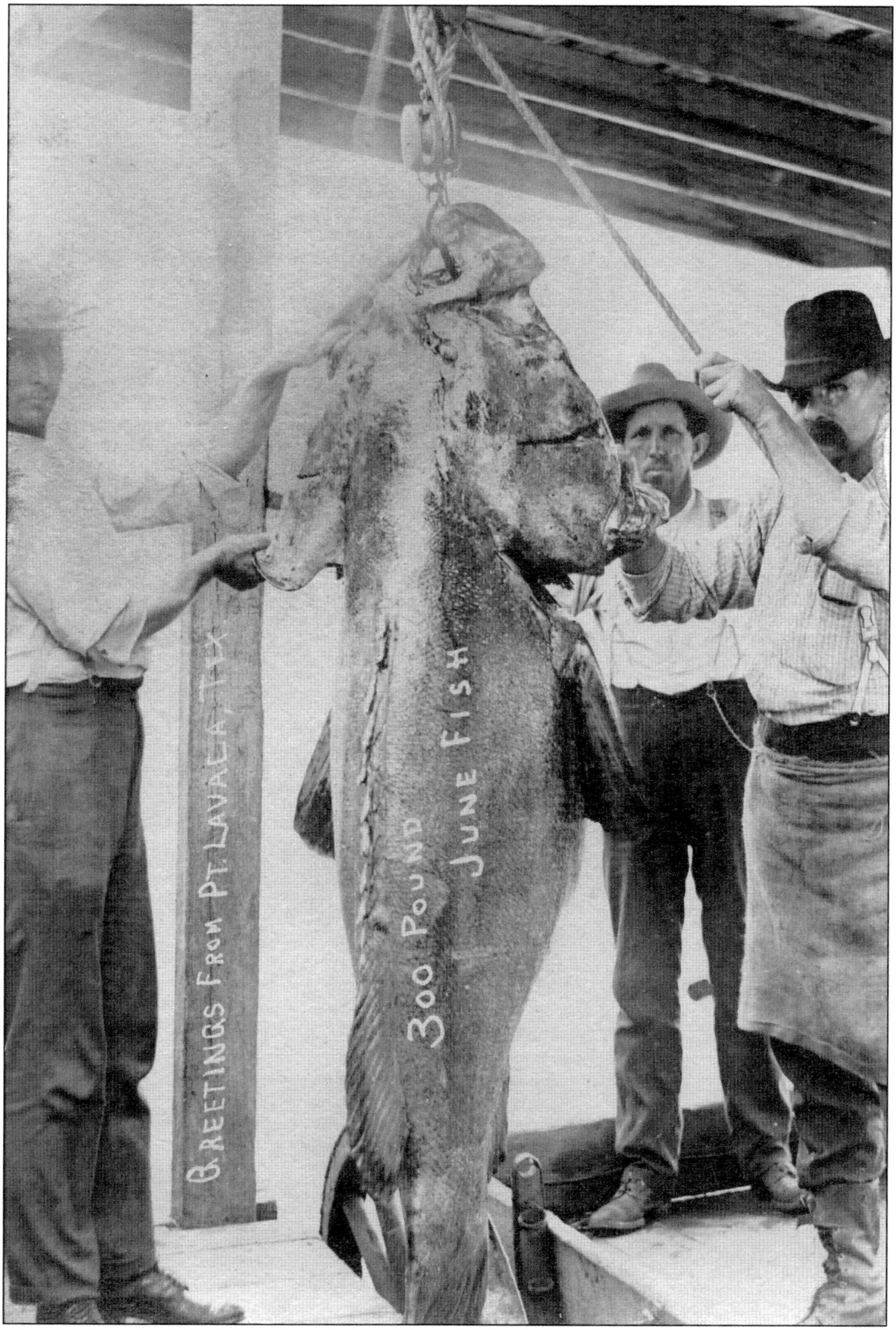

Three men show off the day's catch, a 300-pound grouper, also called a June fish, in the early 1900s.

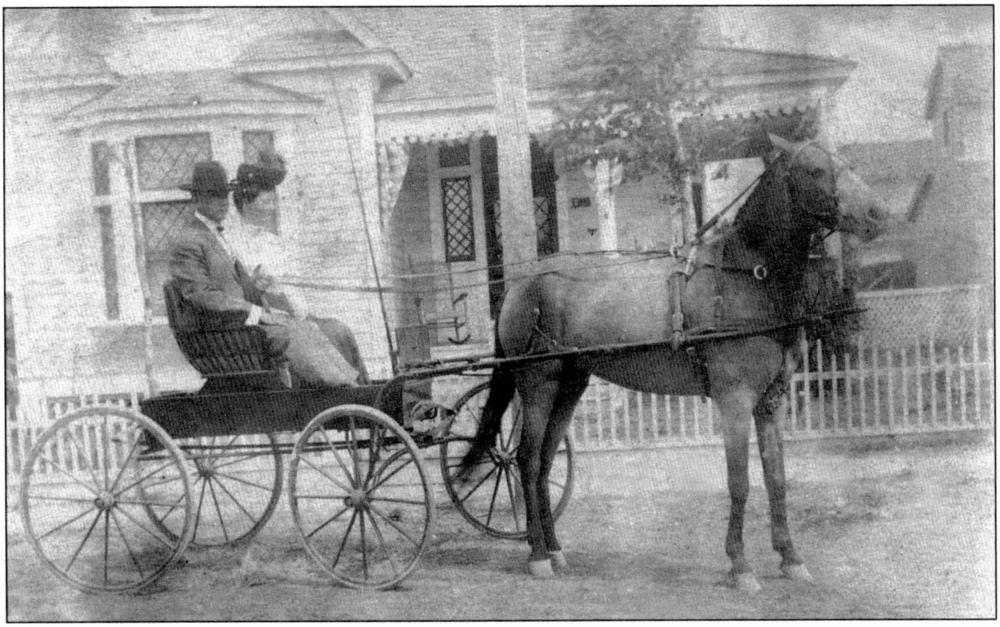

Jim George and his wife go for a ride in their one-horse carriage.

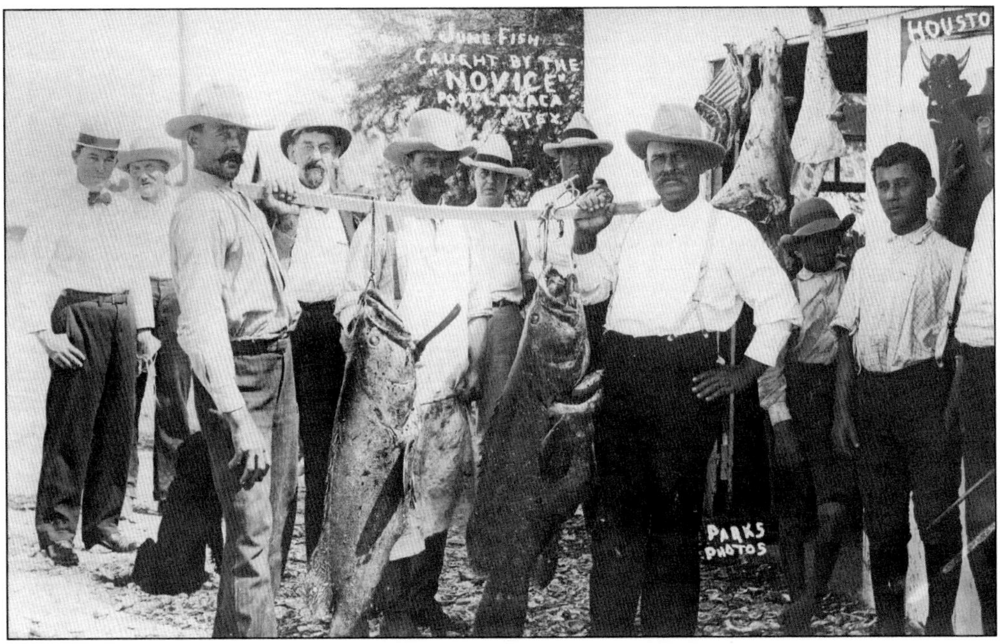

The goliath grouper, also known as June fish or Jewfish, was caught in abundance in the early 1900s. They are now rare enough in Texas waters to be restricted to catch-and-release.

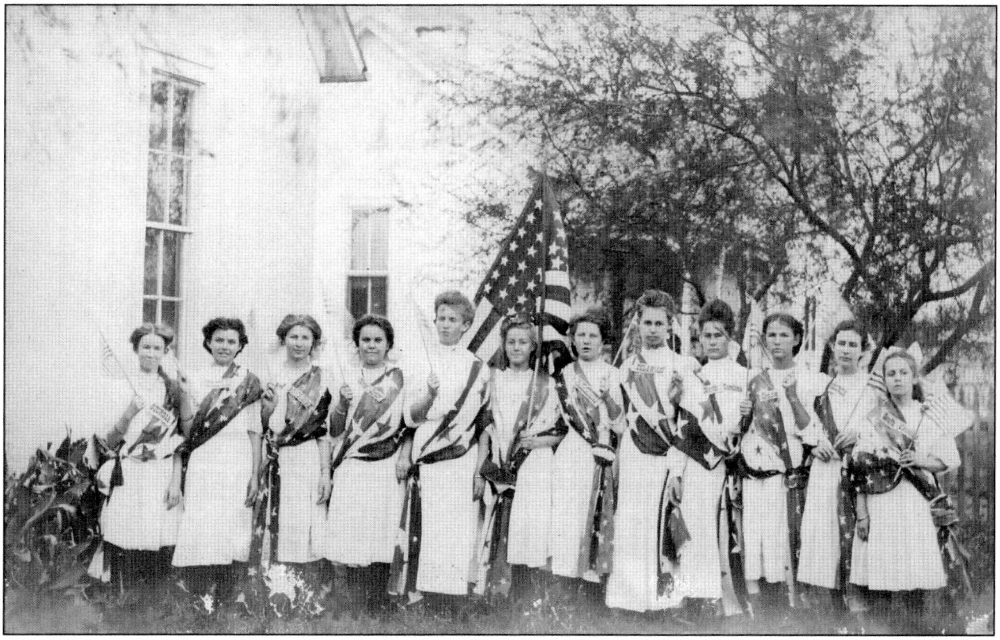

Young ladies from Port Lavaca High School celebrate the states with sashes and flags. They are seen here representing 12 of the original 13 colonies—one girl seems to be missing.

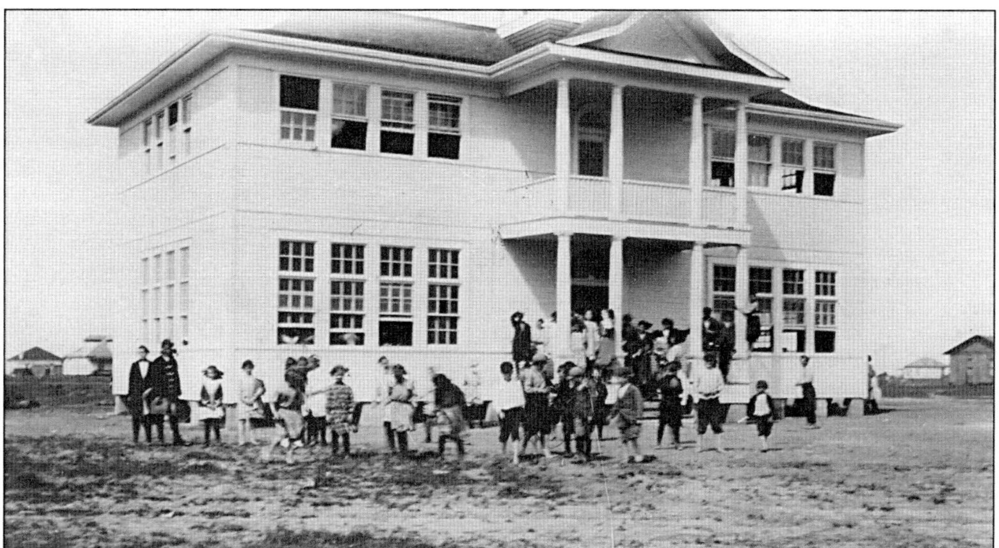

A group of young students stand outside the Seadrift School, which was built in 1910 at a cost of $4,000.

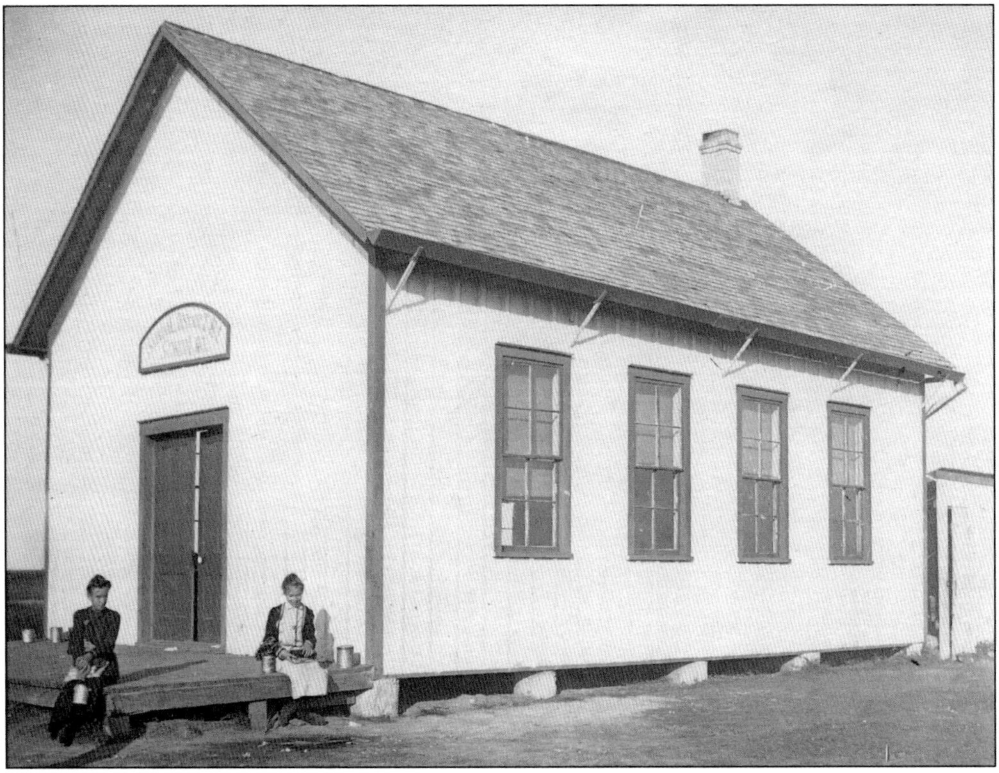

Above, two young women rest on the porch of an early Olivia schoolhouse. Many of the families that settled in Olivia were Swedish, and needed to quickly learn English. The children were taught during regular school hours, and in the evenings, the parents were taught English in the one-room schoolhouse. This building was simply called School No. 1 and was in School District No. 1. The building below may be the same schoolhouse. If it is, windows have been added to the front. The number of automobiles and well-dressed attendees indicate that it is no normal school day.

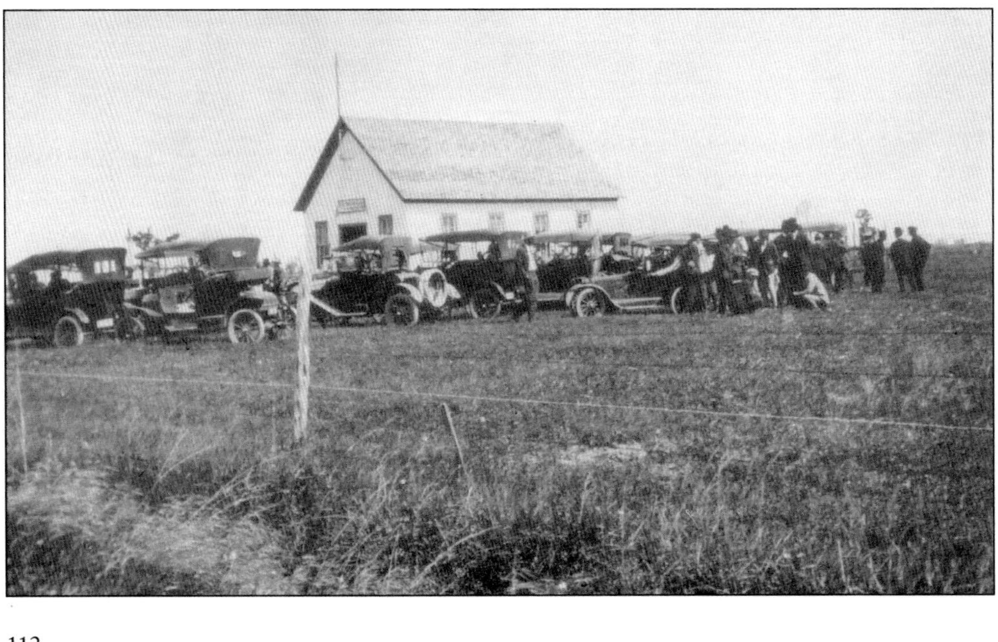

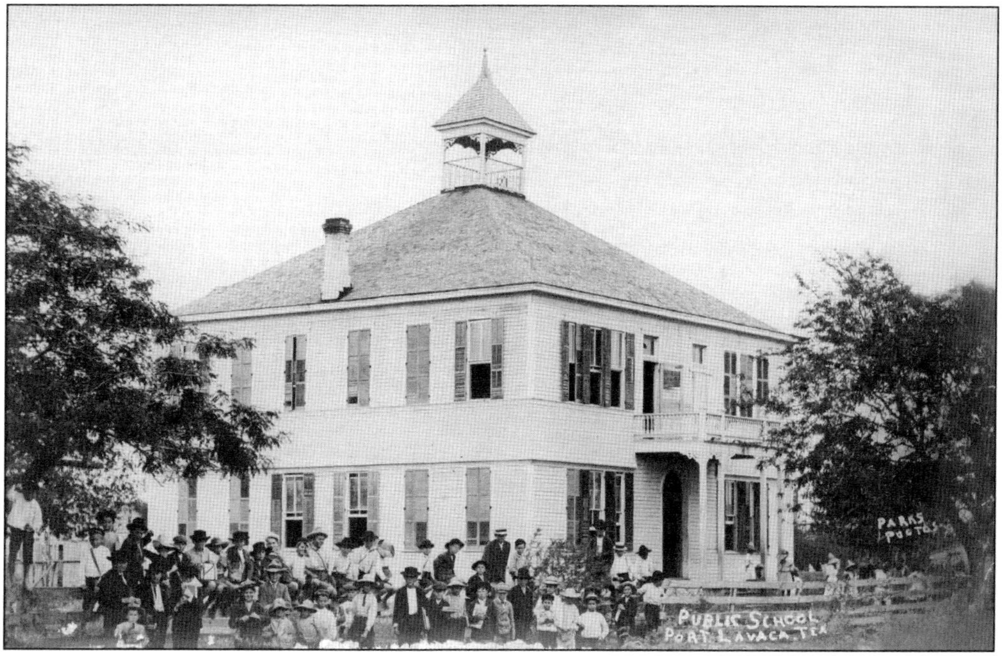

Students congregate at Port Lavaca School, which was built in 1897 on the corner of Main and South Virginia Streets. The school was replaced in 1910 by a new school built on the same site, at which time this building was moved across the street and converted into the Mallory Hotel, which later became the Texan Hotel.

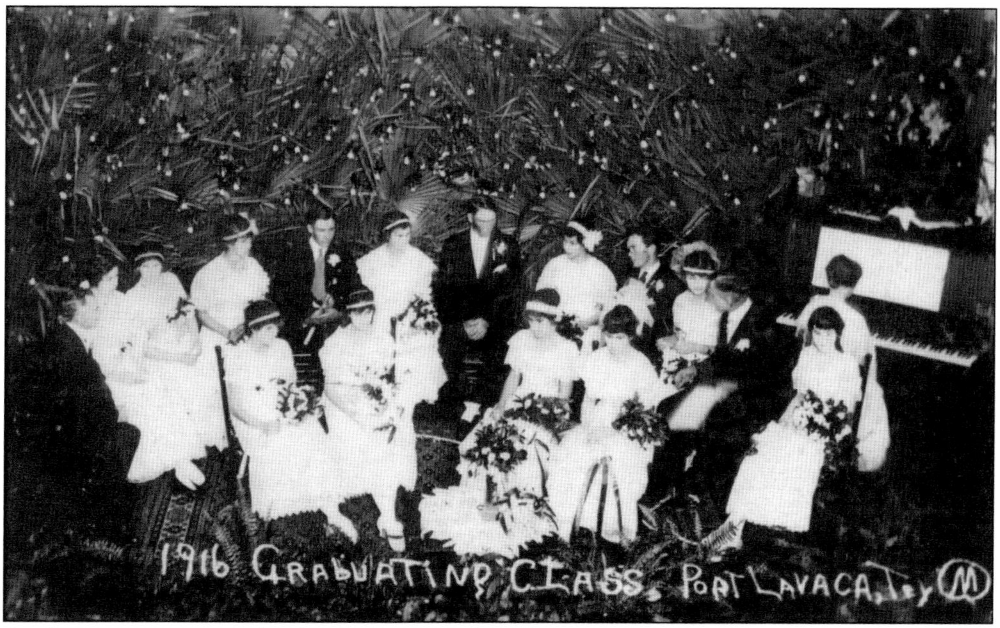

Graduation ceremonies for the 1916 senior class of Port Lavaca High School took place in the midst of palm fronds, flowers, and ferns.

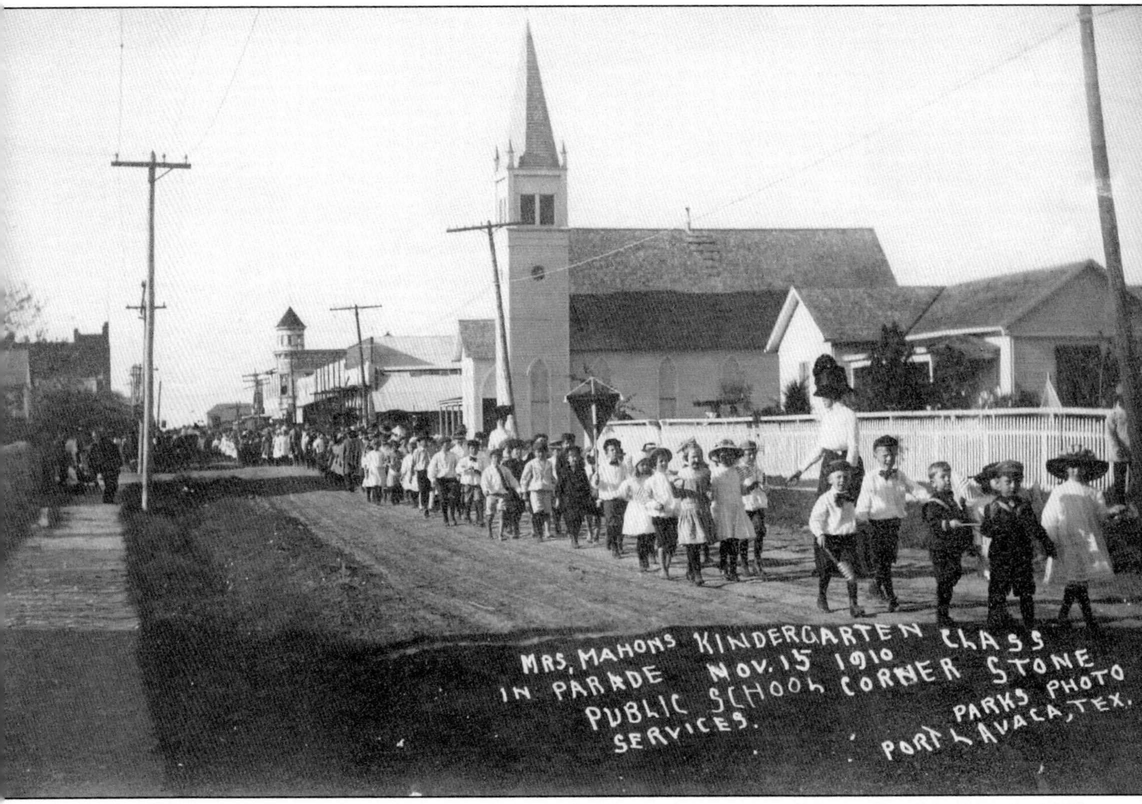

Mrs. Mahon's kindergarten class proudly parades down the street on November 15, 1910. In 1898, the six students in Port Lavaca School's inaugural class received their high school diplomas. Only 10 years later, attendance at the same school neared 250. In 1910, it was replaced by a new, four-story brick school with two water cisterns. This parade may have been held in celebration of the opening of the new school.

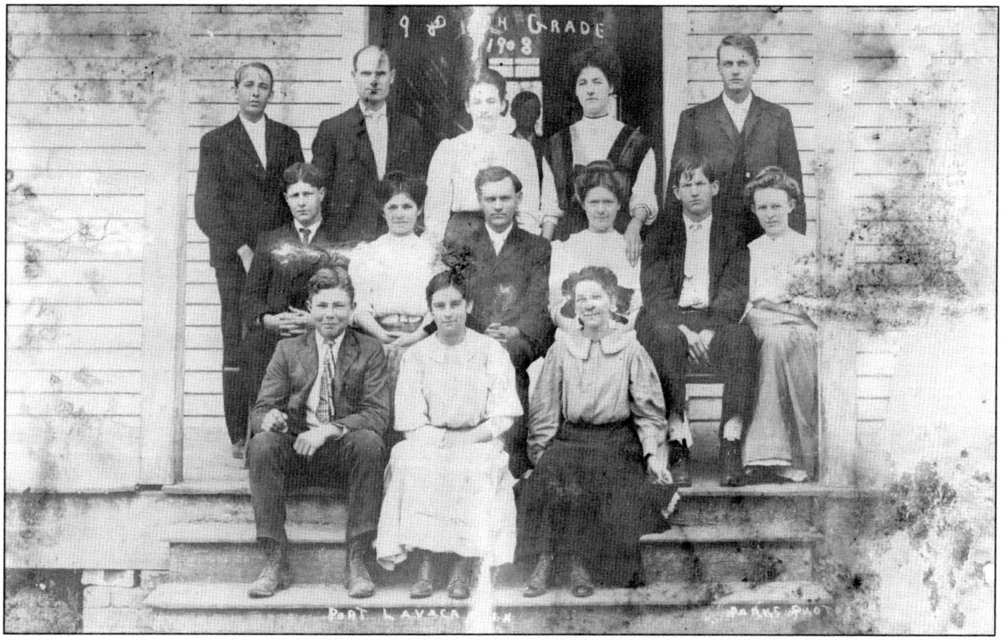

Ninth- and tenth-graders pose on the steps of Port Lavaca School in 1908.

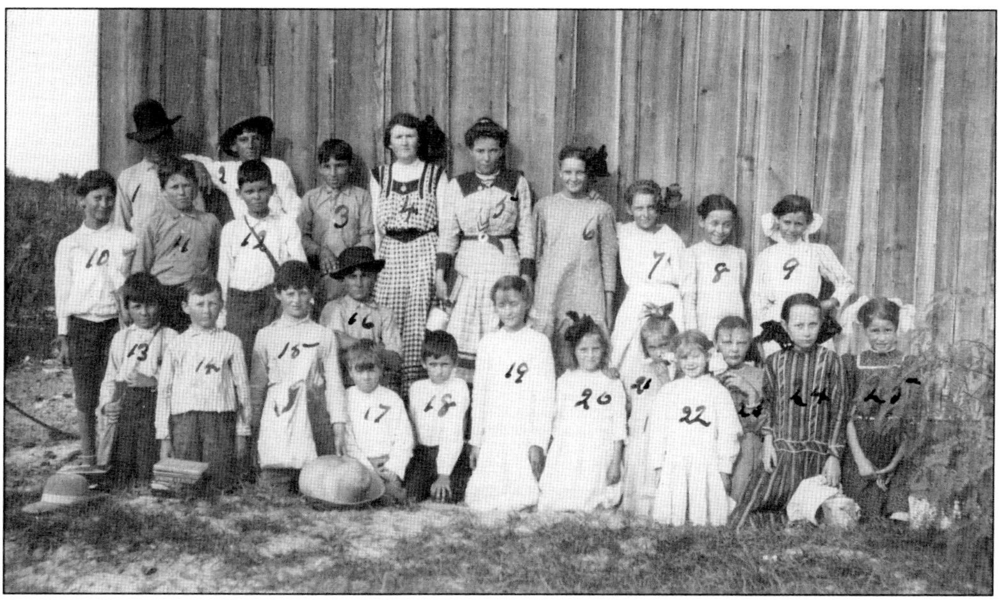
Students from Seadrift School pose for a photograph outside the school on September 28, 1910. The students ranged from ages six to sixteen.

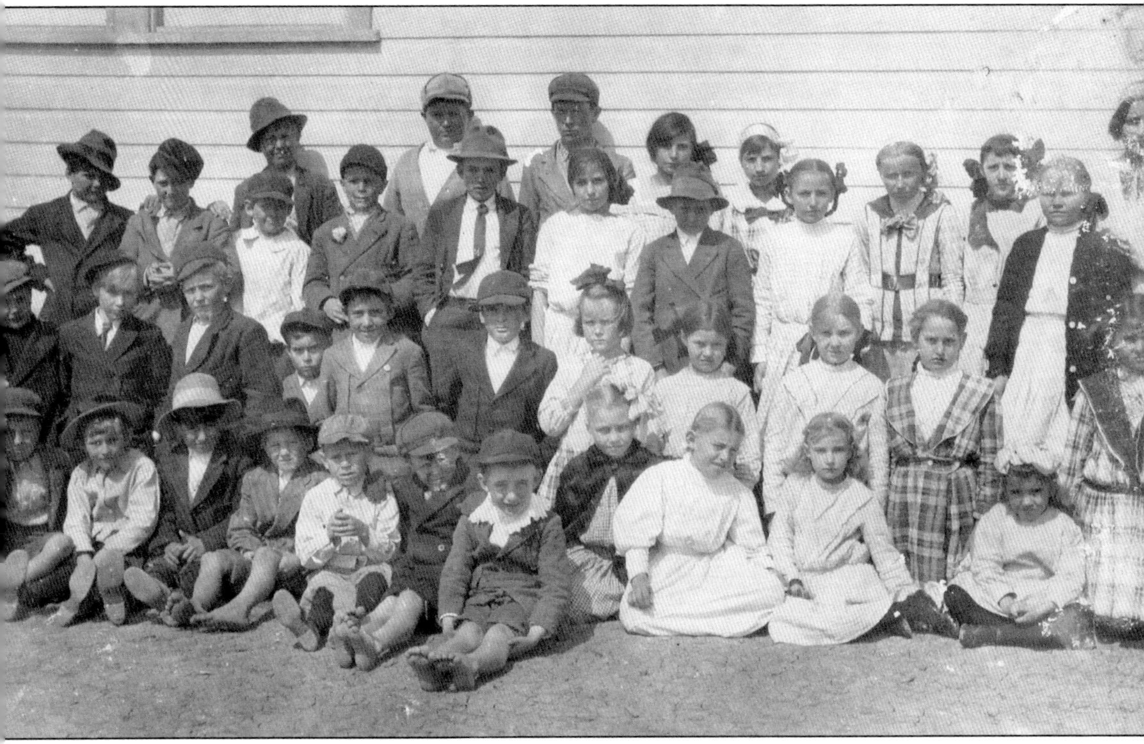

Students from Chocolate School pose for a group photograph in front of their school on March 17, 1913.

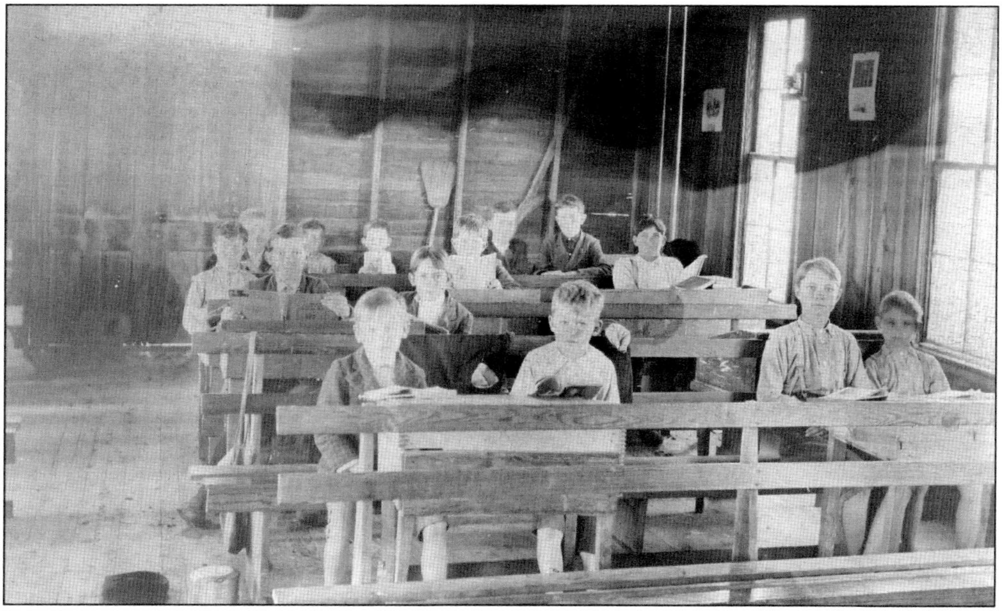

Young students sit for a day's classes at an unidentified school in Calhoun County.

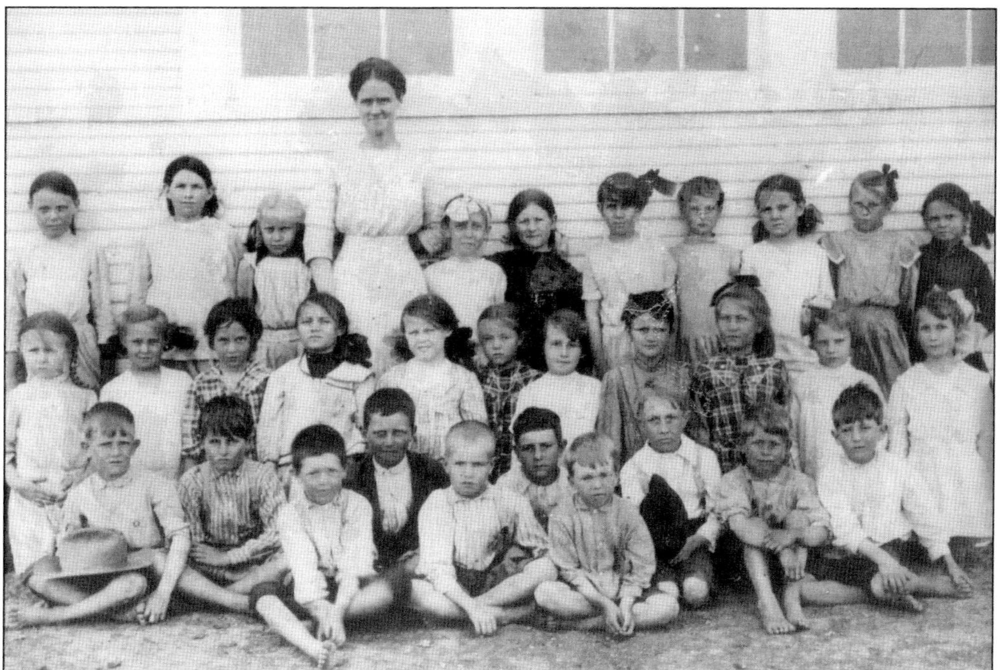

This young teacher poses with her students in the early days, when boy and girls were taught in separate classrooms.

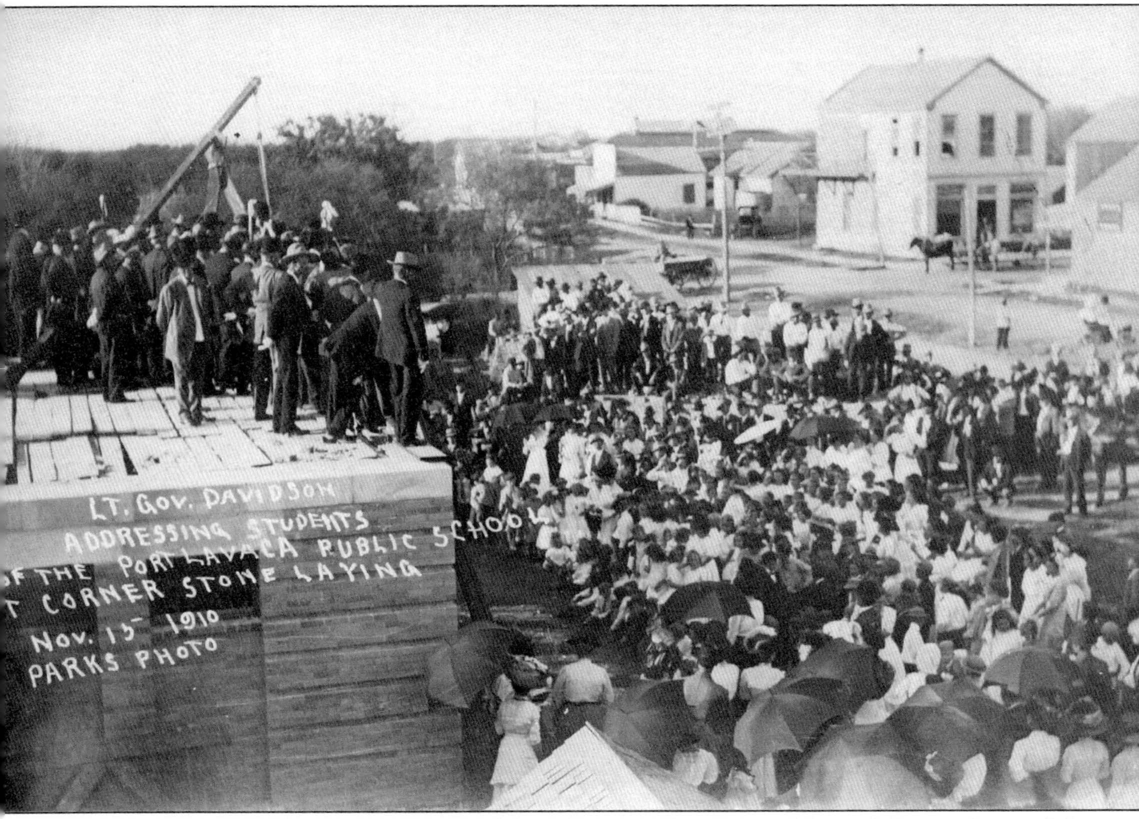

On November 15, 1919, Lt. Gov. Ashbury Bascom Davidson addressed the students of the Port Lavaca public school system at the cornerstone-laying ceremony for the new Port Lavaca High School.

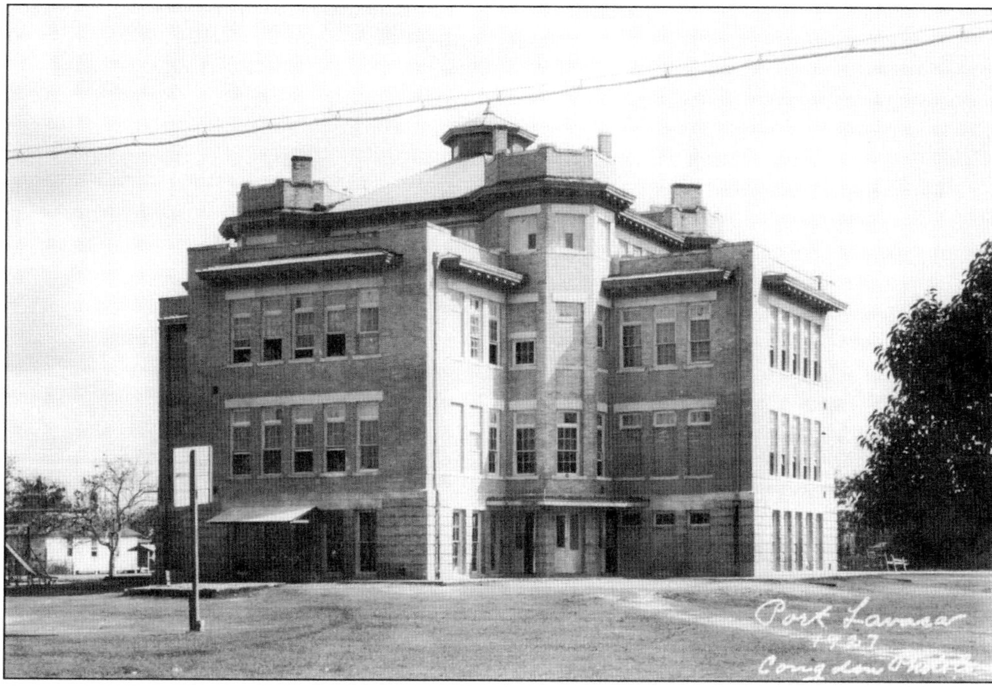

Port Lavaca School is seen above in a 1927 photograph by the Congdon Photo Company of San Antonio. The school, built in 1910, was damaged by a hurricane (below) and then razed in 1948.

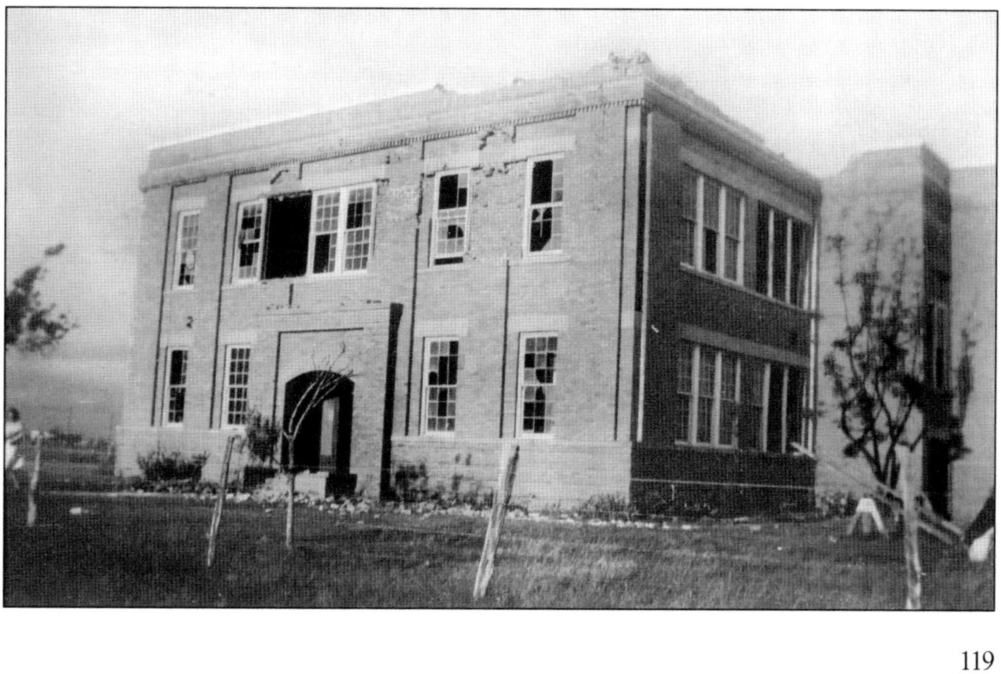

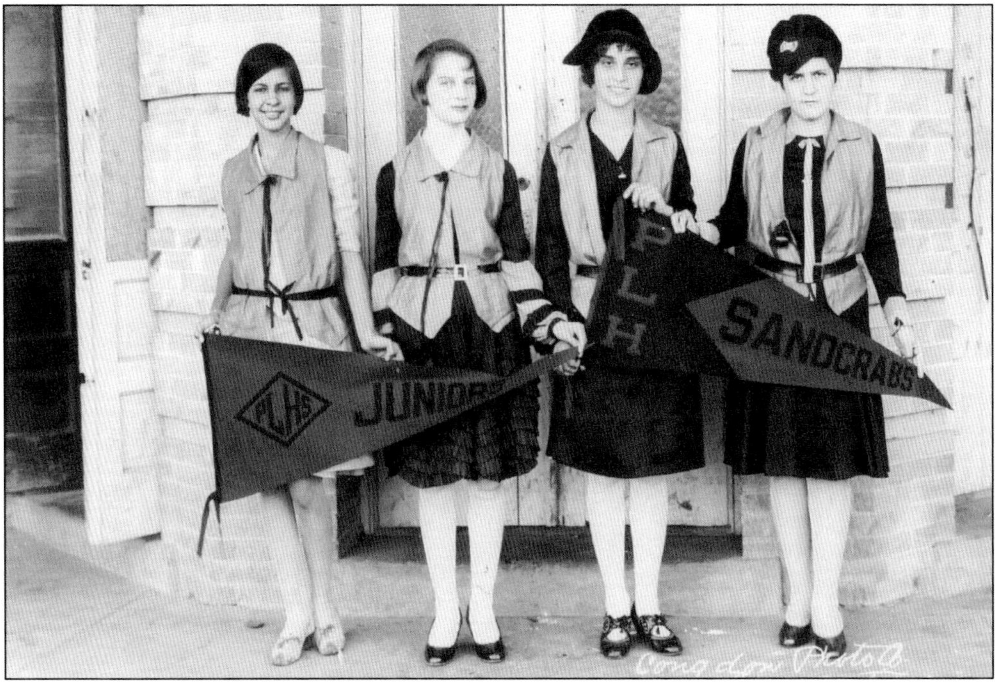

Four Port Lavaca juniors from the class of 1928 stand holding the Port Lavaca High School banner and the Sandcrabs team banner. Today, Calhoun County High School's mascot is still the Sandcrabs. Below, four young ladies pose for the photographer in their best Sunday dresses.

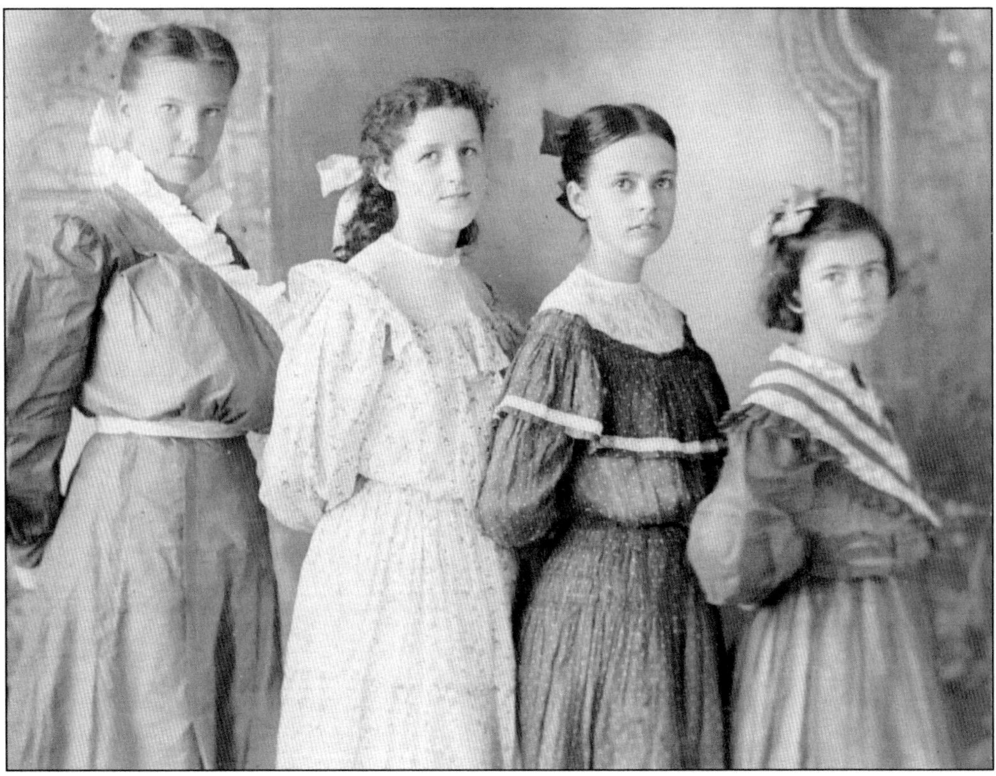

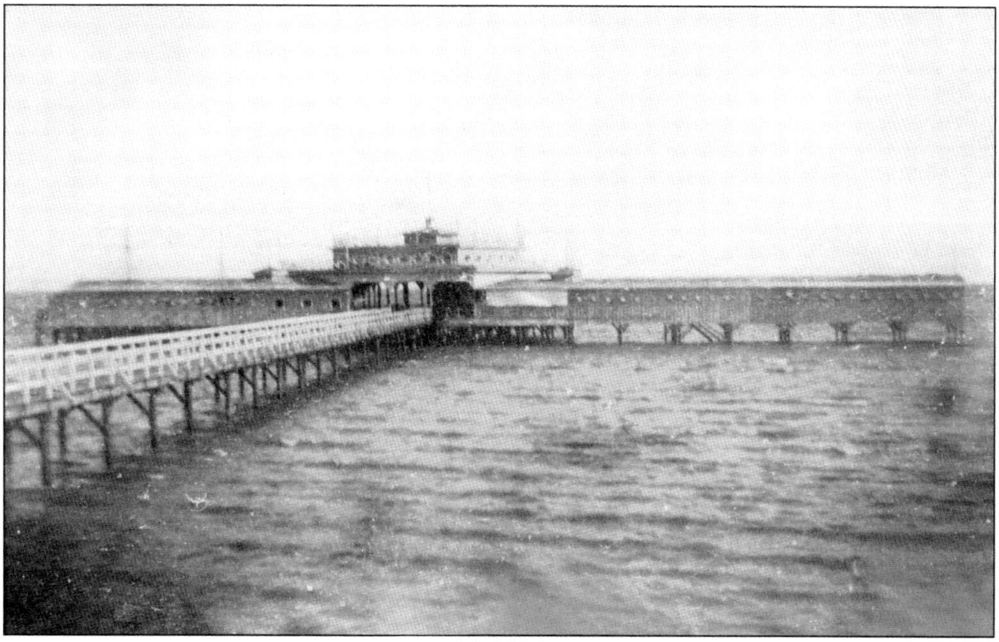

The Port Lavaca Pavilion (above) was one of five pavilions located on Lavaca Bay in the early 1900s. Built around 1916, it was used as a bathhouse and for dance parties and community functions.

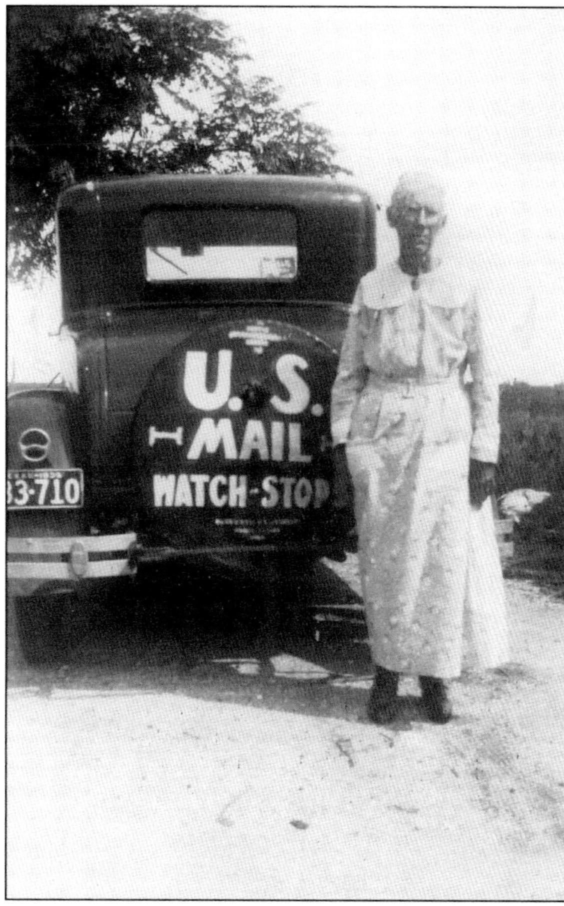

Blanche McMillian stands next to a US Mail car in the mid-1930s. Home delivery did not start in the county until October 1957.

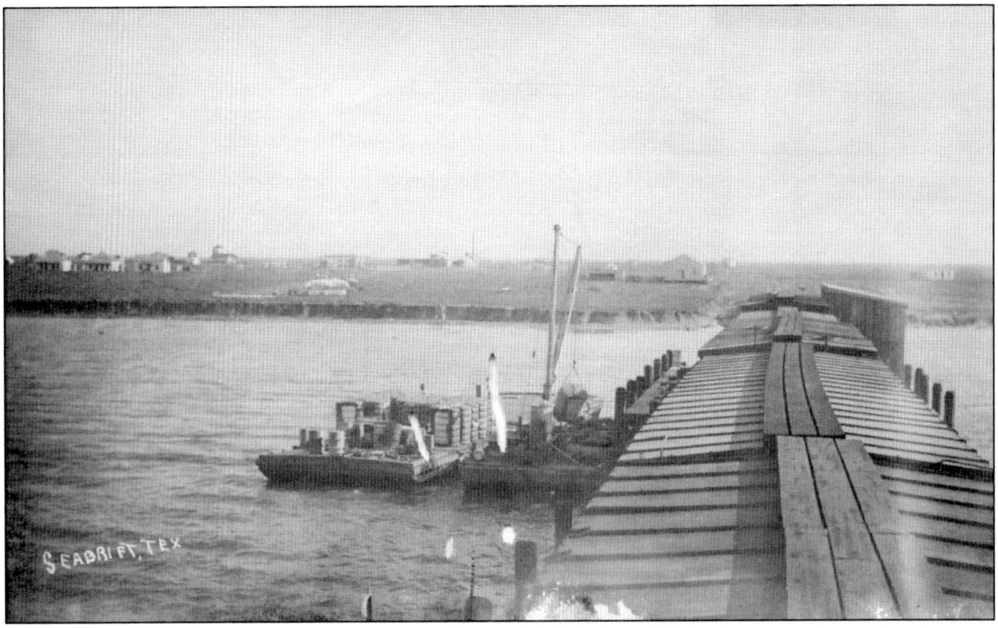

This barge is being loaded with cotton next to the Seadrift pier. Seadrift, on the San Antonio Bay, began as a settlement of German immigrants in 1848. Some of the original settlers included the Dierlam, Bindewald, and Sonneman families. The post office first opened in 1891 and was run by Jessie Dierlam. James Hatch was the first mail carrier. Originally known as Lower Mott, the town was renamed by Mrs. John Dierlam after the detritus that washed up on the shore. Mrs. Dierlam's sister, Catherine A. Coward, had suggested the name of Driftwood.

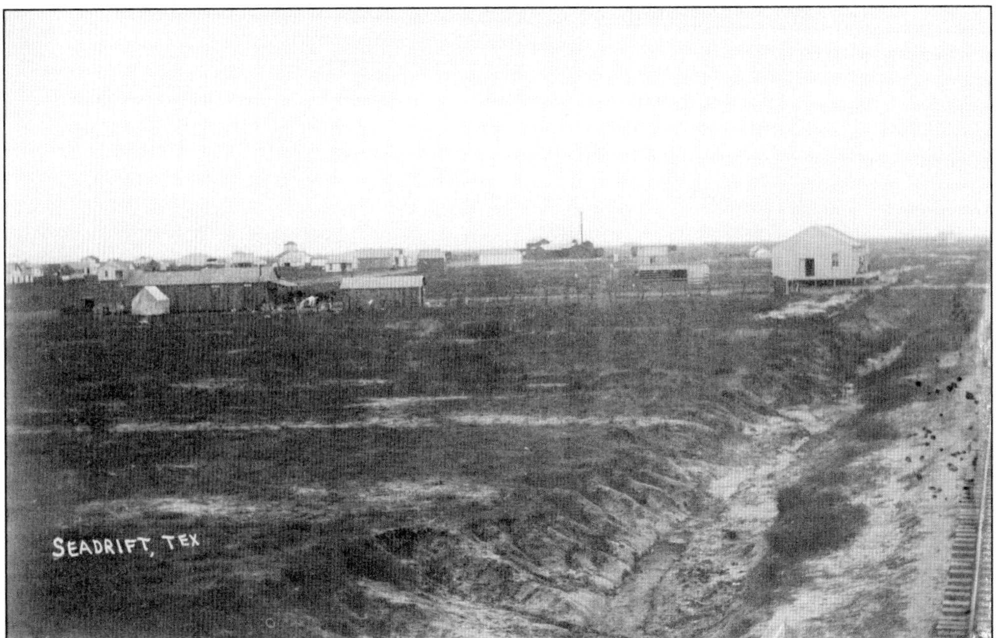

This is an early view of Seadrift. The town's first council meeting was in December 1912. Although it was already a small settlement before this time, it grew after A.D. Powers began promoting the town. W.G. Stewart was the first mayor.

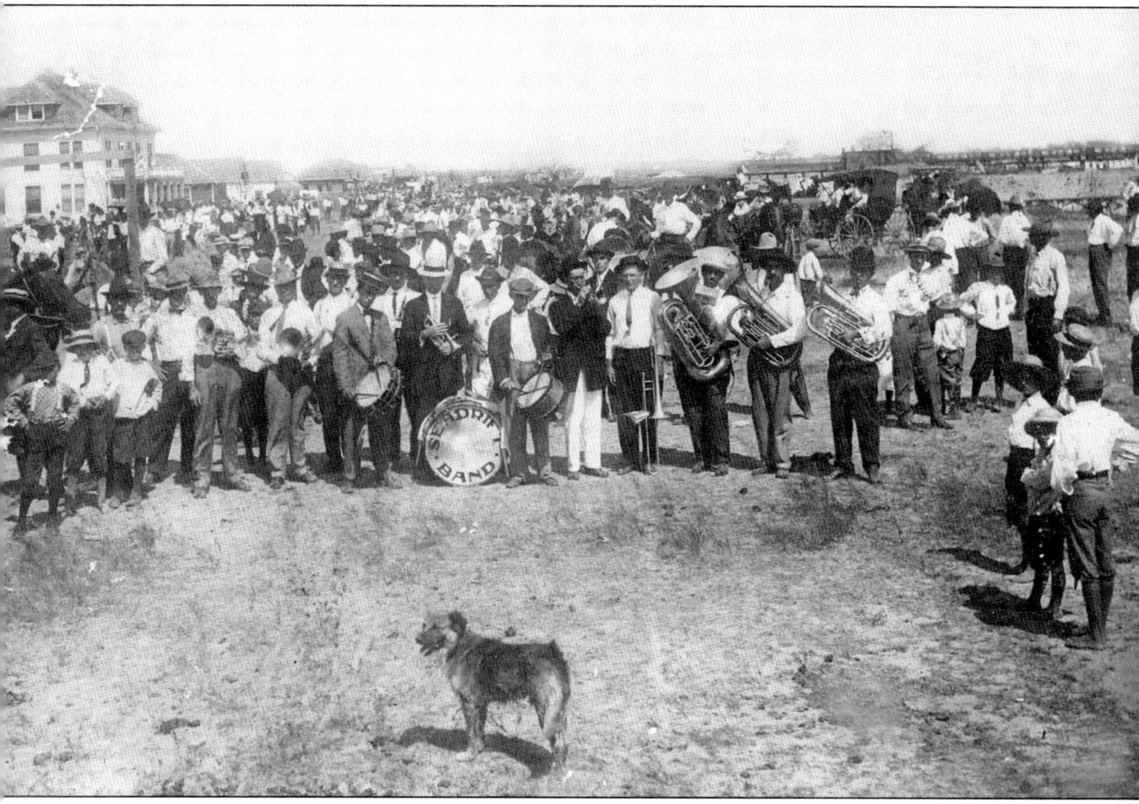

This crowd gathered on San Antonio Bay in 1912 to listen to the Seadrift Band not far from the Lafitte Hotel and the pavilion. Seadrift had its own school, hotels, and rail system. The first city hall was on the bay front and later moved to the bay side of Bay Avenue. By 1914, there were three churches, two banks, four hotels, factories, the telephone, and a local newspaper, the *Weekly Success*. The 1919 hurricane damaged the city hall and it was torn down.

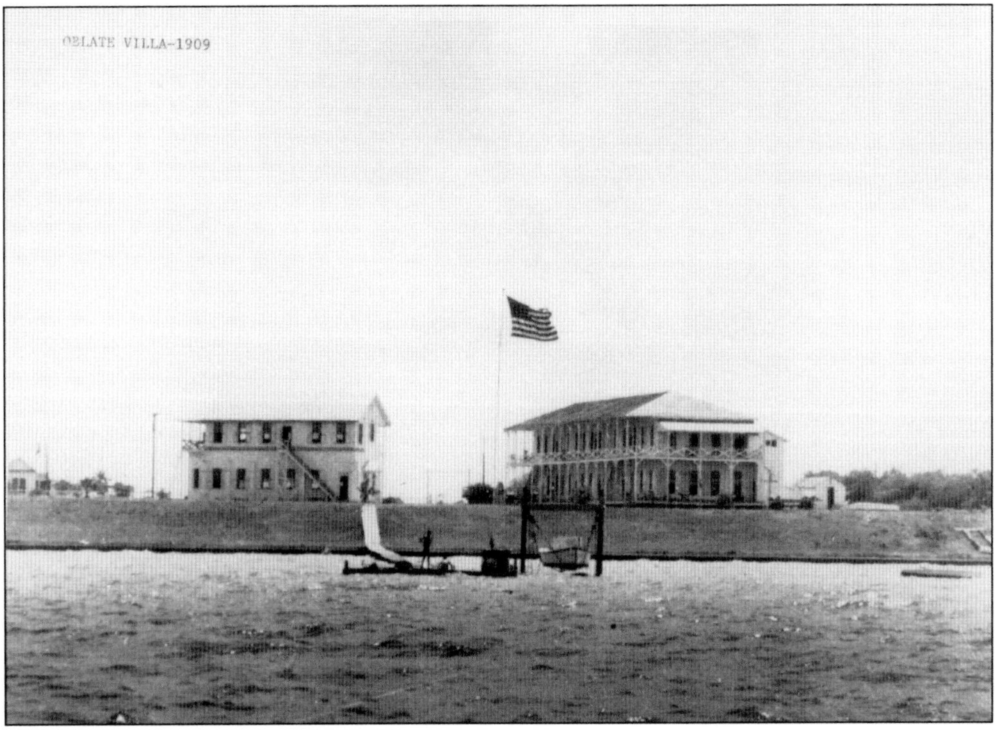

Oblate Villa was built by the Oblates of Mary Immaculate starting in 1910. It served the students of the Oblate Seminary in San Antonio. Every summer, the students in the final phase of becoming priests at the DeMazenod Scholasticate in San Antonio came to the villa for the summer. Hurricane Claudette took a toll on the villa on July 15, 2003.

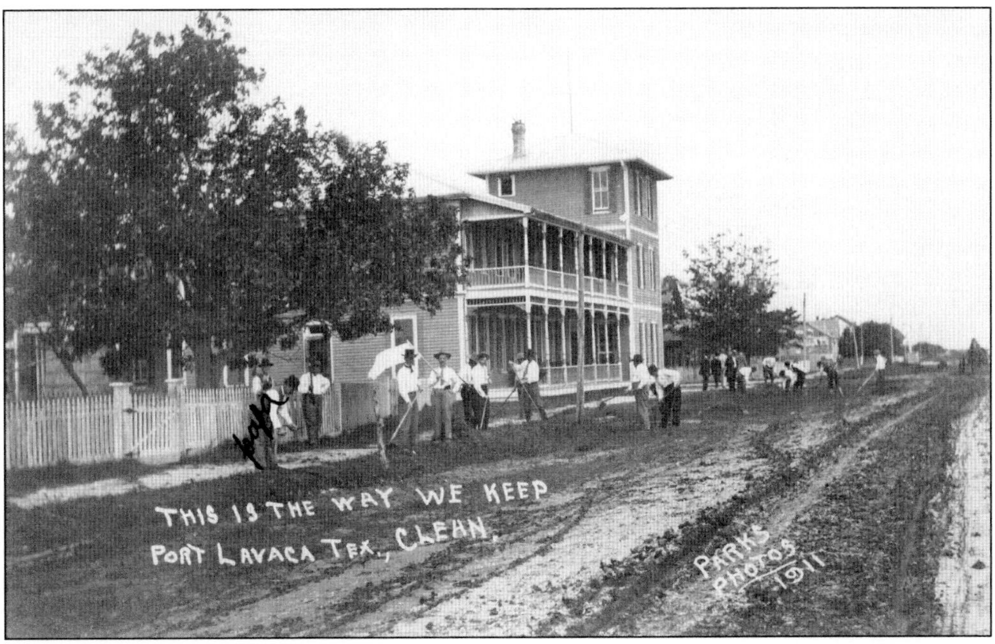

In this 1911 postcard, a group of men work to keep Commerce Street clean, near the Beach Hotel on the corner of Main and Commerce Streets.

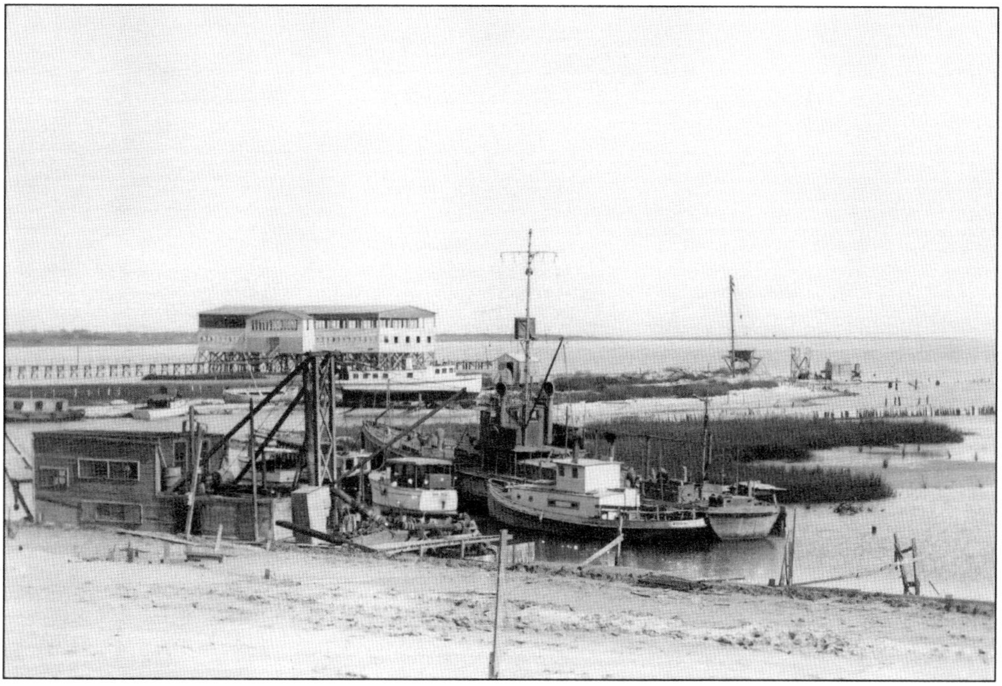

Although there are not photographs of all five pavilions in Port Lavaca, the last structure built is seen above. It was constructed out of the remains of the Port O'Connor Pavilion, which was destroyed in the 1919 hurricane. After Prohibition began in 1920, it was sold and used for some time as a fish and oyster house. Below, a small craft cruises around Lake Placedo near Port Lavaca.

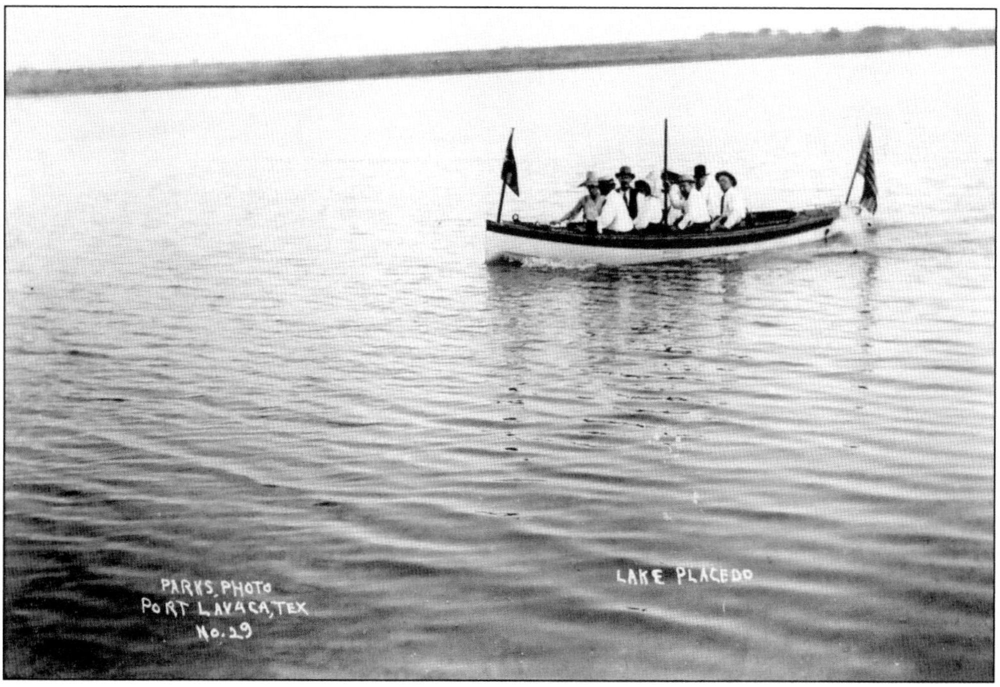

Matagorda Island Timeline

1519 Alonso Álvarez de Pineda sails the Gulf Coast, mapping Matagorda for the first time.

1685 René Robert Cavelier, Sieur de La Salle, sets up a camp on the island when he arrives from France.

1839 The town of Calhoun is established on Matagorda Island.

1844 The customhouse in Calhoun is moved to Galveston Island and the town does not survive.

1847 March 17 – James Power deeds the site for the future town of Saluria to Sommervell, Denison, and Rose.

1848 The first post office is established in the town of Saluria.

1852 A lighthouse is built near Saluria.

December 31 – The first light is lit in the lighthouse.

1857 An additional 24 feet are added to the lighthouse tower.

1859 The first third-order Fresnel lens is placed in the Matagorda lighthouse.

1861 Fort Esperanza is first garrisoned.

1863 Confederate troops abandon Matagorda after a four-day siege of Fort Esperanza.

1864 June – Federal troops withdraw from Fort Esperanza for the last time.

1865 October 15 – The lighthouse tower is dismantled and a temporary wooden tower is erected with a fifthorder lens installed.

1870 The tower is moved to higher ground and rebuilt.

July – A new third-order lens is ordered from Sautter & Company in Paris.

1875 Saluria is destroyed in the same hurricane that decimated Indianola for the first time. They do not rebuild.

1882 Oil lamps are retired from the lighthouse and are replaced with the new kerosene incandescent vapor lamps.

1956 The lighthouse is finally automated.

1977 The lens is removed from the lighthouse by the Coast Guard and is loaned to the Calhoun County Museum in Port Lavaca, where it continues to be on display.

This timeline shows the history of Matagorda Island. Today, it is a wildlife refuge that is extremely important to the survival of many species.

ABOUT THE ORGANIZATION

The Calhoun County Museum was established in 1964 by the Calhoun County Commissioner's Court. Originally housed in the 1896 jail building, it later moved to the Courthouse Annex Building and then to its present location. The mission of the Calhoun County Museum is the acquisition, documentation, preservation, study, and exhibition of artifacts relating to the history, natural history, and maritime history of Calhoun County.

Some of the outstanding exhibits include the Fresnel lens from the 1852 Matagorda Island lighthouse, an eight-foot diorama of the town of Indianola, a collection of items from the *Belle* in an exhibit titled "La Salle Odyssey," and many more items dealing with the life and times of Calhoun County.

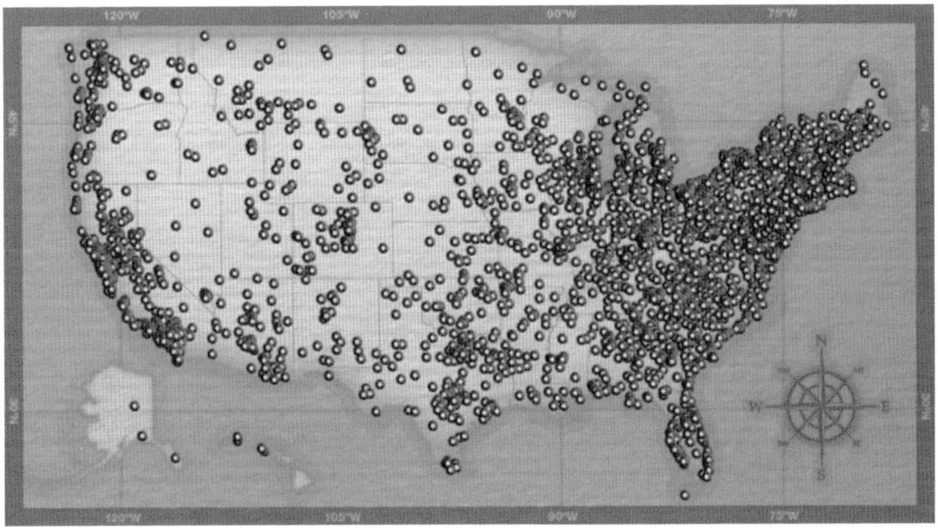